I0893982

RODOLPHE EL-KHOURY

FIGURES

RODOLPHE EL-KHOURY

FIGURES

ESSAYS ON CONTEMPORARY ARCHITECTURE

INTRODUCTION BY GEORGE BAIRD

OSCAR RIERA OJEDA
PUBLISHERS

TABLE OF CONTENTS

INTRODUCTION TO "FIGURES"
BY GEORGE BAIRD

For the past two decades or so, Rodolphe el-Khoury and I have—off and on—been academic colleagues at two architecture schools, first, at Harvard's Graduate School of Design, and then, at the Daniels Faculty at the University of Toronto. During that period of time I have watched with interest as el-Khoury has published critical commentaries on a variety of issues, architectural firms and buildings, in a variety of venues. With the present volume, el-Khoury has assembled a number of them together.

It has been an interesting experience for me, in preparing to write this introduction, to read—and sometimes—to reread the texts in question. First of all, they do not focus on the most famous architects of the era. Rather, they devote serious and thoughtful critical attention to a range of architects and architectural firms in various parts of the world who have substantial professional reputations, but who are not household words. Then too, among them can be found such likely candidates as practitioners in the schools in which el-Khoury has himself taught, such as Office dA, Machado and Silvetti, and An Te Liu, but—and in my view rather less likely—there are also included discussions of the work of notable designers in major corporate firms such as Ralph Johnson at Perkins + Will, and Andrew Bromberg at Aedas. Since I have myself lamented the tendency in architectural discourse in recent decades, to delineate a sharp boundary line between a small number of so - called "stars" who receive a disproportionate amount of attention, as compared with everyone else in the worldwide profession, it has been very refreshing to me to see el-Khoury ignore this boundary line in his own commentaries.

One of the implications of this is that the commentaries address rather diverse architectural issues. In particular, the texts devoted to "Architects" and to "Buildings," tend to shift focus rather sharply from one to the next, giving prominence in each case to issues that are central to the practice of the various architects respectively, or to the designs of the respective buildings under discussion. And one of the consequences of this is that I at least, have not been able to discern in the volume as a whole, an articulation of an architectural position on el-Khoury's part that is a fully unified one.

Now this might be thought of as a criticism, but I want to argue here that it is in an important sense a strength. After all, even so distinguished a critic as Ignasi de Solà-Morales felt impelled to remark in an introduction to a similar collection of texts that it had "seemed impossible" to him "to construct a systematic discourse" from them.[1] And I don't think that doing so has been an objective of el-Khoury. As he states in the text on Office dA, "my aim is define the general terms of the debate, as much as to clarify Office dA's particular position."[2]

I might go even further in this regard, and state that el-Khoury quite consistently attempts in these texts to take the architectural firm or the building under discussion, on its own terms. And he is willing to risk some degree of inconsistency in his own overall position, in order to do so. Hence it is also that his commentaries seem so consistently collaborative. Sometimes he has co-authors; sometimes he discusses projects on which he has himself been a collaborator; but even when he does neither, he is wont from time to time to incorporate opinion from others into his commentaries. This does not mean that he is not ever critical, because he is—I am myself lightly side-swiped in one of the texts—but his criticism is always aimed at a productive expansion of the overall architectural debate, rather than at point-scoring. It is one of the rewards of this distinctive critical method of his that the reader can expect to discover thoughtful discussions of a whole range of consequential aspects of contemporary architects in the pages that follow: formal ones, historical ones, digital ones, environmental ones, plastic ones. Such are the benefits of el-Khoury's heteroclite curiosity. I commend it to you.

[1] *I. de Solà-Morales, Differences (1997).*

[2] *R. el-Khoury, page 227 of this volume.*

ACKNOWLEDGEMENTS
BY RODOLPHE EL-KHOURY

I thank my friends, colleagues, students, and fellow travellers for the support, assistance, inspiration, dialogue, advice, criticism, and countless other ways with which they facilitated my work: Yanina Arabena, George Baird, Nadia Benabid, Andrew Bromberg, Zeynep Celik Alexander, Fares el-Dahdah, David Erdman, Lisa Findley, Sarah Hasan, K. Micheal Hays, Stephan Jaklitsch, Ralph Johnson, Byron Kuth, Robert Levit, Yvonne Levy, Sebastian Lopez, Rodolfo Machado, Randa Malkawi, Christos Marcopoulos, Jürgen Mayer H., Steve McDowell, Carol Moukheiber, Oscar Riera Ojeda, Mark Pasnik, Andrew Payne, Alessandra Ponte, Liz Ranieri, Larry Richards, Richard Sommer, Philippe Samyn, Jorge Silvetti, Paulette Singley, Nader Tehrani, Georges Teyssot, Charles Waldheim and Meejin Yoon. This book would not be possible without their contribution.

This book is dedicated to the memory of Detlef Mertins

- PART ONE
POLEMICS

The essays in this section engage current discussions in architecture. They point to trends, recognize and frame diffuse cultural phenomena, or tease out latent tendencies from a close reading of artifacts. Some also stake a position and deliberately provoke. “Monolithic Architecture” mounts a frontal assault on a persistent idea: it challenges a pervasive tendency to assign critical or emancipatory virtues to avant-gardist formal techniques. The piece on Jürgen Mayer H.’s Metropol Parasol fuels an ongoing debate on digital media, a fragment of which is reproduced from a Facebook discussion.

– STATES OF ARCHITECTURE: SIX PAVILIONS FROM THE SHANGHAI WORLD EXPO*

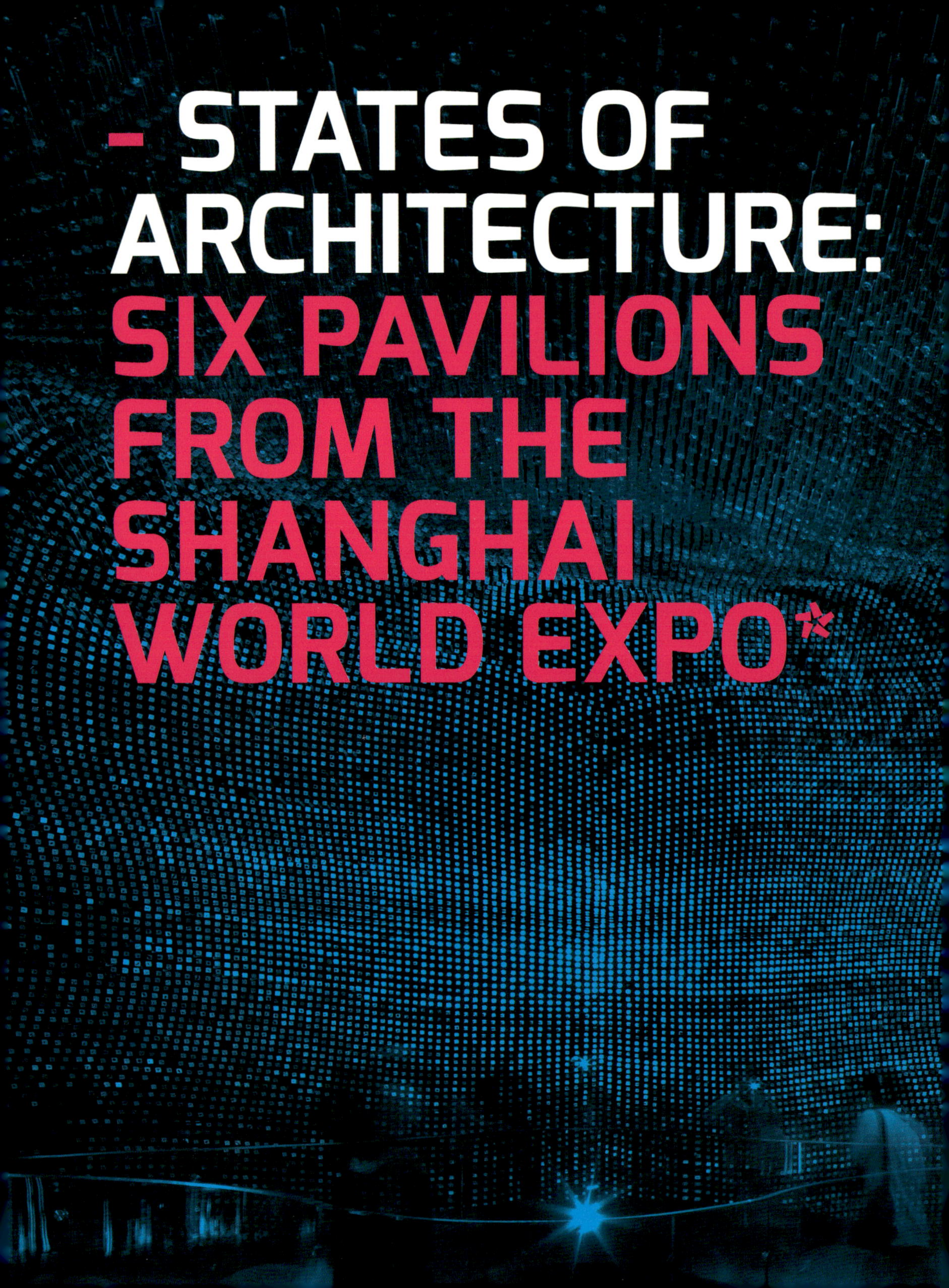

EXCERPTED FROM **STATES OF ARCHITECTURE IN THE TWENTY-FIRST CENTURY: NEW DIRECTIONS FROM THE SHANGHAI WORLD EXPO**, OSCAR RIERA OJEDA PUBLISHERS, 2011.

* WRITTEN IN COLLABORATION WITH ANDY PAYNE

SINCE THE FIRST WORLD EXHIBITION held in London in 1851, world fairs and expositions have been an important locus for the intersection of architectural invention, technological innovation, and the flows of transnational capital. Distinguished nineteenth-century examples of this phenomenon include Joseph Paxton's "Crystal Palace," constructed for the London exhibition, and the Eiffel Tower, constructed thirty-eight years later to serve as the entrance arch for the world exposition celebrating the centennial of the French Revolution. Mies van der Rohe's Barcelona Pavilion, constructed as the German Electrical Industries Pavilion for the world Expo held in Barcelona in 1929, and Iannis Xenakis/Le Corbusier's Philips Pavilion, constructed for the world Expo held in Brussels in 1958, speak to the persistence of this phenomenon in the century that followed.

Apart from its being the largest exhibition of its kind in world history (with an estimated 70 million people slated to attend), three things may be thought to distinguish the Shanghai Expo from its nineteenth and twentieth-century precursors. First, this is arguably the first time that the global economy—of which world expos have always served as the anticipatory icons—is not merely a promise, but a realized fact. Second, it is unique among such exhibitions in taking the urban condition as its explicit theme. Finally, in this exposition the technological enthusiasm so very apparent in earlier expos is subject to a decidedly bioconstructive inflection, one informed not merely by concerns that architecture orchestrate a more "sustainable" relationship between natural and technological systems, but also by a biomimetic impulse inspired by contemporary advances in the chemo-mechanical simulation of animate processes.

That Shanghai should serve as the host for the first world exhibition to explore the technological and cultural vicissitudes of a now globalized urban condition at the moment of China's emergence as a significant player in the new global economy is surely no accident. Shangai has long served as a privileged site for commercial and cultural exchange between East and West. It was, we might say, a global city avant la lettre, and its significance as a world city with both a rich cosmopolitan past and a bright economic future is likely to increase as the economic and cultural consequences of globalization unfold.

Titled "Better City/Better Life," Shanghai Expo features contributions by more than 190 countries and 50 international organizations of one sort or another. In addition, there are several themed pavilions. Surveying the pavilions in their entirety, at least three themes or preoccupations begin to emerge: the first of these themes is biomimicry (a theme that must be related to a broader vitalist or neo-vitalist ethos in contemporary architecture). The second theme concerns the potentials of the architectural surface. Three things may be thought to characterize this second preoccupation: a neo-picturesque conception of the building as image rather than form; a sensualist aesthetic of wonder rather than of Kantian disinterest; and an eschewal of any conception of the building façade as the syntactical assemblage of compositional elements in favor of an aesthetic of the micro-element whose indifferent repetition produces a textural or atmospheric field. The third overriding theme concerns the recalibration of the relationship between built object and landscape, a recalibration that seeks to render this relationship at once more pliable and more equivocal. In addition to the prevalence of these themes, one can observe the recurrence of a strategy that involves wrapping an informal constellation of at once programmatically and volumetrically diverse elements in a homogenous and regularly patterned membrane. This strategy serves to mediate between demands for programmatic complexity and spatial variety, on the one hand, and the need to offer an at once coherent and iconic presence to the street, on the other. In what follows, we will elaborate on these themes and strategies, showing how they emerge in various ways throughout the projects represented in this volume.

LEFT. Finnish Pavilion

RIGHT. Finnish Pavilion, interior court

"In this exposition, the technological enthusiasm so very apparent in earlier expos is subject to a decidedly bioconstructive inflection, one informed not merely by concerns that architecture orchestrate a more 'sustainable' relationship between natural and technological systems, but also by a biomimetic impulse inspired by contemporary advances in the chemo-mechanical simulation of animate processes."

BIOMIMICRY

What is the "life" in "Better City/Better Life"? The historian and theorist of scientific culture, Eugene Thacker has described the Western conception of life as developing in three major episodes corresponding to three distinct models: life as soul (Aristotle), life as meat (Descartes), and life as pattern (the cybernetic conception of life as organized information). The idea of life arising from the cybernetic homology between living systems and information systems has had a strong hold on the contemporary architectural imagination for several decades (in no small part owing to the ubiquity of computer aided design).

This cybernetic conception of life has powerfully influenced the contemporary conception of the building as an animate or quasi-animate entity. Since the early nineties, that conception can be said to have advanced in three stages: the first stage (represented by the work of architects like Bernard Cache and Greg Lynn) imagined the building form as the empirical trace of a process of virtual morphogenesis. The second stage, represented by architects like MY Studio/Höweler + Yoon, Khoury Levit Fong, and Mark Goulthorpe, exploited the potentials of embedded technologies to reconceive the built work as artificial sensorium. At the third stage, largely enabled by digital parametric modeling, the building is conceived, in conformity with Thacker's third paradigm (life=pattern), as the aggregate produced by the patterning of micrological elements.

These stages are less consecutive than cumulative, since strong residues of the earlier stages can be observed in even the most daring and radical examples of the later ones. In the Shanghai Expo, vestiges of all three are apparent, although it is perhaps the fascination with the patterns produced by the dense but carefully regulated distribution of a micro-element across a surface or field that produces the most novel and ingenuous expressions of this vitalism. It is here, also, that these vitalist preoccupations begin to encroach on our second theme, surface.

The treatment of both the interior and exterior surfaces of the UK Pavilion are exemplary in this regard. The Seed Cathedral, situated at the center of a deftly terraced landscape, consists of a steel and timber composite structure pierced by 60,000 fiber optic filaments, 20 mm square in section, which are encased in aluminum sleeves. By day, the filaments draw

daylight inward to illuminate the building's interior, while at night light sources within the rods illuminate them so that the whole structure glows. Perhaps one of the most fascinating dimensions of this surface is its capacity to be affected by changes in the surrounding milieu. Not only do the filaments on the exterior skin move like hair when touched by even the gentlest of passing breezes, their sensitivity to changes of light allows them to register, through changes in the luminosity of the filament tips that stud the interior skin, the movement of clouds overhead.

This strategy of employing a dense patterning of micro-elements to form a continuous and evenly variegated surface or constellation of surfaces has sometimes been viewed as a counter response to the postmodern tendency to understand the architectural artifact in semiotic terms, as a kind of visual symbol or sign. However, in the Korean Pavilion, the repetition of the micro-element threatens to collapse the difference between ornamental form and semantic content, geometric pattern and syntactic sequence. In this building, the exterior surfaces are produced through the patterned alteration of two types of pixel. The first type consists of white panels bearing a relief of Han-geul letters rendered in a range of sizes; the second type consists of works by the Korean artist Ik-Joong Kang, renowned for his massive art walls made from hand painted tiles. The alteration of these panels produces a kind of pixilation of the building's surface, transforming its complex figure into the armature for a Borgesian landscape populated by symbols flickering enigmatically between pattern element and semiotic cipher.

SURFACE: FROM FAÇADE TO INTERFACE TO SPECIAL EFFECTS MACHINE

Our discussion of the biomimetic impulse at play in the works populating this exhibition has already signaled to the prominence of surface in the contemporary orchestration of architecture's effects. As many of the pavilions show, digital technologies have had a significant role to play in this development. That role concerns not merely a significant extension of the range of what is feasible, it also concerns a fundamental shift (or sequence of shifts) in our conception of what a surface is and how it mediates our relations with one another and with our surroundings. We might describe that shift as involving the transformation of our conception of the surface as façade into a conception of the surface as interface, a movement, then, from surface as the instrument of social and spatial differentiation to surface as the conduit for mediated connection. More recently another paradigm has emerged: the surface as special effects machine. Interestingly, the first significant example of this surface strategy was another piece of exposition architecture, Diller and Scofidio's Blur Pavilion for the Swiss Expo in 2002. Inspired no doubt in part by the Blur Pavilion, artificially produced clouds, mists, and spectra of various sorts are plentiful in recent architecture, and that plenty is very adequately represented in the submissions to this exposition. An interesting example is the Corporate Pavilion, whose surfaces are outfitted with an array of sensors and actuators that allow them to respond to the site's immediate conditions in a way productive of both aesthetic and ecological amenity. For instance, misters embedded in the building's external skin respond to increases in heat by emitting a cloud of cooling vapor. The vapor serves to both augment environmental performance and to enhance the foamy character of the façade.

Such effects are not exclusive to electronic media. The Spanish Pavilion achieves similar ecological goals and atmospheres with a meshwork of tubular steel and 8,524 wicker shingles. Intricately layered natural fibers deployed in a complex curvilinear form here modulate light and shade to define and shelter gathering spaces.

PREVIOUS PAGE AND ABOVE. South Korean Pavilion

FOLLOWING SPREAD. Corporate Pavilion

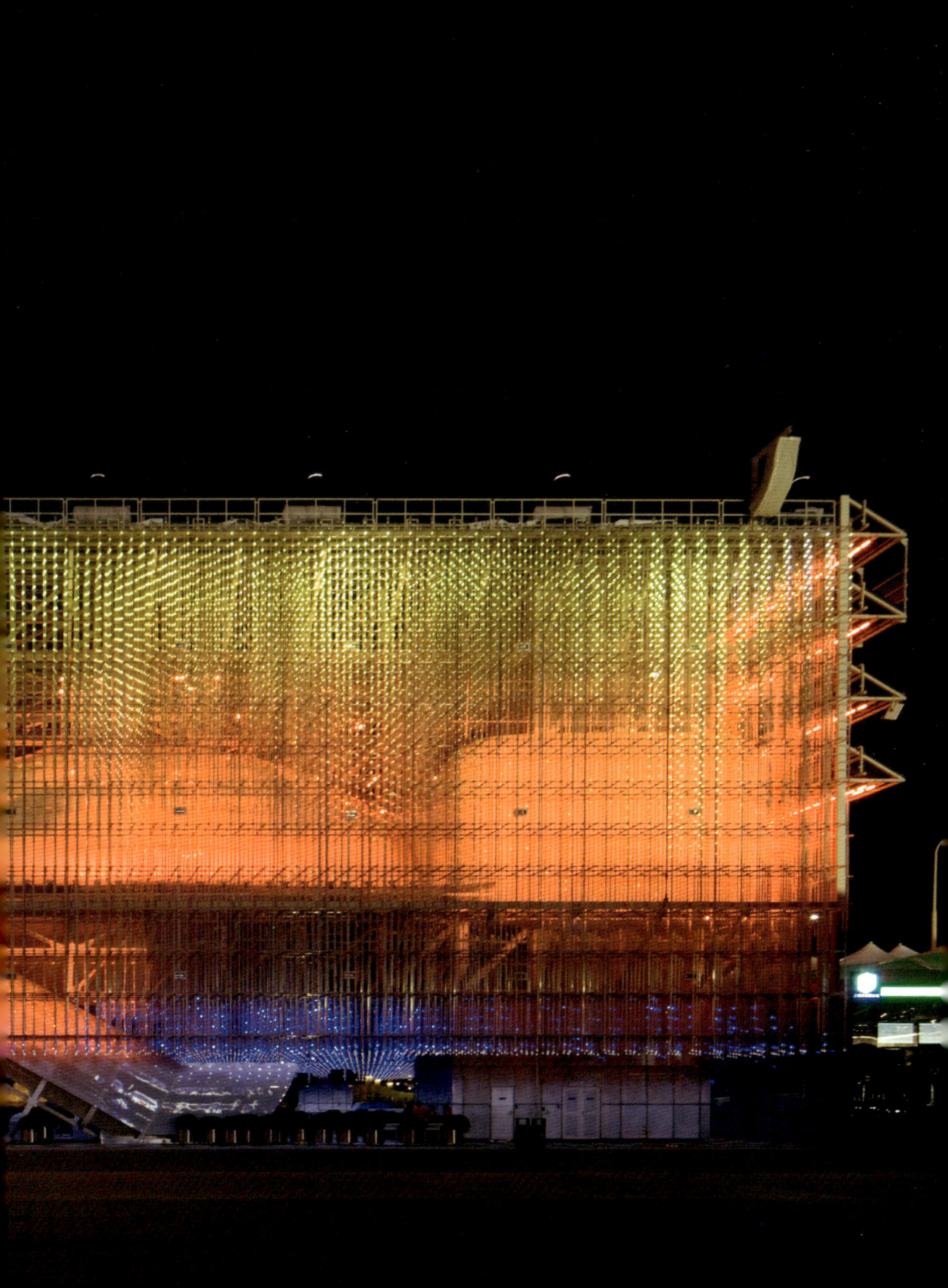

BUILDING AS LANDSCAPE/LANDSCAPE AS BUILDING

Landscape architecture has enjoyed an unprecedented prominence in recent discussions of architecture, serving not only as a disciplinary pursuit in its own right, but also as a model for reimagining the future of built architecture and urban design in view of new cultural and ecological circumstances.

This prominence is the result of a variety of factors, among which are to be numbered landscape architecture's traditional role as mediator between the natural and the artificial systems and elements that comprise the human environment. Not surprisingly, then, the cybernetically inflected vitalism that we observed in our brief discussion of biomimetic strategies is also a factor in the contemporary prominence of landscape, where it is associated with the application of terms and paradigms originating in systems ecology to the interpretation and construction of the built environment.

If the prominence of landscape in a wide array of pavilions can be indexed to this cyber-naturalism, it is also symptomatic of an interest in reimagining the relationship of building to site in such a way produce novel interlacings of interiority and exteriority, object and milieu. In order to give some sense of the variety of strategies deployed in aid of these interests, we will briefly discuss three pavilions: the Expo Pavilion, UK Pavilion, and the French Pavilion.

In what might be seen as a discrete nod to the tectonic features of the pavilion as a building type consisting of a constellation of vertical members topped by a textile canopy, the Expo Pavilion is in essence a colossal roof structure lofted on fifty giant masts whose support is buttressed by six steel and glass framework shells. Reminiscent of the lightweight construction of Frei Otto's design for the German Pavilion of Expo 1967, the structure frees sightlines and pedestrian movement while serving as both a hovering icon of virtuoso engineering and a monumental diagram of the distribution of program across the site. In addition, spacious lateral slopes flood the floor levels with light and air. The result is a building both maximally open to and embedded in its surroundings.

LEFT. French Pavilion, garden courtyard

The UK building can be thought to orchestrate an entirely distinct approach to the relationship of building to landscape, one wherein the interaction of building and site is defined by a clear differentiation of roles. The pavilion is a kind of two-part invention, in which the first part consists of the Seed Cathedral whose ingenuous surface effects have already been described, and the second part consists of a carefully terraced landscape comprised of surfaces covered with artificial grass. In sharp contrast to the hard ground surface of the adjacent sites, these surfaces are designed to continue the texture of the Seed Cathedrals interior and exterior surfaces as well as to offer a welcoming public space for visitors to sit and view the building.

Despite the conspicuousness of a cosmopolitan spirit fueled by global capital and technological virtuosity, expressions of national pride are a constituent feature of world expositions, and the Shanghai exposition is no exception. Perhaps the most architecturally consequential of these nationalist expressions is to be found in the French Pavilion, where a celebration of the restrained sensualism that has traditionally distinguished the Gallic expression of neoclassical values finds a surprisingly contemporary expression.

As was the case with the UK Pavilion, the relationship between building and site is clearly differentiated. The familiar type of the courtyard building with a classical French garden at its center, a type which arguably finds its apotheosis in Claude Perrault's library with interior court, is here subject to an unexpectedly picturesque inflection, reconceived as a succession of atmospherically and programmatically distinct episodes unfolding along a continuous ramp that twists around the court garden before terminating in a roof garden. That succession reveals a taut dialectic between the symmetry and decorous regularity of the court garden and the dense mélange of media presentations and atmospheric effects that animate the galleries strung along the ramp. The French spirit of the pavilion is also revealed in the intricately carved topiary that extend from the roof garden into the court below.

ABOVE. French Pavilion

/ THE PAVILIONS

UNITED KINGDOM

Working with the Kew Gardens Millennium Seed Bank, Thomas Heathwick Studio designed a pavilion consisting of two main elements, the Seed Cathedral, a biomorphic icon situated at the center of the site, and the multi-layered 6,000 m^2 landscape that surrounds it. Designed to be a direct manifestation of the thing its exhibits (a collection of thousands of seeds culled from China's Kunming Institute of Botany, a partner in the Millenium Seed Bank Project), the Seed Cathedral is a steel and timber structure pierced by 60,000 fiber optic filaments, 20mm in section, which pass through aluminum sleeves. The dense aggregation of these filaments then form both the exterior and the interior surfaces of the building. From the outside the building resembles nothing so much as a giant sea anemone. From the interior it appears as a kind of cave or grotto illuminated by a hovering galaxy of luminious studs, each containing one of the seeds. By day, the filaments draw daylight inward to illuminate the building's interior, while at night light sources within the rods illuminate them so that the whole structure glows. The filaments also serve as devices for making the cathedral highly responsive to even the smallest events in its immediate environment. Not only do the filaments on the exterior skin move like hair when touched by even the gentlest of passing breezes, their sensitivity to changes of light allows them to register, through changes in the luminosity of the filament tips that stud the interior skin, the movement of clouds overhead.

The second part of the pavilion is a generous, multi-layered open space paved with an artificial grass that is both an extension of the visual idiom of the building's internal and external skins and a sharp contrast with the surfaces that pave adjacent sites. The open space gives room for visitors to stop and rest, but also provides multiple unobstructed views of the Cathedral. Canopied and naturally ventilated entrance and exit sequences provide a circulation zone along three sides of the site. That zone contains three installations by the London-based design firm Troika: Green city, Open city, and Living City.

RIGHT. UK Pavilion, interior

SOUTH KOREA

The South Korean Pavilion looks like a low-resolution picture of a building. It is clad with panels of varying size designed and conceived as physical pixels that aggregate into larger figures or breakdown into individual bits.

The design, by Seoul-based Mass Studies, is consistent with current trends that capitalize on the potentials of digital parametric modeling and fabrication techniques to aggregate infinitely varied building blocks into complex architectural constellations. The method imitates processes in which morphological complexity in nature grows from the accretion and variegation of simple constituent parts. It also captures and translates into a memorable image, the informational constitution of architecture, the extent to which contemporary buildings are shaped and produced by digital media.

The orchestration of pixels and figure is also related to the Korean culture and language. The form of the pavilion is based on Han-geul, the Korean alphabet, with graphic symbols aggregated and translated into special constructs. The building envelope is clad in a variety a square panels—physical pixels that coalesce in myriad combinations. The white variety features Han-geul symbols. The colored so-called "art pixels," are 45 cm x 45 cm aluminum panels created by Ik-Joong Kang, a Korean artist known for his mosaic-like murals.

The intricately woven patterns of Han-geul and art pixels create a variety of effects that are both atmospheric and symbolic: visitors are immersed a rich texture of shifting colors, light and patterns while they decode the ever-shifting programmed messages that animate the elevation with back-lit Han-geul pixels.

Within the three-dimensional matrix of concatenated symbols the pavilion offers a variety of space for small-group meeting and large public gatherings including a 40 m x 77 m landscape extending under the pavilion's lifted volumes. The ladscape is an abstract translation of a typical Korean city, complete with a miniaturized mountain and river for the visitors to enjoy while queuing for the programmed spaces above. Much like the rest of the building this public room bathes in the atmosphere of digitality, saturated with flickering pixels, both virtual and physical.

PREVIOUS SPREAD. UK Pavilion
LEFT. South Korean Pavilion

SPAIN

A basket-like structure envelops the open and enclosed spaces of the Spanish Pavilion. It shapes the building and defines its character while sheltering from the sun, dust, and noise. The intricately textured surface is a tubular steel structure with a complex curvilinear geometry that is clad with 8,524 wicker panels arranged in a shingle pattern. The alignment of digital technology with artisanal craft here makes a persuasive case for the recovery of vernacular charm and efficiency with high-tech means and ingenuity.

The pavilion, designed by Benedetta Tagliabue of Miralles Tagliabue Architects, speaks eloquently about the coordination of low and high-tech means in ways that take advantage of new methods of fabrication in a new global economy. The tubular steel structure is modeled and fabricated with the help of sophisticated software that rationalizes its complex double curvatures for efficient production and assembly. The wicker panels belong to the basket-making field, a thriving artisanal traditional with a global reach.

The steel structure with its curvilinear inflections enables the large spanning sweeps of the sheltering wall. The infinitely varied wickerwork, creates with the richness, intelligence, and unparalleled intricacy of handmade products an atmosphere that is reminiscent of Hispanoarabic architectures with its play of light and shade, transparency and opacity. The combined effects of freeform contours with intricately layered natural fibers, a sustainable material par excellence, create a unique architecture that is both traditional and progressive, demonstrating new possibilities for responsible and efficient uses of resources in sustainable and livable cities.

RIGHT. Spanish Pavilion, interior

FOLLOWING SPREAD. Spanish Pavilion

FRANCE

The French Pavilion aims to recreate the sensory world of France with installations targeting all the senses for a fully immersive experience. The building stages within a stately package a series of experiences in a continuous multimedia circuit featuring highlights from French cinema classics, samples of perfumes, and ambient noises of Paris, to name just a few of the many effects that create the French ambience throughout.

The building primarily consists of a continuous ramp that rises within a structural shell around a square court and terminates in a roof garden. Intricately carved topiary cascade from the roof into the courtyard covering the interior elevations in a thick layer of living ornament.

The living wall, along with other eco-friendly features rhetorically integrated into the spatial and decorative makeup of the building overtly state the environmental dedications of the building. The precisely etched topiary is most effective in demonstrating the potential of living systems as building material while embracing the long established French tradition of a geometricized and rationalized nature.

The green court, physical and "spiritual" core of the structure is in constant visual focus from the gently ascending galleries. Its regularity and symmetry contrast with the animated and ever-changing ambiance of

ABOVE. French Pavilion, night view

FOLLOWING SPREAD. Expo Axis

the galleries. It anchors the building in solemn tranquility that evokes the classicism of the Grand Siècle.

A concrete basket-like structure, exterior counterpart to the topiary wall, packages the building in a homogeneous and regularly patterned wrapper. The parametric compression of its diagrid toward the top—perhaps a reference to proportional inflections in French classical architecture—yields subtle variations in component geometry and assembly that speak the sophistication in CNC parametric modeling and fabrication.

EXPO AXIS

This is one of the five permanent structures. It is meant to become a public amenity for the new urban district that is slated for development on the Expo site. The design is by the Stuttgart-based firm that won an international competition for this prestigious commission. The building is one the most important of the exposition, marking the entrance and defining the main axis of the site. It is also most ambitious in terms of technological innovation and shear magnitude.

The building is a tour de force of engineering. Its tensile roof structure spans 100 meters, pushing the envelope of what is feasible with the technology. The roof membrane is propped on a series of colossal masts and held in tension with massive anchors that attach to the structure underneath. The funnel-shaped anchor resonates with the geometry of the Sun Valleys: oversized glass and steel masts that bring light to the lower decks and provide shelter under their flaring caps.

The juxtaposition of the funnel-shaped anchors and masts offers a striking composition where fabric in tension and glass and steel in compression are rhetorically compared and contrasted.

BSA is partnered with Knippers Helbig Advanced Engineering Stuttgart for the innovative design and engineering. Together they continue a German tradition of lightweight construction that developed with Frei Otto's groundbreaking works. Much like the German Pavilion at the World Exposition 1967 in Montreal and the Munich Olympic stadium—formative precedents that defined the genre—the Expo Axis how advanced computation and material research align to produce structures of increasing elegance and efficiency.

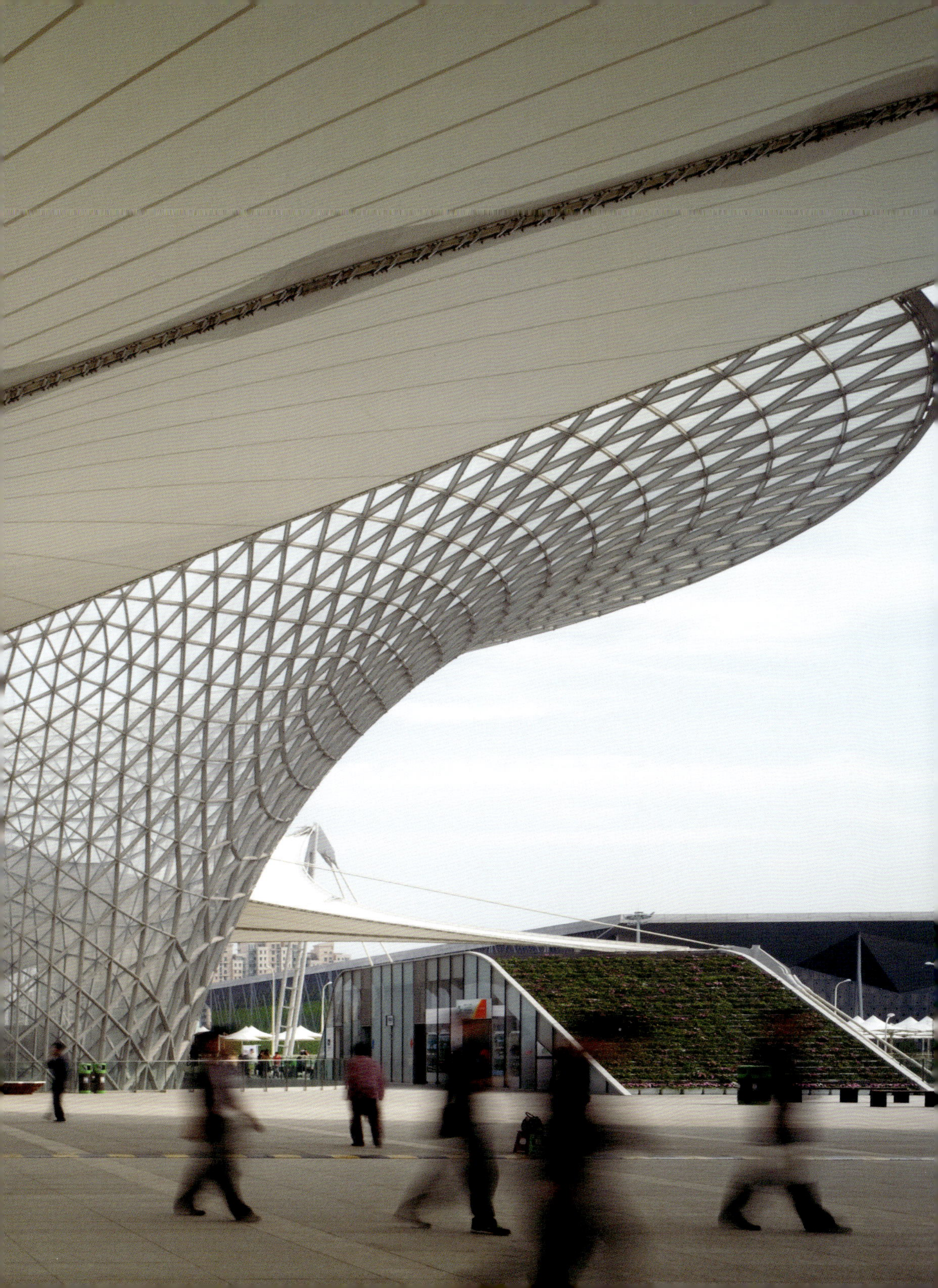

CORPORATE PAVILION

A dense infrastructural matrix envelops a collection of irregularly shaped spaces, unifying diverse programs and volumes into a rectangular block. This is a recurrent compositional strategy at the Expo and a compelling model for urban buildings in general. It is a way to transition from increasingly complex programs and interior configurations to a consolidated mass and iconic presence on the street.

The building pays homage to the groundbreaking Centre George Pompidou of 1976 with its exposed infrastructure and ductwork. In lieu of massive structural members and conduits the Corporate Pavilion presents a filigree of infrastructure. While the Centre Georges Pompidou flaunted technology in the form of colossal machinery this pavilion appeals to a different technological paradigm: information technology and miniaturization.

The building is enveloped in a mist of technology: a cloud-like distribution of miniaturized structure, electronics and digital bits. This steel and silicon filigree features an array of sensors and actuators that enable the building envelope to respond to ambient conditions and accordingly enhance its environmental performance. Embedded misters for instance produce an actual cloud of cooling vapor that regulates the ambient temperature. This climate-control device responsively boosts the environmental performance of the building while visually enhancing the foamy character of the façade.

Embedded LEDs transform the building into an active digital display controlled by computers that alter the appearance of the building in a variety of automated or programmed ways, further underscoring the shit from the iconography of the machine to the atmospherics of the information age.

RIGHT. Corporate Pavilion

– METROPOL PARASOL: ANIMATES PUBLIC SPACE AND ONLINE DEBATE

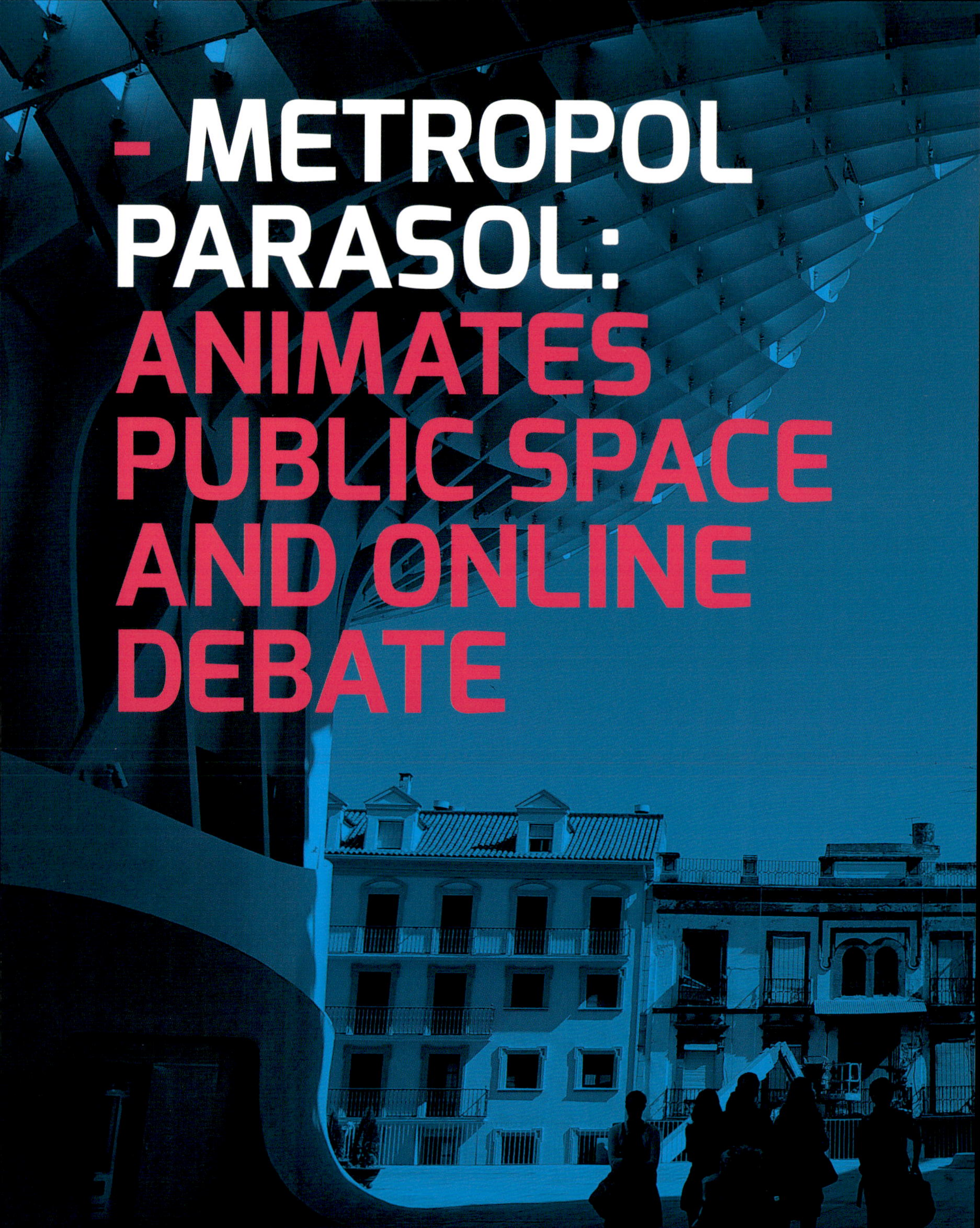

ORIGINALLY PUBLISHED IN AZURE, JULY/AUGUST 2011.

SEVILLE HAS A NEW LANDMARK: a multi-level, action-packed structure that occupies the main public square, Plaza de la Encarnación. Architect Jürgen Mayer H. designates the buildings he designs for the intensification and orchestration of public life in various European cities "Urban Activators"—and Seville's Metropol Parasol is surely his most ambitious one. Mushrooming above a concrete base housing such public amenities as an archaeological museum, a farmers market, an elevated plaza, and bars and restaurants, this colossal shade is a futuristic architectural folly whose rooftop offers the best view of the historical city.

Even before it was completed, this engineering tour de force—made of 3,400 polyurethane-coated timber panels held together by 3,000 joints—won sustainable design awards and instantaneous iconic status as soon as images of it began appearing on design blogs. When I posted on Facebook a photo of the barely finished structure with a construction crane silhouetted against a gorgeous Andalusian sky, it provoked a range of impassioned responses. Surprisingly, a public customarily critical of extravagant architectural intrusions in dense urban cores is wholeheartedly seduced by the canopy's playful inventiveness. The specialists are more ambivalent, displaying a mixture of resentment and admiration at the fact that such a wildly unorthodox and expensive project could gain the necessary institutional, political, and financial support while far tamer innovations generally fail to gain traction. "How could such an insane timber cloud get built in the main square of a traditional European city while my mildly quirky door handle is deemed too odd and costly?" A perhaps justified sentiment, it only points out Seville's visionary ambition and faith in architecture.

Metropol Parasol's crate-like structure is another point of contention. It reads as a literal adoption of a technique widely used for the rough approximations and rapid prototyping of complex forms: a digital low-resolution sampling method that enables the fabrication of cardboard mock-ups with CNC laser cutters. To the layperson, the crate may seem ingenious; to the pro it's all too vulgar: an oversized version of the ubiquitous laser-cut models that litter the design studios and classrooms. So close is Metropol Parasol to this crude artifact of digital production that one Facebook commentator likens it to Claes Oldenburg's oversized reproductions of familiar objects. Notwithstanding the paradoxical notion that Metropol Parasol may be an ironic imitation of a model that represents Metropol Parasol, the fact remains that the naked presentation

ABOVE. Metropol Parasol, rooftop

of the means of digital productions is seen a letdown: too much of an artifact and lacking in art.

In 1887, the Eiffel Tower offended for similar reasons, not because it was radical or strange but because it reproduced the all-too-familiar language of utility. Architecture is expected to transform and elevate such bare fact with artful elaboration. The literal presentation of the digital

sampling technique in Metropol Parasol may be too "easy." But much like the naked iron of the Eiffel Tower, its brutality is likely to become iconic. And no matter how familiar and ubiquitous the laser-cut waffle model, this supersized iteration still captures most eloquently the digital aesthetic in the tension between the ineffable form and its rational quantification. Metropol Parasol is a landmark for Seville as much as a monument to the digital.

TRANSCRIPT OF DEBATE ON FACEBOOK, BEGINNING APRIL 15, 2011:

RODOLPHE EL-KHOURY
Jürgen's tour de force in Seville ... gorgeous!

JONATHAN MANZO Is this a permanent or temporary installation?
April 5, 2011 at 4:36pm · Like

PHIL HENRICKS that looks amazing
April 5, 2011 at 5:36pm · Like

VAIRA HARIK Darn! I was in Seville last March and didn't see it!
April 5, 2011 at 6:02pm · Like

NADIA BENABID How beautiful!
April 5, 2011 at 6:08pm · Like

RODOLPHE EL-KHOURY *@Jonathan:* temporary installation? at that scale? more like Seville's attempt at a "Bilbao effect."
April 5, 2011 at 6:34pm · Like

MARK ANTHONY That is stunning!!!
April 5, 2011 at 9:09pm · Like

AZIZA CHAOUNI magnifique!
April 5, 2011 at 10:15pm · Like

SATU MAARIA Hanhirova wild!
April 6, 2011 at 2:15am · Like

KEVIN WEISS It is undeniably beautiful! For me it does put into question the difference between architecture or sculpture.
April 6, 2011 at 7:30am · Like

RODOLPHE EL-KHOURY Kevin Weiss like the Eiffel Tower?
April 6, 2011 at 9:55am · Like

KEVIN WEISS dirigables will dock here?
April 6, 2011 at 11:38am · Like

JOHN SHNIER I think it looks transparent ... that is at this point the trope of egg-crate rhino undulating fastened plates ... while it is no doubt "remarkable" in its context ... it is dated and therefore its beauty is somewhat lost on me ... overruled by its somewhat heavy-handed caracture of digi-architectural form ...
April 6, 2011 at 7:13pm · Like

JOHN SHNIER or ... in otherwords ... like a giant first-year laser cut object
April 6, 2011 at 7:14pm · Like

KEVIN WEISS John No Holds Barred Shnier
April 6, 2011 at 7:17pm · Like

RODOLPHE EL-KHOURY *@John:* true. And that's precisely why it's so good: the naked fact of digital production monumentalized. Brilliant.
April 6, 2011 at 7:25pm · Like

JOHN SHNIER well .... c'mon;
April 6, 2011 at 7:28pm · Like

JOHN SHNIER @Rudy I think the pictures of Genghis Kat are far more beautiful ...
April 6, 2011 at 7:36pm · Like · 1

RODOLPHE EL-KHOURY The Eiffel Tower reference is appropriate—not only to challenge Kevin's implicit dismissal. It was widely condemned when it was built as an unmediated expression of the crude facts of steel construction. Jürgen went through different versions, all more intricately detailed before reducing

the design to the "indexical" crate. It was actually a process of refinement that led to this—Jürgen, when do I get my fee
April 6, 2011 at 7:48pm · Like

KEVIN WEISS I suppose the analogy of Eiffel can be furthered. The tower was meant to be the naked fact of engineering yet the base arches which are arguably what makes the thing elegant were a cave in to more conservative aesthetic values. Perhaps the uneasiness of the object is that there is no tension. John's harsh "first year" statement makes sense in regards to this.
April 6, 2011 at 7:59pm · Like

JOHN SHNIER Just saying Rudy, that Office dA's early restaurant interiors demonstrated this technique ten years ago. I remember seeing earlier images of this project ... if it is as you say the result of the original being paired down to the "naked engineering truth" then a more appropriate analogue would be say the re-presentation of the Statue of Liberty ... minus the figurative ... wrapping. But I suspect that in that case, the naked truth would be far more compelling, as the skeleton of the Statue of Liberty is both more interdependent than and more abstract with respect to what it is stripped from than what the featured project here might be.
April 6, 2011 at 8:16pm · Like

RODOLPHE EL-KHOURY *@john:* here is one of several earlier versions:
http://img17.imageshack.us/i/encarnacion5.jpg/
April 7, 2011 at 12:10am · Like

JOHN SHNIER yup ... he earlier iterations were perhaps 1 or 2 degrees of separation from the naked truth ... as this thread suggests ... whether we are more beautiful naked than cloaked is an open ended discussion ... thanks for sharing the link and congratulations to Jürgen for his achievement ... as I said remarkable in its very presence.
April 7, 2011 at 12:42am · Like

SHANE WILLIAMSON I am with Rodolphe on this one. I like the Claes Oldenburg take on the egg crate.
April 8, 2011 at 2:22pm · Like

JOHN SHNIER hmmm. I thought of Oldenburg as well ... except for me there is an important distinction here ... when Oldenburg did a giant rubber hamburger it WAS a hamburger; this is a large tectonic structure with egg-crate-like qualities; it is not an egg crate nor does it represent anything other than the tectonic of an egg crate which may be a referent to a tectonic or structurally trope ... as such it may succeed in fulfilling an objective that at least in some part is about space making and form making. This it does with great bravado ... but it does so in my mind without the whimsy, or irony that my be attributal to a giant sculpture that

attempts to represent or simulate its "other" self. It is what it is ... to me its biggest success that it actually exists as an extra ordinary project.
April 8, 2011 at 3:45pm · Like

SHANE WILLIAMSON Yep, I knew that when I mentioned Oldenburg that I was opening myself up for this very valid criticism. My thoughts are that the laser cutting is pretty much like a hamburger It's not an object but it's certainly a well worn trope in our world.
April 8, 2011 at 3:53pm · Like

JOHN SHNIER that I can most certainly agree with—and hence my very first comment.
April 8, 2011 at 3:55pm · Like

JOHN SHNIER I am still flummoxed that something like that can be built in the middle of a place like Seville but anything close to that ambition here would be a non-starter unless it were indeed by Oldenburg ... and then with our luck, we would get the very worst Oldenburg one could imagine ... what ever that might be.
April 8, 2011 at 3:56pm · Like

RODOLPHE EL-KHOURY @John: How about a laser-cut egg-crate model of an Oldenburg sculpture blown up to 1:1 scale?
April 8, 2011 at 6:32pm · Like

JOHN SHNIER which sculpture? if it is actually of a giant egg crate ... I'm in!!!!
April 8, 2011 at 6:36pm · Like

ROBERT LEVIT I don't get the either the Oldenburg or Eiffel Tower analogy. The whole point of the Oldenburg is that it is a giant version of an ordinary object —burger, clothespin, etc.—you can't have a giant version of an egg crate assembly, it dosen't have a proper size to begin with so you can't have a giant version in the same way. If you want to argue that it is habitually a certain size in model-making production it is a habitual practice apparent to a much narrower audience than the giant sized objects Oldenburg transformed.
April 11, 2011 at 7:54am · Like

ROBERT LEVIT It would be a more appropriate comparison if the egg crate were used to make a giant hamburger. The loopy shapes of Jürgen have no proper size that can be shrunk or enlarged—they just are whatever they are.
April 11, 2011 at 7:55am · Like

ROBERT LEVIT I also don't think the idea of a naked digi form makes much sense either. There is no such think as a naked digi form. There are conventions of modeling and drawing associated with digi form and its translation into physical models, which means the building is like a representation of architecture used

in the studio. It is a built representation. It is not like the Eiffel Tower because the constraints on this form of representation are so few compared to those of structurally engineered forms. Conservative or not, the arch, and frame of the Eiffel Tower have to resolve much more than the egg crate or the tesselation patterns of flattened curvature in mesh models. The problem with the digiform that Rodolphe speaks of is that like such phenomenon as the Voronoi/Delaunay triangles patterns of recent popularity, their virtue and finally weakness for architecture is that they are so flexible as to provide no discipline, no intellectual interest to the solution of a problem. The mud of mud pies. Compare the egg crate or the general behaviour of Voronois to the unique geometrical solution used in the Beijing Watercube.
April 11, 2011 at 8:07am · Like

ROBERT LEVIT So, the Digi form that Rodolphe talks of reminds me of the ways in which architects used to be so excited by the confused tangle of unhidden lines in a digital model that such skeins appaeared on the cover of their books. It is not much different that the translation of an architect's scribble into built form (think of early Coop Himmelblau). Not to my mind anything like the Eiffel Tower or like the Watercube. So either you like such things or not. The concrete construction of an architect's arbitrary musings. Regardless of how many times it is redrawn.
April 11, 2011 at 8:12am · Like

ROBERT LEVIT BTW I am not sure why the question of whether something has been done before matters. Ten years ago or 200, the question is whether it bears repeating.
April 11, 2011 at 8:18am · Like · 1

SHANE WILLIAMSON ".... it is a habitual practice apparent to a much narrower audience than the giant-sized objects Oldernburg transformed."—agreed.
April 11, 2011 at 8:37am · Like

RODOLPHE EL-KHOURY Robert, the egg-crate form is a product of the sampling technique that defines the digital: slices of data at specified frequencies instead of the contiuous flow of the analogue. The egg-crate is simply low-resolution —crude—sampling and definitely an artifact of the digital.
April 11, 2011 at 12:57pm · Like

ROBERT LEVIT It is and it isn't. It and tesselation preceded the digital. Think of topo models from the 80s. In any case to the extent it is tied to curvature it is a frictionless product like the tessalation of rendering meshes. Just as any dot array can be used to generate a Voronoi. There is no friction between pattern and figure—no problems.
April 11, 2011 at 1:06pm · Unlike · 2

RODOLPHE EL-KHOURY The laser-cut models you are refering to, which indeed have a very narrow audience, are but one manifestation of digital sampling techniques. The low resolution sampling in Jürgen's project is in my mind both, a brute and naked expression of the digital means of production and a symbol of the digital.
April 11, 2011 at 1:10pm · Like

RODOLPHE EL-KHOURY Robert, no forms are entirely new; they still can flourish when they resonate with new technology or ideas.
April 11, 2011 at 1:18pm · Like

ROBERT LEVIT Ah, you are trying to enlist me Rodolphe by describing the convergence of the naked expression of means AND the symbolic expression of this means. My argument against all claims on behalf of uncamouflaged insturments.

But it is a means that is so flexible, just as with the b-spline, which has a complex mathematics underlying it, the flexibility of such math, like that of the mesh or egg crate gives rise to such hugely flexible results that the forms pose no intellectual challenges no matter how complex the under-the-hood computation may be.
April 11, 2011 at 1:23pm · Like

SHANE WILLIAMSON The fact remains that this is an extraordinary parasol regardless of its underlying methodology, no? Even with methodology considered, I can think of nothing comparable in scale or execution which, again, makes it extraordinary.
April 12, 2011 at 3:30pm · Like

JOHN SHNIER I certainly would agree with Shane's comments ... but would add that thought its formal conceits are much different and without bringing up programme (other than its role as a parasol, it strikes me that from a certain perspective, urbanistically, this project is a riff on the Social Urban Condenser propositions solicited by the Krier brothers, that proliferated and were so influential in speculating on urban form in the 70s .
April 14, 2011 at 9:58am · Like

JOHN SHNIER ... and I suppose, it may or may not matter (?) whether or not it's appearance is in part generated by parameters that take into consideration how it might optimize its form to enable that it act effectively as a parasol/umbrella
April 14, 2011 at 6:29pm · Like

RODOLPHE EL-KHOURY *@john:* it's more than shade. it's a mixed-use program with shops, restaurant, and public amenities.
April 14, 2011 at 6:48pm · Like

JOHN SHNIER as was Krier's urban condensers ... they actually contained housing and mixed use ... not merely shopping and look-outs ... not that there is anything wrong about shopping and look outs. One of the main questions a project like this raises is "why displace any portion other ground plane?". What does this say about the trajectory of public space? This is an interesting question as well ... is the ground place saturated as a public urban realm; does elevating public space literally elevate the public ... ennoble people and create a shared privileged experience that. Does elevating truly elevate ... sometimes something can be just cool ... or as you said when you openned up the thread, "simply gorgeous" but as this thread suggests, our responses are not content to accept that simplicity ... or if we are content to do so ... we do so even as we may feel provoked or inspired to talk about it.
April 14, 2011 at 9:25pm · Like

NADER TEHRANI @ schnier and rudi: Not a hamburger! Its a waffle, in need of syrup. Or should I say soaked in syrup? Soaked so much, that, in turn, it has inflated. I saw some reference to Office dA above ... dated indeed, so 90. Still, as I tried to argue to Jürgen, the piece offers no resistance between the part and whole, the whole project that we attempted to undertake. There is no attempt here to reconcile the the relationship between the configuration of its parts to the overall figure. In that sense, it is "easy," even if hard to achieve at a technical level. Still, I am impressed at how impressed I am with it, despite all my earlier suspicions. The surreal still has an impact, or is it scale? What is unacceptable however, are the socks on the legs. It undermines the very idea of the piece! If the parasol is to read as a single, it has to meet the ground without mediation, even puncture the base. The socks are a no go!
April 17, 2011 at 6:12pm · Like · 1

ABOVE. Metropol Parasol, aerial view
LEFT. Metropol Parasol, viewed from a side street

– RE-FASHIONING THE ROOF: WEATHER AND SOCIAL FORM*

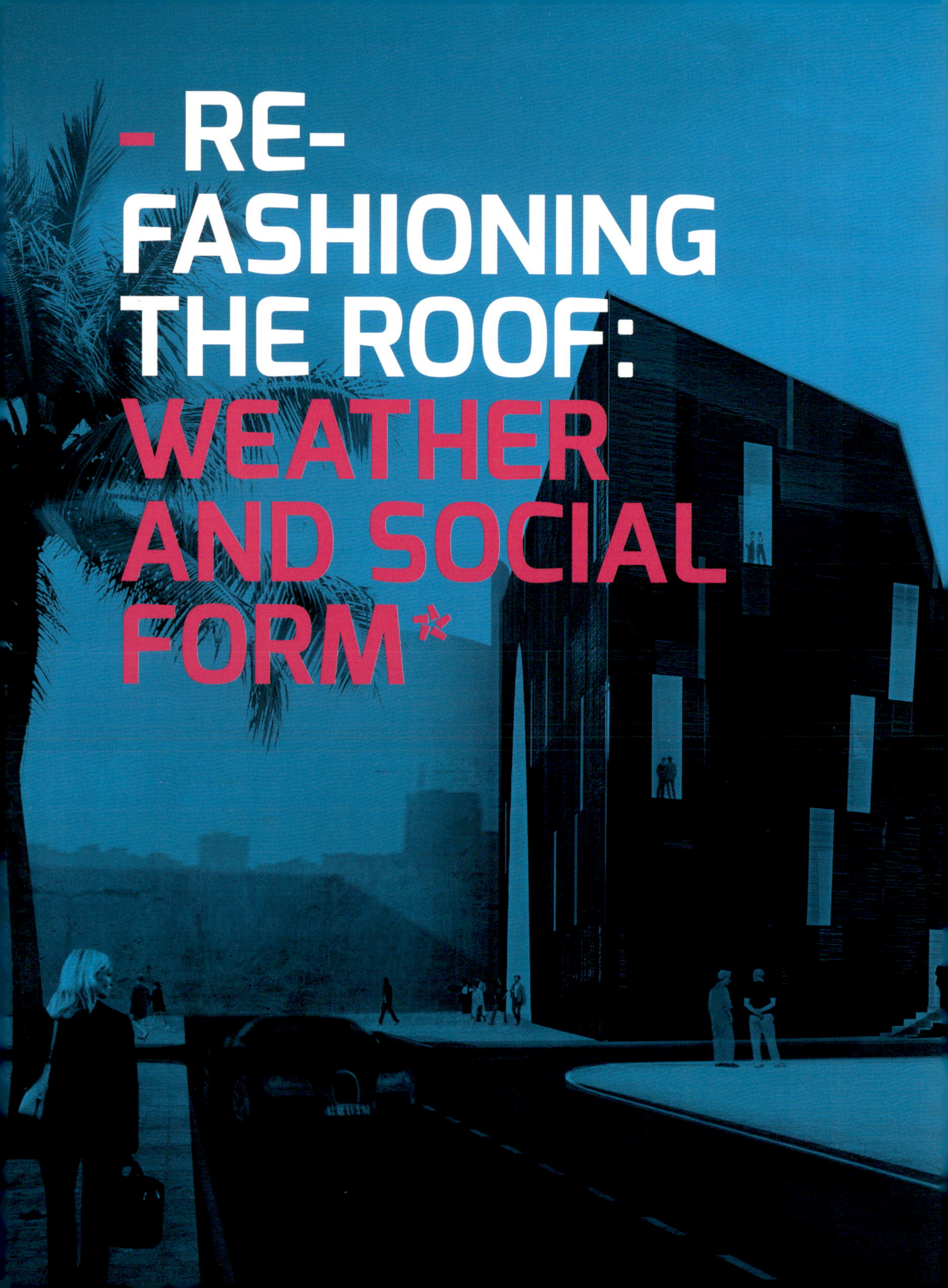

ORIGINALLY PUBLISHED IN NEERAJ BHATIA AND JÜRGEN MAYER H., **ARIUM: WEATHER AND ARCHITECTURE**, HATJE KANTZ, 2010.

*WRITTEN IN COLLABORATION WITH ROBERT LEVIT

THE FORM OF THE ROOF IN ARCHITECTURE is a remarkably embattled arena: a site of orthodoxies, censure, and rebellions. This thought is verified simply by turning one's attention to the pitched roof. But let us for an instant put aside polemics and recall that the roof has historically been shaped by, amongst several other forces, its responsiveness to weather. Modern technology which solves various problems of climate and humidity control by means of new building materials and methods has underplayed this environmental link, allowing the flat roof to prevail for reasons that are symbolic as much as functional. A growing environmental awareness is now drawing the roof out from the aesthetic conformism of flatness into figures of greater visibility. The roof is increasingly valued, not merely as a repository for expensive air-conditioning machinery but most importantly as an environmental interface that manages and exploits the energies unleashed by weather.

Weather and climate have significant roles in shaping our work. Their influence is most legible in the articulation of various roof structures designed to capture, modulate, filter, amplify, and channel air and light.

Liwan Bayrut is shaped by two superimposed thin-shell concrete vaults that are joined like Siamese twins at an occulus-like aperture where their surfaces intertwine in a spiraling ramp. The bottom vault extends the public realm deep into and through the building. The top one inverts the sheltering form of the dome into a bowl-shaped theater. Its figure gathers people in a form oriented towards the pleasures of the sky. Its orientation and shape optimize the performance of photovoltaic cells embedded in its south facing slope while sheltering the opposite's face and its integrated stadium seating from the low angle of the late afternoon sun. The draped and curved form draw together figurative and social ambitions with environmental and technological innovations: the roof is an iconic form (dome/bowl/theater), a place of social action (gathering and performance), an efficient solar interface combining active and passive devices (solar energy collection and shading), and a feat of structural technique (the bowl is a tensile net of steel and concrete).

In a proposal for the city of Phoenix, we developed a ceramic football-shaped tile as the versatile core of citywide shading strategies.[1] Light yet robust, it is designed to be strung like beads on cables and suspended over public space in a variety of structural configurations and shading scenarios. The strung ball-tiles can hang by cables from concrete columns along sidewalks as well as in park settings. They can also shade public alleys or small urban squares by attaching directly to the sides of buildings. The perforated ball-tiles come in a variety of designs and colors to achieve multiple compositional and environmental ambitions. Variations include embedded photovoltaic cells, motion sensors, and LEDs allowing tiles to function as autonomous and responsive light sources. At night they glow in patterns of color controlled interactively by sensors responsive to movement and any number of programmable inventions. In this project the materiality of the ceramic ball-tiles and their simple molded production coincide with the economy and simplicity of vernacular traditions of molded roof tiles. These tiles are able to draw upon experiences of common familiarity while doing so in a manner that refashions this familiar material according to up-to-date and emerging technologies—technologies that are themselves reshaping our experience of ourselves as an urban public.

In the Malana Learning Center, Hawaii, we capitalized in a similar fashion on vernacular forms and means of construction to economically achieve ambitious environmental, social, and symbolic goals.[2] We deployed an array of prefabricated butler-building-framed canopies into a vast superstructure that softens weather conditions and envelops the building and spaces below in a microclimate. The superstructure is fine-tuned to regulate sunlight, wind, sound, and water and deforms to better perform in particular situations: it folds down into a vertical sunshade along the eastern elevation and gently bends into an acoustical shell above the stage, dramatically framing the open-air theater—the social heart of the institution. The saw-tooth pattern, layout, and orientation of the roof is meant to optimize shading, ventilation, and waterproofing/collection while still yielding views to the mountains and northern sky, the most dramatic features of the site.

The project for Beirut's Martyrs' Square also proposes a weather modulating roofmostlydevotedtoshadingthehistoricsquare.Theprojectisateemingarray ofmetalpanelsthatfloatoverheadsupportedonlightbranchingcolumns.The pattern of the roof tiles shifts from precise regularity to chaotic aggregation.

RIGHT. Shading infrastructure for the city of Phoenix

[1] *The shading proposal for Phoenix is a project by Khoury Levit Fong and Kuth Ranieri Architects submitted to an international ideas competition.*

[2] *The proposals for the Malama Learning Center, Hawaii, and Martyrs' Square, Beirut, are projects by Kuth Ranieri Architects and Rodolphe el-Khoury submitted to international design competitions.*

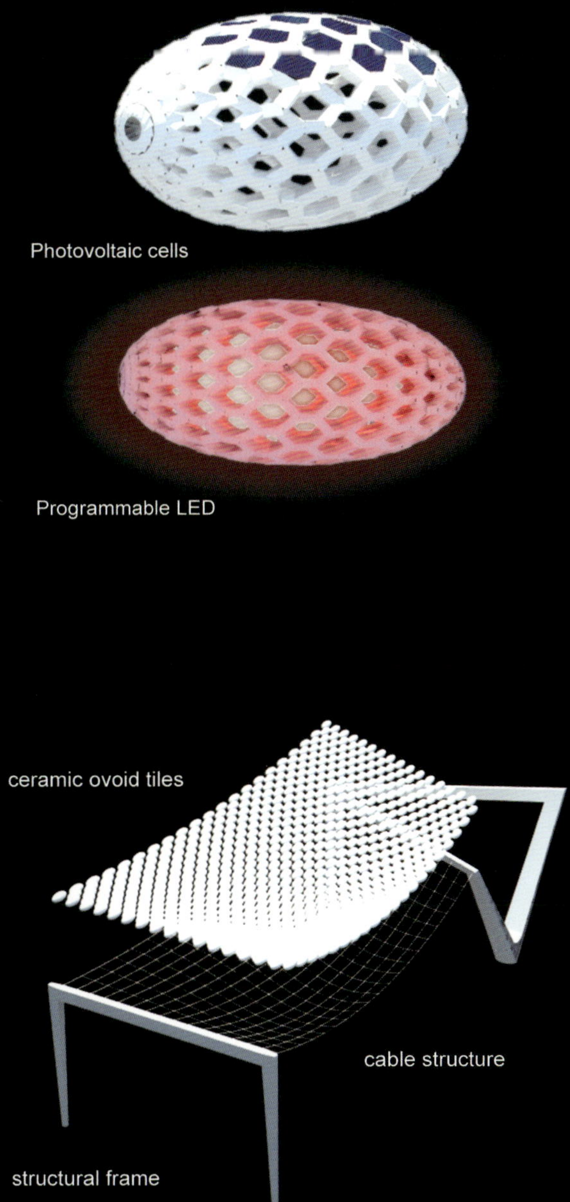
Photovoltaic cells
Programmable LED
ceramic ovoid tiles
cable structure
structural frame

"A growing environmental awareness is now drawing the roof out from the aesthetic conformism of flatness into figures of greater visibility."

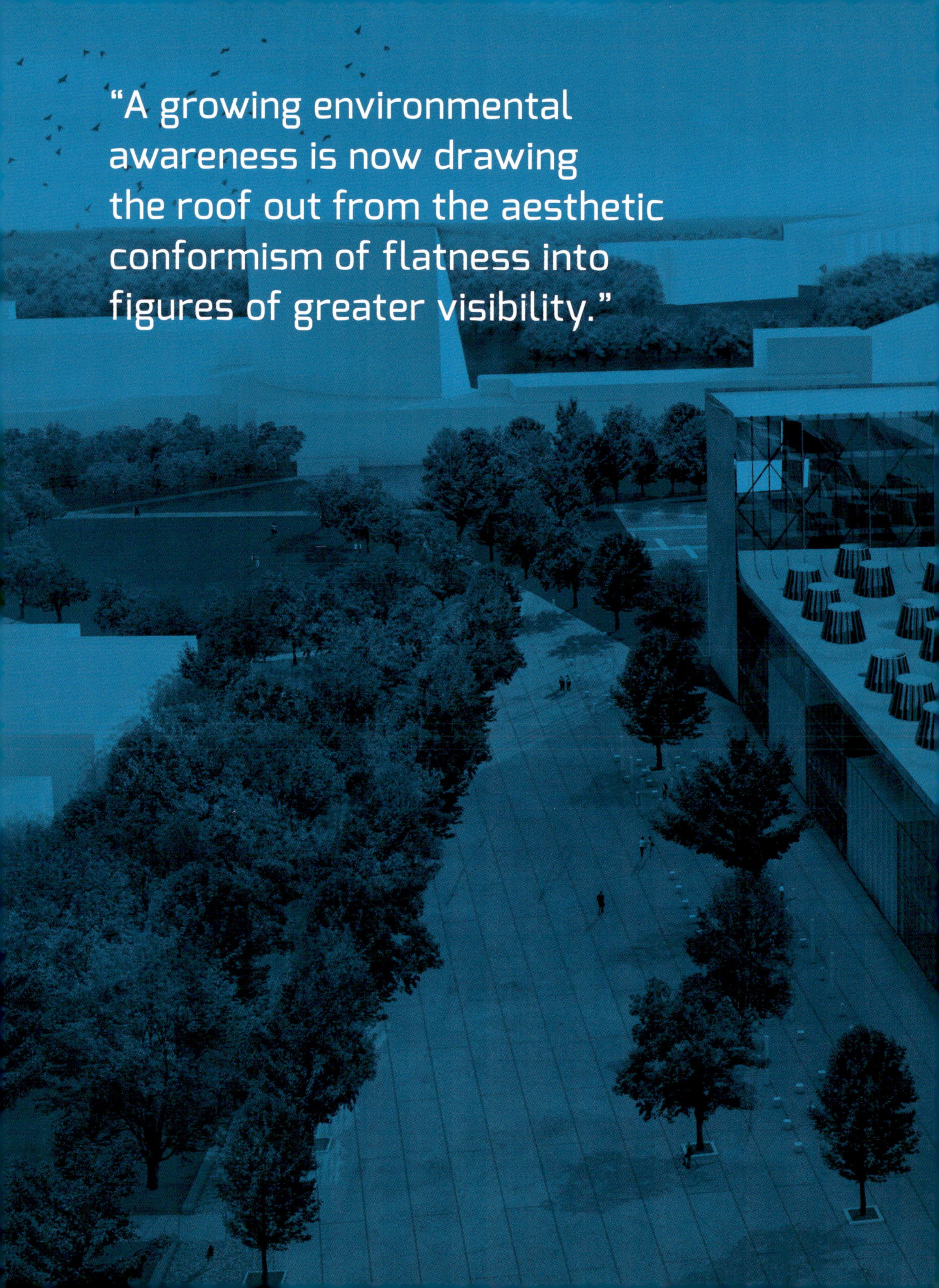

ABOVE. Shading infrastructure for the city of Phoenix

Moments of calm order coincide with programmed amenities that benefit from optimized and sustained protection from sun and rain while turbulence disrupts the programmatic and environmental logic of the roof to expose symbolically charged instances such as archeological vestiges and memorials open to the sky. The roof permits the freedom of social forms to occur in an architecture that is itself a framework open as much to the social world as it is to the weather from which it selectively shelters us. At the busiest intersection, the canopy opens into a larger circular swirl that defines an urban room, reproducing in the very device of its patterning the figure through which to encompass the gathering of the urban crowd.

Now, let us turn to some polemical questions:

Enemy camps have formed around the question of the roof in modern architecture. Le Corbusier's "five points" created a new world on the roof: more than habitable, his roof, solariums, pools, and concrete landscapes were a theater for his figures of Mediterranean health.

But also the flatness became an emblem in itself of modernism's distinction from historical idioms of architecture even if one suspects that flatness, as in many generational battles, simply leapt over a (parental) generation to identify with the geometrical purity of neoclassical grandparents. In any case, at some point, the use of roof figures became an impossible breach of conscience for generation after generation of architects. Alvar Aalto figured out a way around the dilemma, extruding his figured plan forms and cutting at angles to create unprecedented profiles. Whatever iconic value Aalto derived from these operations, and however they might invite censure from an ethic still dictated by modernist phobias about symbolic form, he could always counter that his forms were derived from the more acceptable circumstances of plan form.

Today, roof and profile are back, but often enough through the exercise of a willful arbitrariness. The refashioning in consciousness of symbol as logo lends a patina of contemporaneity to formerly censured forms of iconicity. By borrowing from the world of logos and branding architects also accept, even delight in the pleasures, and finally, in the limits of the arbitrary form (Big, Plot, OMA). Authorial expressionism, such as that of Frank Gehry, presents a corollary phenomenon to the arbitrary logo-like profiles of shape architecture. Artistic expression, arbitrary in its own fashion, shares with logo what for modernist ethics is a freedom from conventional symbolic forms and from historical idioms of architecture.

The interest that logo architecture and expressionist practices take in the return of the roof profile is something that we share. However, we are also invested in the roof as a habitable realm, a condition that played so central a role in Le Corbusier's "five points." And even more pointedly we are committed to the relationship between roof and climactic setting that withdrew in favor of a disavowed conformity to stylistic orthodoxy. In Liwan Bayrut we have made a building figure in which a very plastic roof form is created. This form possesses the iconicity of the logo, yet it is not arbitrary. It is a theater, a roman bowl, structural in character (a tensile net), and energy efficient in its geometry and orientation. It is an intense social form whose shape is the shape of the roof. Its archaic familiarity and its technical modernity combine with its provision for a real social invention germane to a contemporary institution.

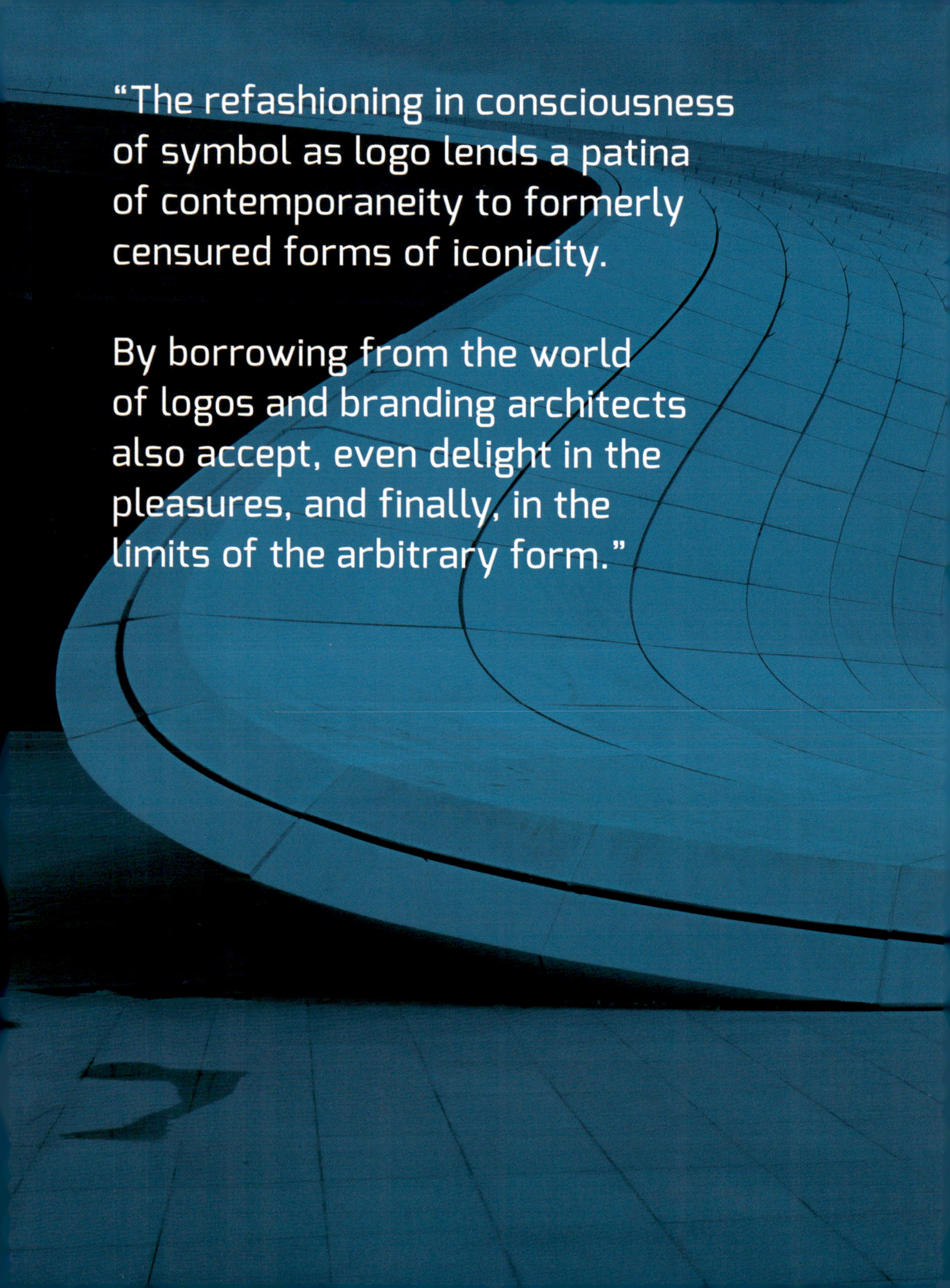

"The refashioning in consciousness of symbol as logo lends a patina of contemporaneity to formerly censured forms of iconicity.

By borrowing from the world of logos and branding architects also accept, even delight in the pleasures, and finally, in the limits of the arbitrary form."

ABOVE. Martyrs' Square: canopy for bus station

Likewise in the Phoenix sun-shading infrastructure and in Beirut's Martyrs' Square we have sought to combine technical innovation with iconographic intent. And, we eschew what we consider an erroneous distinction between socially and environmentally performative architectural form and symbolic form, which means that we consider these works to

be equally committed to an environmentally responsible shaping of social experience as they are to providing symbolic forms of the social world they hope to make. In aligning these goals our work escapes from the collapse of practice into the immaterial discursive forms of the logo and of technique into a self-unaware and thus benighted form of technicality.

- NEXT: IT'S ABOUT TIME

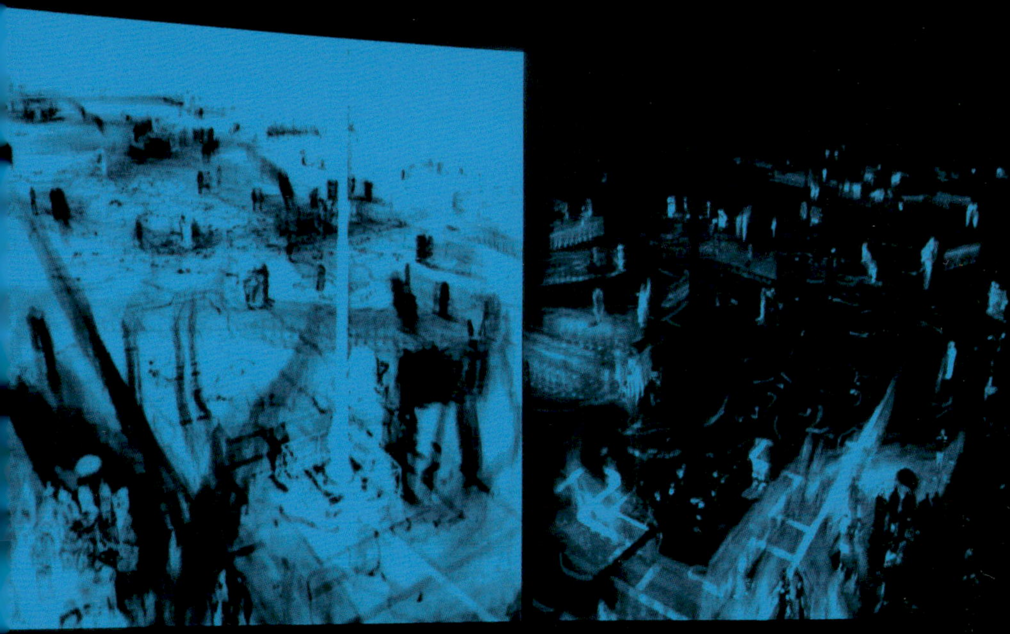

ORIGINALLY PUBLISHED IN **NEXT MEMORY CITY—TORONTO: VENICE**, INTERACCESS, 2002.

THE CURATORS OF THE CANADIAN EXHIBITION in the 2002 Venice Architecture Biennale have taken a risk. The work they selected by Michael Awad, Eve Egoyan, and David Rokeby would make a lavish, winning contribution to any art show, but their frugality with literal architectural content is bound to raise more than a few eyebrows.

The architects are the most conspicuous omission. With the notable exception of Awad, the show features artists who have had but a marginal investment in architecture. The fact that they are interested in the city as subject matter doesn't bring them any closer to the discipline than a Manet or a Canaletto.

The unconventional choices may be taken to reflect an ambition for interdisciplinary breadth. But this is not the kind of show where architects hope to expand their scope with timid excursions beyond disciplinary boundaries. This one brings artwork, done by artists, to an architectural arena. It confronts architecture directly with something external, alien.

The virtual spaces of video and sound installation are familiar and, of course, welcome in a show on architecture. They are by now regular extensions of the "built environment." In a media-saturated world, the assumption that architecture primarily deals with physical objects is no longer tenable. It is increasingly hard to think of buildings independently of magazines, television shows, video games, and surveillance cameras that alter and process them for consumption. The urbanity delivered in sitcoms like *Seinfeld* and *Friends* often precedes and inevitably inflects the experience of the "real" city. These shows have in fact been credited for the urban renaissance in North American cities; like a TV commercial, and far more effectively than buildings, they have sold the city to suburban consumers.

ABOVE. Michael Awad, Chinatown

ABOVE. Stills from David Rokeby's video projection

The pieces by Awad, Egoyan, and Rokeby inent new forms of mediation to construct a different experience of the city. They demonstrate a capacity to design and control the reception as much as the production of the urban environment. The show suggests a series of potential shifts in architectural discourse—from fabrication to inhabitation, things to phenomena, promising a refreshing relief from the tyranny of the object and of formal innovation.

This is not to underestimate the formal ambitions of the show. The curators/artists have capitalized on the curving perspective of the Canadian Pavilion to orchestrate an animated sequence of visual and aural effects. The rhetoric of the avilion and the installation combined deliver a riveting mise-en-scène of urbanity. An architectural tour de force in its own right that speaks of the dynamic and complex nature of cities, if not of Toronto and Venice specifically.

But if there is a critical edge to this show, beyond a skillful deployment of unconventional media in the staging of urban atmospherics, it would have to be sought in the temporal rather than spatial features—features that are not readily recognized as architectural.

There are no buildings to speak of in Michael Awad's Chinatown. They have vanished behind the iconic red-and-white streetcars of Spadina Avenue and some pedestrians in the foreground. The monumental figure of Plaza San Marco is outstaged in David Rokeby's video projection where only moving objects are highlighted by means of digital processing. The installation by Eve Egoyan and Rokeby is strictly aural. Any building here would have to be inferred from the acoustical qualities of the soundscape.

Where static building masses are muted, evanescent characteristics of the living city are emphasized. This is most evident in Awad's work. His innovative technique reverses expectations inherent to photography—whose camera obscura origins are partial to immobility: anything moving is in sharp focus while the static is blurred beyond recognition. This is a consistent device in the show that defamiliarizes the ephemeral and fluid features of the city by imparting to them the kind of presence and solidity that is expected of architecture. The device is particularly effective in enhancing the perception of change in Rokeby's "Seen." All change, even as minute as in a pigeon's flight across the square, is picked up and registered in pyrotechnic trajectories. "Seen" is a documentation of time rather than space.

"It is now possible to expand on recent investments in program, event, and scenario, to think of time as a workable medium where one could manipulate the vital but elusive fluidity of the city."

This show must then be recognized as a provocation: an assault on the hegemony of space, and the concomitant occularcentrism. It challenges the domination of space as both, the self-evident medium and all-inclusive subject of architecture.

Time has made sporadic and not so challenging appearances in architectural theory and practice, such as in radical instances of the picturesque and the cubism-inspired experiments of modernism. But only recently have new media and technology begun to provide the tools that would allow designers to engage it dynamically. With Awad, Egoyan, and Rokeby, it is now possible to expand on recent investments in program, event, and scenario, to think of time as a workable medium where one could manipulate the vital but elusive fluidity of the city.

In an age where space offers no resistance to communication, and when efficiency is measured in lag time and processor speed, architecture is poised for the conquest of time, the next frontier.

ABOVE. Still from David Rokeby's video installation

- BEIRUT/ TOKYO

ORIGINALLY PUBLISHED IN **PROJECTING BEIRUT: EPISODES IN THE CONSTRUCTION AND RE-CONSTRUCTION OF A MODERN CITY**, PETER ROWE AND HASHIM SARKIS, EDS. PRESTEL, 2007.

"THE CITY I AM TALKING ABOUT OFFERS this precious paradox: it does possess a center, but this center is empty." The city is Tokyo and the statement is Roland Barthes's. I quote it from his quasi-utopian account of Japan in *Empire of Signs*. I say utopian because Barthes does not approach the Orient as a reality that can be contracted historically and politically to the West, but rather as a reserve of features whose inventive manipulation allows him to entertain the idea of an unprecedented symbolic system: the center of the European city is always full, it is the site of truth, where the values of civilizations are condensed. In Tokyo, where the urban traffic is forced into a perpetual detour around the imperial residence, and in the visible form of invisibility that conceals the indifferent monarch, the "sacred nothing," Barthes can entertain the notion of a voided center, a city where "the system of the imaginary is spread circularly, by detours and returns the length of an empty subject."[1]

Barthes's utopia may well have been realized in Beirut, quite fittingly in a city which has historically negotiated—and frustrated—the extremes of Orientalist fantasy. In Beirut's city center, where once the busiest and densest structures stood, now lies an empty field. For the last few years it has attracted crowds of curious Beirutis and held the attention of international media. Visitors to the city center have yet to exhaust their fascination with this dusty field. Some are supposedly interested in the ancient artifacts that archaeologists and bulldozers have recently found. Others are interested in the development of the Central Business District; they come to survey what PR slogans have promoted as the largest construction site in the world. In fact, Beirut's BCD project is dwarfed by dozens of other developments across the globe. Do not be fooled by the subterfuge: their curiosity for the excavated past and the speculative future is an alibi for a morbid fixation on the scene of the absent center. The combined effects of thoroughly destructive warfare and equally uprooting reformulations of property law and zoning ordinances—namely, the forces of capital—have created a tabula rasa at the very heart of the city. This cleared ground has no discernible physical differentiation: all traces of streets and building masses are now erased. Also obliterated are the property lines, zoning envelopes, and other invisible but no less "real" demarcations which customarily determine or inflect urban morphologies. The homogeneity and superficial neutrality of this clear slate may have been compromised when the archaeological strata were exposed in the recent surveys. But the excavations finally participated, perhaps most effectively, in the systematic erasure

[1] *R. Barthes, Empire of Signs, Richard Howard, trans. (1982), 30-32.*

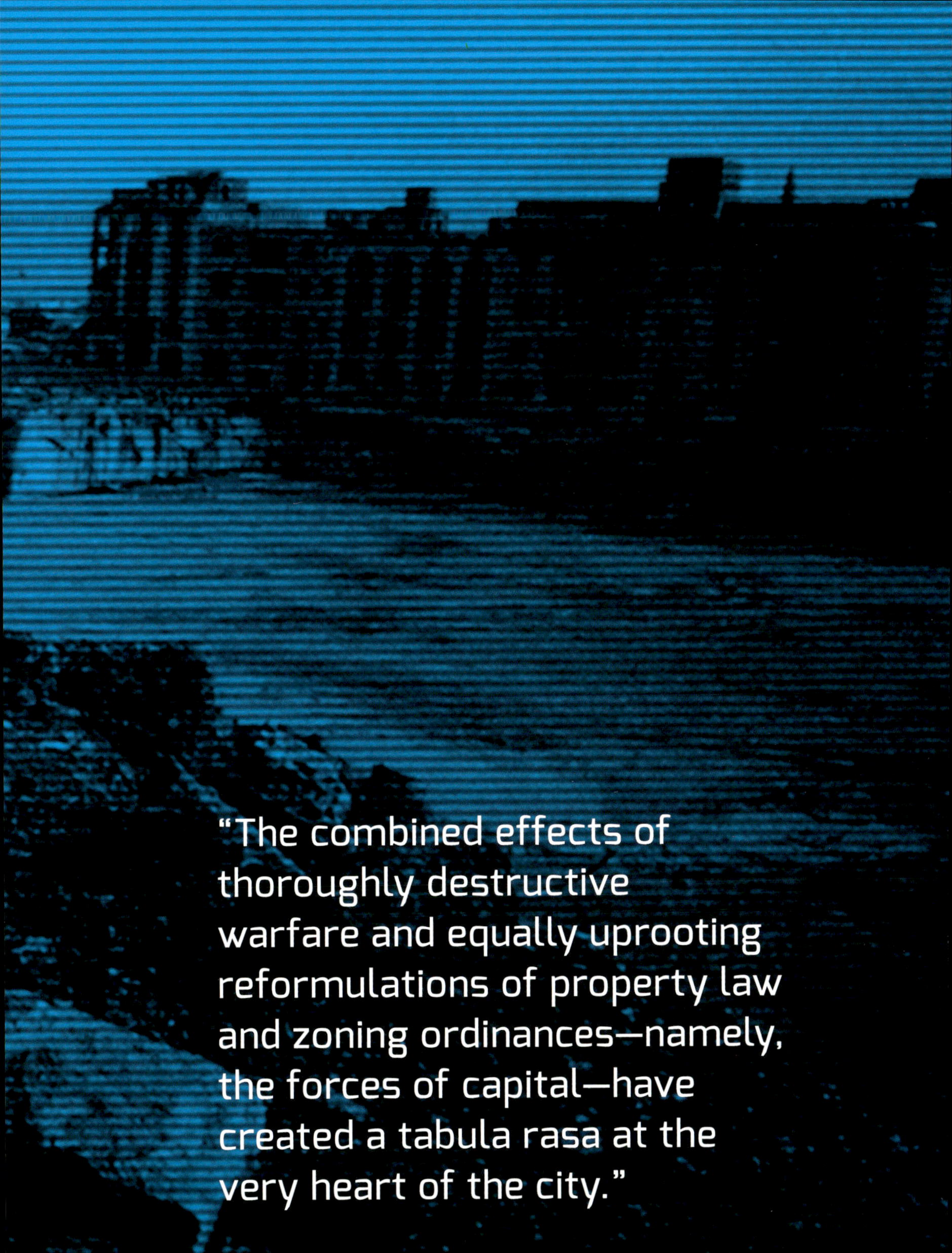

"The combined effects of thoroughly destructive warfare and equally uprooting reformulations of property law and zoning ordinances—namely, the forces of capital—have created a tabula rasa at the very heart of the city."

of modern Beirut by challenging the primacy of the surface, eventually replacing one ground with several others: by the time the survey is complete, the valuable artifacts collected, and the trenches filled up, the new ground will be artificial, and therefore arbitrary, abstract, and more vacant still (Fig 1).

Keeping in mind that the war period saw more building construction than actual destruction, and if reconstruction entails the systematic deployment of efforts and resources in the transformation of Beirut, we may then argue that the most radical if not substantial project in this process has already been realized in the "deconstruction" of the center. By deconstruction I mean literally a systematic dismantling of preexisting structures (physical, political, and legal); deconstruction also refers to the symbolic assault on the plenitude of the center. To go downtown, or to the city center, Barthes reminds us, is "to encounter the social 'truth,' to participate in the proud plenitude of 'reality.' " [2] This ritual persists in Beirut's city center but only in its inverted form. In today's Beirut, we go downtown to encounter another truth in the spectacle of a sublime emptiness.

The ritual engagement with the center, be it the positive participation in logos or the negative but still gratifying encounter with the sublime, may be altogether lost once this site is reclaimed for development. In fact, Beirut has survived for twenty-two years without its downtown and its centrifugal energy and is not about to waste its momentum, despite the efforts of planners, legislators, and investors. So no matter what we build on the site, be it the developer's fantasy of a miniature Manhattan where enclaves of wired office buildings will rival the inscrutability of Tokyo's walled precinct, or the nostalgic reconstruction of a vanished historical district where simulation can only hasten cultural degradation, losses will linger and indifference will grow.

But as long as this terrain vague persists in its vagueness, vacancy [3], and vagrancy, our Beirut could very well be Roland Barthes's Tokyo: we may see in the emptiness of the evacuated center the possibility of difference, of mutation, of a revolution in the propriety of symbolic systems. At the site of Beirut's sacrificial immolation, we may recognize an opportunity for the remorseless detournement of a negative yet liberating violence.

Beirut is dead; long live Beirut.

[2] *Ibid. 30.*

[3] *See I. de Solà-Morales, "Terrain Vague," in Quadems.*

ABOVE. Excavation for the reconstruction of the Beirut Souks

ABOVE. Downtown Beirut today

– MONOLITHIC ARCHITECTURE

ORIGINALLY PUBLISHED IN RODOLFO MACHADO AND RODOLPHE EL-KHOURY, **MONOLITHIC ARCHITECTURE**, PRESTEL VERLAG, 2005.

ONCE WHEN I WAS SIX YEARS OLD I saw a magnificent picture in a book, called *True Stories from Nature*, about the primeval forest. It was a picture of a boa constrictor in the act of swallowing an animal. Here is a copy of the drawing (image). In the book it said: "Boa constrictors swallow their prey whole, without chewing it. After that they are not able to move, and they sleep through the six months that they need for digestion." [1] I pondered deeply, then, over the adventures of the jungle. And after some work with a colored pencil I succeeded in making my first drawing. My Drawing Number One. It looked like this:

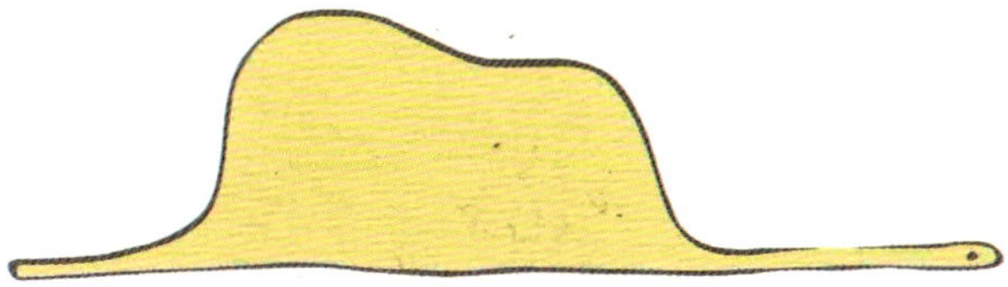

I showed my masterpiece to the grown-ups, and asked them whether the drawing frightened them. But they answered: "Frighten? Why should any one be frightened by a hat?"

My drawing was not a picture of a hat. It was a picture of a boa constrictor digesting an elephant. But since the grown-ups were not able to understand it, I made another drawing: I drew the inside of the boa constrictor, so that the grown-ups could see it clearly. They always need to have things explained. My Drawing Number Two looked like this:

[1] *A. de Saint-Exupéry, The Little Prince* (1982), 7-8.

A number of recent architectural works have converged on features and issues that, in our view, merit investigation. Some of these works have already acquired notoriety, due primarily to their strong physical presence in important urban settings. Most are still under construction or were never actually implemented in built form. Nevertheless, they circulate in drawings and model reproductions, yielding sporadic jolts of critical controversy with occasional appearances in various architectural journals. These buildings, at first glance, seem to have little in common; in fact, their blatant differences in shape, material, scale, and program could hardly warrant an exhibition claiming aesthetic coherence. Indeed, any attempt to identify common formal or stylistic traits across the emphatic individuality of these buildings is at best a contrived artifice and, more probably, a coercive imposition of conformity upon highly individuated expressions.

Yet, these buildings coincide in their extreme economy and simplicity of overall form and consistency of external appearance; also common is their capacity to deliver tremendous eloquence with very limited formal means. Some adopt straightforward, elementary configurations, while others limit more gestural impulses to a clear and single utterance. Sometimes, they construct their clarity with one or two bold spaces; more characteristically, they contain considerable planimetric and sectional complexities within strict volumetric restraint. All have a monolithic character that ostensibly defies current preoccupations with arbitrariness, shapelessness, fragmentation, and heterogeneity.

ABOVE. View of the unfinished obelisk which remains in its pharaonic quarry near Assuan, Egypt

ABOVE. Paul Virilio, World War II observation post on the Normandy coast. Reproduced from Paul Virilio, Bunker archéologie (Paris: Centre George Pompidou, 1975), p 103.

Such emphatic simplicity and consistency in the composition of the exterior evokes various episodes in the history of architecture. Yet, a consistent unorthodoxy in the treatment of building types, programs, materials, and technologies marks important distinctions and denies any particular or clear pedigree. It may be tempting to seek distant relatives to monolithic architecture among some (neo)classical, modernist, and (neo)rationalist architectures or even in non-Western building practices. But besides a common investment in the power of primary forms, obvious formal and ideological differences within monolithic architecture and with respect to such precedents problematize linear genealogies. For instance, this architecture does not articulate the part in relation to the whole as dictated by classical doctrine, nor does it avoid inconsistencies between exterior and interior character and disposition. Quite the contrary, most of the buildings gathered in this volume insist on such disjunctions, and, unlike much twentieth-century architecture, they are not compelled to externalize the complexity of the program in individuated iconographic or volumetric components, nor do they shy away from a mannerist confusion of structure and ornament. More critical is the distinction between the taciturn elementarism of modernism and the monodic poetry of the architectural monolith, between negational silence and rhetorical laconism. The simplicity of the architectural monolith does not aim at abstraction, nor does it share the minimalist aspiration to nonreferential objecthood. Rather, it seeks to maximize the expressive potential of common architectonic configurations by condensing their figurative allusions into one eloquent gesture.

ABOVE. Dominique Perrault, Bibliothèque Nationale de France, 1989, model. Reproduced from Dominique Perrault, Dominique Perrault (1994), p 52.

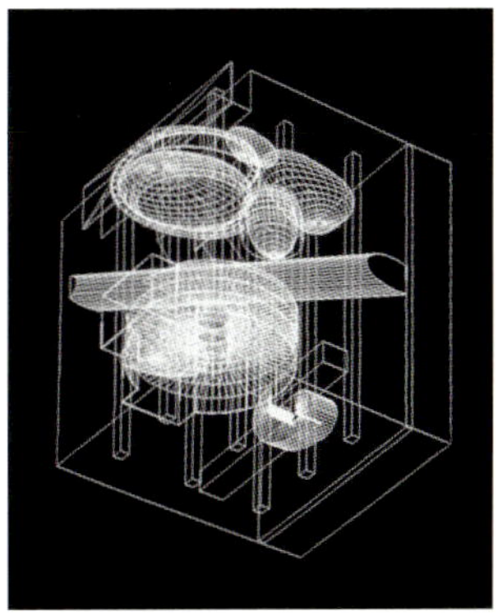

ABOVE. Rem Koolhaas, Bibliothèque Nationale de France (1989), computer-generated axonometric drawing. Courtesy Office for Metropolitan Architecture.

"The simplicity of the architectural monolith does not aim at abstraction, nor does it share the minimalist aspiration to nonreferential objecthood. Rather, it seeks to maximize the expressive potential of common architectonic configurations by condensing their figurative allusions into one eloquent gesture."

In short, a disdain for stylistic rigor, historical veracity, structural rectitude, or other claims at transcendence and authenticity clearly positions this architecture in the contemporary cultural arena, among other postmodern contestants that have embraced the schizophrenic tensions of culture and society. Monolithic architecture thrives in the unprecedented conditions of today's megalopolis. Its strategic schematism is calibrated to the specific urban and suburban conditions of late capitalist environments. It is sometimes tailored to the company of dignified buildings in so-called historical districts, places whose auras have the unfortunate tendency to inspire degrading spectacles of simulated authenticity from traditionalists and avant-gardists alike. However, the radical composure of monolithic architecture is most often customized for the challenging environments of consumerism. With its assumed gravity, it is meant to sober the strident gesticulations of neighboring buildings in congested city centers and to generate with its stubborn presence a sense of urbanity in more depleted surroundings.

Questions concerning success or failure at these ambitious tasks will be left aside for the moment, since there is no objective way to verify or falsify claims about the instrumentality of monolithic character in the construction of urbanity. In the context of this discussion, problems of representation are also of greater relevance than issues of construction and usage per se. We prefer to focus on tectonics rather than technology, and we will consider the program in its capacity to generate form and not in terms of functional efficiency. We wish to examine these buildings in their most radical aspect, as paradoxical representations: radical, in the sense that they self-consciously elaborate their monolithic character into an aesthetic strategy and carry it out to its extreme realization; paradoxical, in the sense that they undermine their own fixity and solidity when their lapidary countenance stands as something totally other with respect to internal and external realities, program, and context.

The stark muteness of the architectural monolith may have an alienating aspect; its hermetic consistency does not readily inspire sympathy nor facilitate empathy. But unlike the dumb boxes of commercial architecture—as epitomized by the American shopping mall—whose characteristic blankness is due to neglect, insensitivity, and financial economy, architectural monoliths are more egocentric than introverted, arrogant rather than aloof. Their external economy is achieved at the cost of formal and material excesses and calibrated for intended effects. We were struck

ABOVE. Christo and Jeanne-Claude, Wrapped Reichstag, 1971-1995

by their sudden and ponderous apparition among the volatile fragments of the collaged landscape, intrigued by their unexpected and sometimes scandalous pedigree (who would have expected Peter Eisenman to father such a fascinating "monster" as the Max Reinhardt Haus?). We have acquired a taste for their uncanny beauty and have also come to recognize their critical potential in reasserting the object in current architectural production at the moment of its proclaimed dispersal and evaporation in multicultural societies, digital technologies, and virtual realities.

RIGHT. Musical instrument cases

"The monolith that is not one stands out as a glitch, a disturbance within the dialectical logic and the corollary axiological dichotomies that continue to regulate the theoretical discourse in architecture and persistently sanction the emancipatory virtues of the formless as opposed to the totalizing and repressive authority of the 'formed,' the small to the big, the fragmented to the coherent,the transparent to the opaque, the irregular to the orthogonal."

ABOVE. "The Dawn of Man." Still from Stanley Kubrick (director), *2001: A Space Odyssey* (1968). Reproduced from Stanley Kubrick (director), *2001: A Space Odyssey* (MGM/UA Home Video).

ABOVE. Future Systems, The Green Building, 1990: montage. Photo: Richard Davies. Reproduced from L'Arca, September 1991, 62.

We like to consider the insistent and unapologetic "object-ness" of these buildings as a challenge to some conceptual habits and compositional clichés in the aesthetics of today's institutional avant-garde. The monolithic architectures examined in this volume and corollary exhibition blatantly transgress some of the formal principles now automatically associated with critical, emancipatory, or progressive architectural practices without having to retreat to conservative ideological positions or having to indulge a nostalgia for solidity, stability, and organic unity in relation to context. Simultaneously solid and hollow, uniform and heterogeneous, impregnable and permeable, foreign and familiar, the monolith that is not one stands out as a glitch, a disturbance within the dialectical logic and the corollary axiological dichotomies that continue to regulate the theoretical discourse in architecture and persistently sanction the emancipatory virtues of the formless as opposed to the totalizing and repressive authority of the "formed," the small to the big, the fragmented to the coherent, the transparent to the opaque, the irregular to the orthogonal.

We have gathered here a variety of buildings and projects under the banner of "monolithic architecture" in order to demonstrate different instances of its paradoxical representations. We do not intend to prescribe a coherent aesthetic from an exemplary body of work; we have faith, rather, in the diversity within the collection to keep stylistic claims and totalizing "isms" at bay—we are now all too aware of the marketing logic underlying the packaging of recent "isms" to indulge the complacency of their institutional legitimation. Desire, personal predilections, biases in taste no doubt have inflected the choice of examples and color this volume with a particular sensibility—a certain "style," one might argue. However, the investment—and the fascination—lies in the aberrant status of the architectural monoliths themselves, their extraordinary appearance in contemporary practice and within the oeuvre of particular architects. We present them as a set of isolated, but parallel anomalies rather than as the converging symptoms of a new tendency.

In the recent past, a number of exhibitions and publications have proposed various formal systems in an attempt to deal with the changing conditions of culture and society on the level of architectural representation. Such proposals have ranged from prescriptive demonstrations of compositional strategies and zeitgeist-invoking arguments about new styles and new spirits to theoretical critiques of representational codes and conventions. Operating with the persistent assumption that an authentic work reflects a real condition (material, cultural, or social) that is otherwise shrouded in ideology and inaccessible to consciousness (without the mediation of art), these proposals have promoted various architectonic systems by virtue of their reflective perspicacity: certain forms, modes of construction, or tectonics are better suited than others because their specular power can pierce through ideological veils to get at the "real." The real may be an unalienated essence that is symbolized organically in a regionalist idiom or, more fashionably, a heterogeneous nexus of contradictions and discontinuities which is translated in the conflictual fragments of an architectural collage. Regardless of content, ideology, and politics, the theoretical legitimations of the various styles coincide in their insistence on overlapping architectonic configurations with structures and narratives in nature and culture.

We make no such claims for architectural monoliths. Rather, we tend to view them as opaque spots in the field of representation, opaque in the sense that they are not readily transparent to any particular homology with social formations or allegory of political engagement.

ABOVE. Superstudio, landscape with figures, 1970: montage. Reproduced from Colin Rowe and Fred Koetter, Collage City (1978), p 42

ABOVE. Herzog and de Meuron, Signal Station

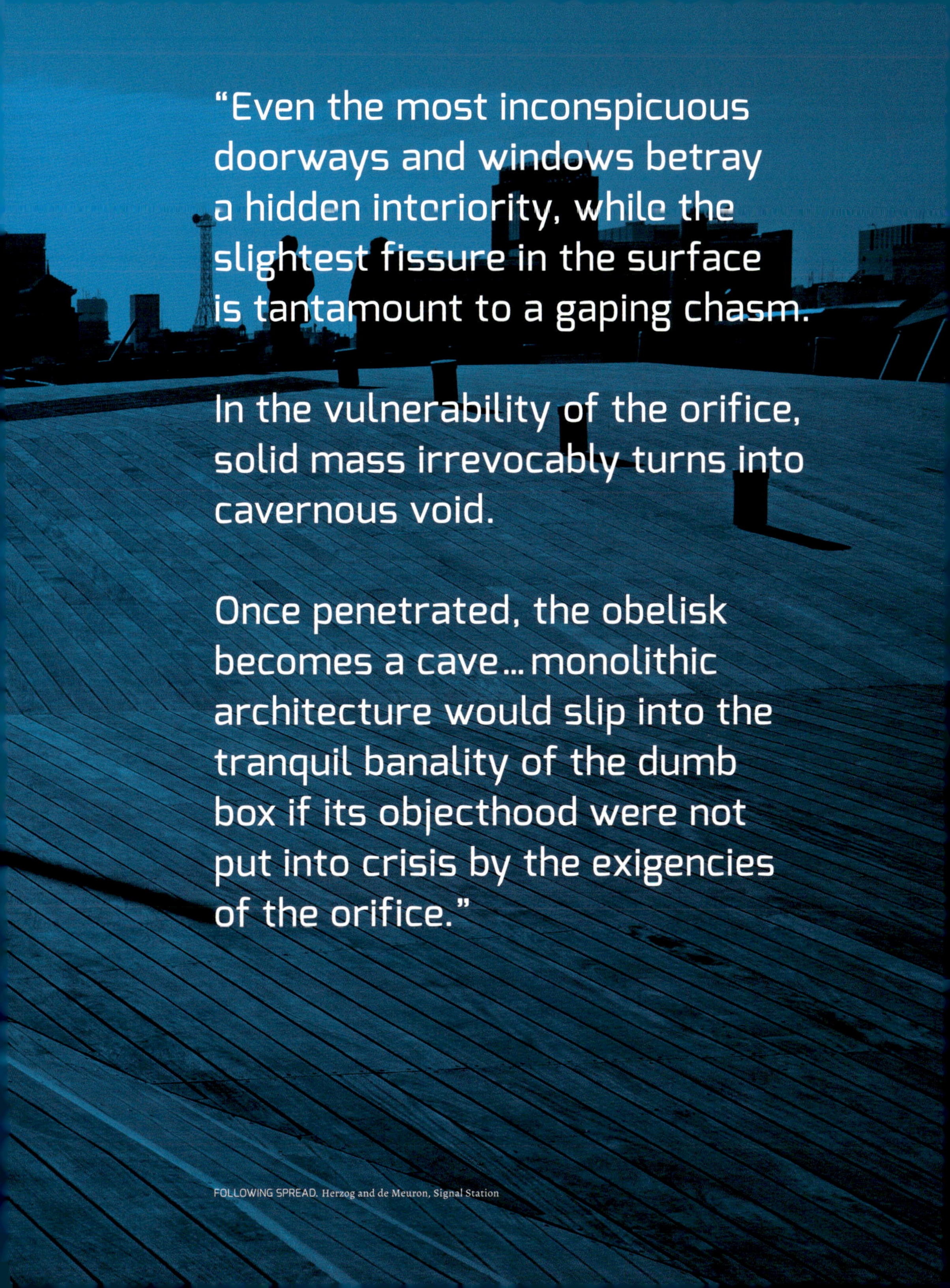

"Even the most inconspicuous doorways and windows betray a hidden interiority, while the slightest fissure in the surface is tantamount to a gaping chasm.

In the vulnerability of the orifice, solid mass irrevocably turns into cavernous void.

Once penetrated, the obelisk becomes a cave… monolithic architecture would slip into the tranquil banality of the dumb box if its objecthood were not put into crisis by the exigencies of the orifice."

FOLLOWING SPREAD. Herzog and de Meuron, Signal Station

- PART TWO ARCHITECTS

The essays in this section examine the work of architects or firms over an extended period or at a defining moment in their history. The aim is to situate their project in the field, to frame their contribution to the contemporary debate while also clarifying the terms of the discussion. What is offered here is not a critique of the work per se as much as a critical framework for entering the work.

- ANTI-AESTHETIC: ATELIER ARCAU

ORIGINALLY PUBLISHED IN **BEYOND CONTEXT: THE WORK OF ATELIER ARCAU ARCHITECTS**, OSCAR RIERA OJEDA PUBLISHERS, 2014.

STEEL BAND, an office complex at the outskirts of Vannes is the home of Atelier Arcau. The architectural firm who shares the premises with a number of other companies conceived it as a built calling card. The buildings demonstrate the core commitment of the firm: sensitivity to context, integration with landscape, and sustainability. The architecture also conveys a distinct sensibility that paradoxically emerges from an indifference to issues of form, to individual language and signature style.

Atelier Arcau finds its clear and characteristic voice while stating the raw facts of architecture: material, structure, and organization. Everything about this building speaks to the bare reality of commercial office space planning and steel frame construction; design is here enabling a bold conceptual and material clarity instead of packaging a polished product.

The elevations of the taller wing, by now a staple image of Atelier Arcau's architecture, achieve their memorable effect with the blunt expression of floor-plate stacking and serial repetition, the commonplace exigencies of an office building's constructional and organizational logic. The stacking effect is enhanced by the receding weather enclosure, a self-effacing glass plane that retreats far behind the edges the steel frame to expose the stacked floor pates. A brise-soleil consisting of perforated metal sheets of irregular trapezoidal shapes, wedged between projecting horizontal steel plates completes the blunt expression of raw materiality. The panels are randomly distributed and re-shuffled at each level with ostensible disregard to compositional order. The arbitrariness underscores the primacy of the horizontal plane and the stacking logic that "reboots" the horizontal datum at each floor level. The orange color adds a playful touch without diminishing the rough and indexical character of the material: it is the chemical byproduct of the rusting process that is designed to sheath Corten steel with its staple protective coat.

The interior exhibits the same indifference to alignment and composition with light fixtures randomly strewn across the ceiling and a straightforward layout for furniture and partitions. Spatial configurations barely deviate from the generic loft condition save for a double-height section that marks the lobby with a generosity of scale. As a by-product of the stacking process it is more index than symbol, an expression of the building's logic rather than a willful shaping of space.

ABOVE. Pronic Municipal Headquarters, country side north façade: floating volume on french bocage

Steel Band projects a palpable disdain for the flourishes we associated with Design—with a capital D—in favor of unmediated delivery of raw amenities such as generous day lighting and shoebox loft spaces that are amenable to standard furnishing. This is a far cry from the vanguard's preoccupation with form and the intricately variegated patterns now afforded by parametric modeling and CNC fabrication. It is equally distant from the minimalist commitment to refined detailing. No effort is here invested in smoothing over the crude reality of building construction and its sometimes-messy manifestation. In fact Atelier Arcau capitalizes on this mess: the screen of Steel Band looks like it is made of scrap metal sourced from a salvage yard and is all the more powerful for it.

The randomly patterned elevation is recurrent device in Atelier Arcau's work. We see it in the irregularly spaced wood slats that shade a linear low-slung building at a training center in Quimper, and again, among several other instances, in the cladding pattern of Salorge, the administrative headquarters for the municipality of Pornic. Occasionally it is a direct consequence of irregularly dimensioned rooms, a blunt expression of a complex program behind an irregular envelope; often it is an alternative to willful composition. The obvious precedent for such patterns is the music-inspired mullions at Le Corbusier's La Tourette. But whereas Yannis Xenakis' pattern aimed to represent a rhythmic idea, Ateier Arcau's randomness in an index of the messy reality of a building's materiality, programming, and use.

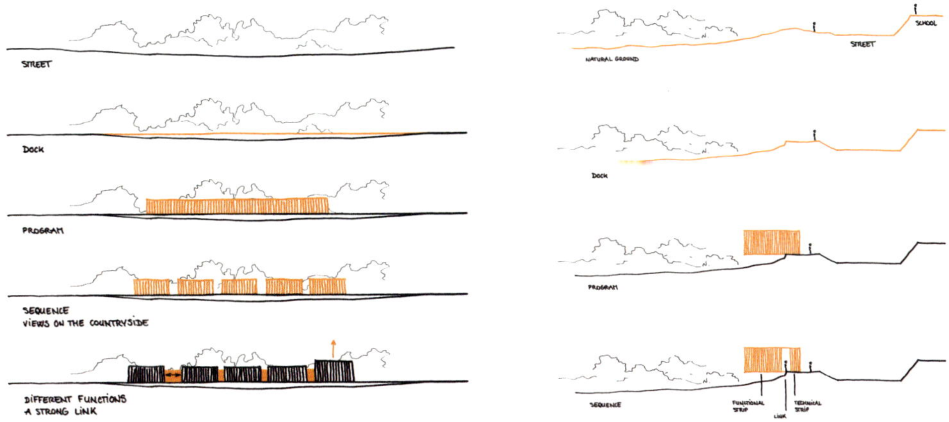

ABOVE. Pronic Municipal Headquarters, conceptual sketches

BELOW. Pronic Municipal Headquarters, main floor plan and south west elevation

"Design is here enabling a bold conceptual and material clarity instead of packaging a polished product."

The core architectural project of Atelier Arcau lies in the unsentimental embrace of this reality. It is a project that surely benefits from the office's long-dating expertise with infrastructural buildings. Examples such as UVED, a power plant in Brest, and Architectural Digest, a waste treatment plant in Ploufragan, are part of an impressive collection of buildings developed on frugal budgets that achieve a laconic poetry in raw efficiency.

Railway Sentinel is another example where Atelier Arcau transfigures the banality of industrial artifacts by tuning in to the raw power of infrastructure. The building, a simple linear volume clad in Corten steel, translates and elevates the logic of the railroad tracks into a utilitarian monument by forgoing formal elaboration in favor of relentless repetition and exacerbated linearity.

The linear plan, perhaps the most persistent motif in the oeuvre of Atelier Arcau suggests a mechanistic extrusion. Much like the staple random pattern on the elevation, the linear assembly indexes an anti-compositional cast: a plan-making process resulting from the sequential aggregation of parts. The assembly-line logic of aggregated parts extends even to public buildings where utility can hardly provide an alibi for raw pragmatism. The City Hall of Ambon is an instance where linear organization and serial repletion are thematized to an extent that points beyond the pragmatic to the rhetorical.

The matter-of-fact, in your face pragmatism points to a vernacular sensibility. And Atelier Arcau's pervasive shoeboxes have an unmistakable affinity, in their disposition, proportions, and dimensions to local barn types. The architecture of Atelier Arcau self-consciously aligns with local building traditions. Indeed Salorge, one of their most celebrated works, literally references a vernacular building type dedicated to the storage of salt. But more consistently and typically Atelier Arcau achieves this alignment by rehearsing a vernacular ethos rather than by adapting its form.

The attention to context is arguably Atelier Arcau's defining trait and the contemporary translation of the Salorge, the eponymous building that inspired labels such as "critical regionalism" may be one of the firm's most explicit investments in Brittany's building tradition. Still, Atelier Arcau's investment in context and commitment to local tradition is consistently ambiguous and perhaps even ambivalent. In contradistinction to their vernacular analogues, Atelier Arcau's barn-like forms are often

ABOVE. Training Center, construction stage: self-service restaurant

ABOVE. Training Center, under the outdoor passageway

ABOVE. Training Center, south façade: random rhythm of wood frame sunshading

ABOVE. Training Center, north façade: broken lines landscape

ABOVE. Training Center, restaurant terrace

ABOVE. Training Center: south façade, landscape integration

on pilotis, floating, un-rooted above the landscape, they are abstract artifacts that embody a regional *mentalité*, more so than an architectural tradition. Something about them is unmistakably Breton, but that same *je ne sais quoi*—shall we say the unsentimental indexicality—is what also binds them, paradoxically, to the universal project of modernity.

The regional character of Atelier Arcau is not a cultivated aesthetic: it is neither an affirmation of a cultural heritage, nor a deliberate resistance to its erosion by global currents. Atelier Arcau's architecture is of a particular place, because buildings such as Steel Band, Architectural Digest, and Railway Sentinel, are blunt and unmediated—anti-aesthetic—expressions of the sites, situations, and material resources that shape them in Vannes, Ploufragan, and Nantes.

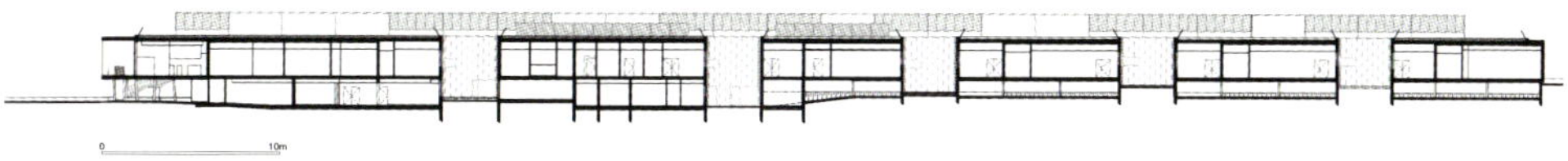

ABOVE. Training Center, transversal section

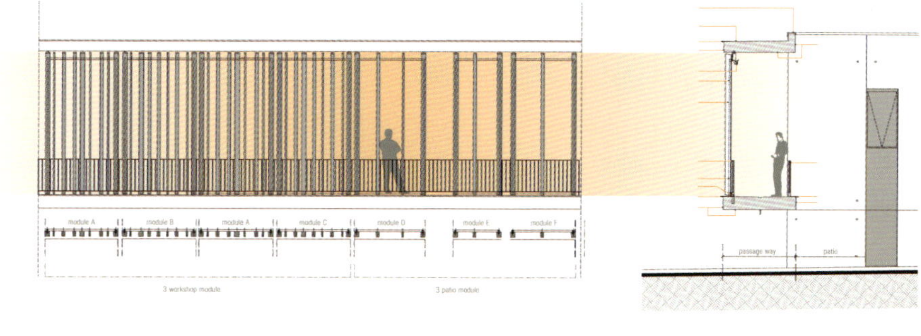

ABOVE. Training Center, outdoor passageway detail

"In contradistinction to their vernacular analogues, Atelier Arcau's barn-like forms are often on pilotis, floating, un-rooted above the landscape, they are abstract artifacts that embody a regional mentalité, more so than an architectural tradition."

ABOVE. Steel Band, double skin complex grid for a web effect

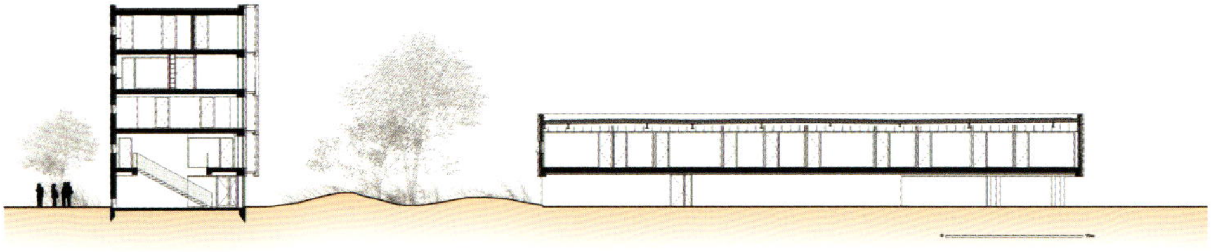

ABOVE. Steel Band, general section

ABOVE. Steel Band, architectural volume through a moving landscape

FOLLOWING SPREAD. Steel Band, view of the baffled broken Corten steel puzzle

- PERFORMATIVE ICONS: RALPH JOHNSON'S

ORIGINALLY PUBLISHED IN **RALPH JOHNSON OF PERKINS + WILL: RECENT WORK**, OSCAR RIERA OJEDA PUBLISHERS, 2012

THIS FIGURAL LEGIBILITY has characterized Johnson's work since his early public buildings in the eighties. It positioned the work critically in relation to both modern functionalism and postmodern pastiche. Johnson's architecture invested in the symbolic resonance of buildings while resisting the tendency to deploy architectural style as a system of fixed signs. For Johnson, architectural signification consists of shaping intelligible and memorable figures from the building's functional and constructional logic.

The courthouse sustains this core principal in Johnson's work. Its constituent parts are innovatively reconfigured as a transition from the scale and character of adjacent civic buildings to high-rise developments to the north. Much like Johnson's staple designs for public institutions, such as the Desert View Elementary School and the Orland Park Village Center, it reconstitutes known typological fragments into new figures that are pregnant with cultural associations and lucid in clarifying the building's organization and relation to context. Only context in this case is taken to include invisible but no less material qualities: environmental influences that have become increasingly important in shaping Johnson's buildings in the last decade.

The most remarkable feature of the building is a south facing atrium with a curving glass curtain wall. The atrium exposes the stacked courthouse to grand public spaces inside and outside the building. It offers the inner workings of the building to public view, in a spirit consistent with the institution's commitment to transparency and inclusiveness in the legal progress. The glass wall also fulfills the environmental ambitions of the federal agency. It is designed for optimal environmental performance, with angles and orientation precisely measured for maximum benefits from wind and sun exposure.

The wall performs well beyond its technical means. Its sweeping arc translates the climatic processes that shape it into an intelligible and memorable image: a posture that embodies a susceptibility and openness to environmental influence. The curtain wall figures a receptive attitude, an openness that resonates with the building's transparency—the literal transparency of the clear glass panes as much as the phenomenal transparency of the organizational diagram.

LEFT. Los Angeles United States Courthouse

RIGHT. Los Angeles United States Courthouse, diagram of constituent parts

BELOW. Los Angeles United States Courthouse, diagram of constituent parts

Johnson builds the civic character of the courthouse by figuratively capturing and monumentalizing its environmental logic. Herein lies his main contribution to the current discussions around sustainable design: in the capacity to tease out a symbolic resonance from environmental performance.

Take, as another example, the Al Shark Tower project. The environmental agenda is here stated more explicitly with the literal greening of the building. A strategy for a sustainable rapport with Dubai's desert climate here favors a permeable building envelope with passive cooling and ventilation capabilities. The design strategy which includes a layer of living plant material as part of a breathing skin generates a unique building form with a continuous spiraling garden carved into the mass of the high-rise structure. A process designed for efficiently regulating environmental recourses is pushed beyond its performative logic to yield a cultural surplus. Sustainability shapes the building into an intelligible icon.

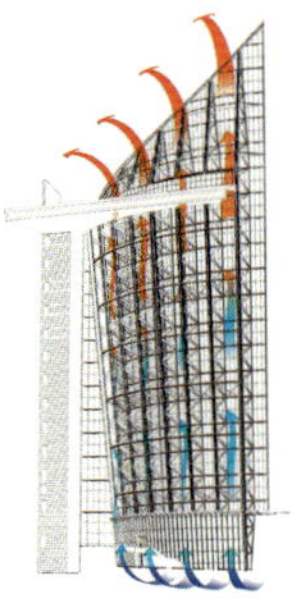

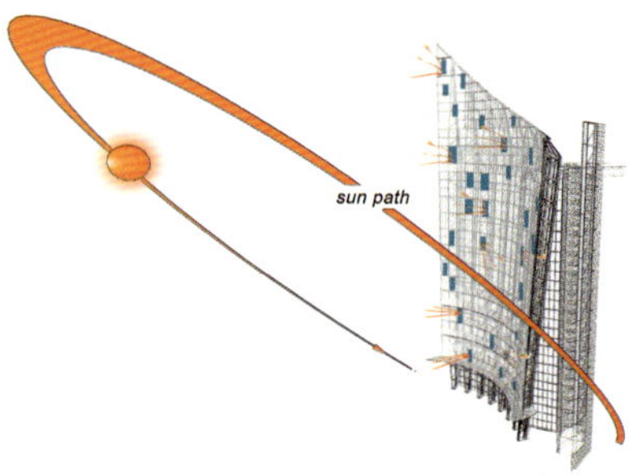

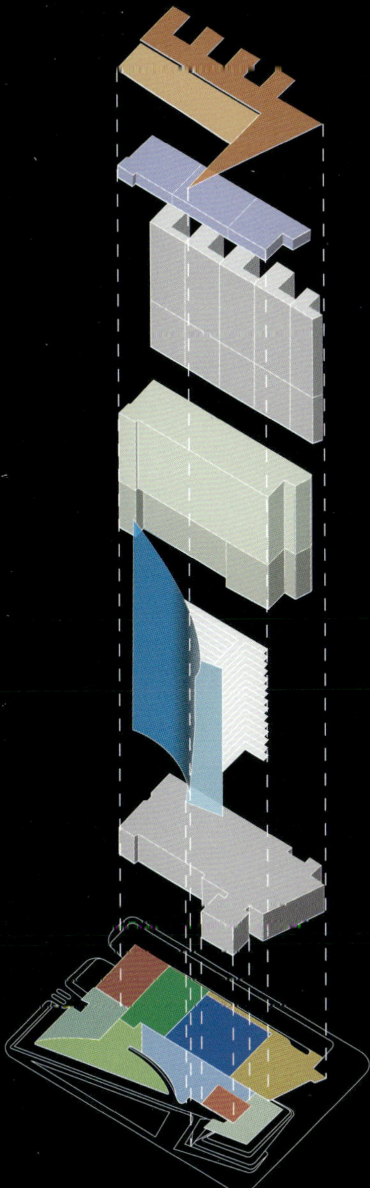

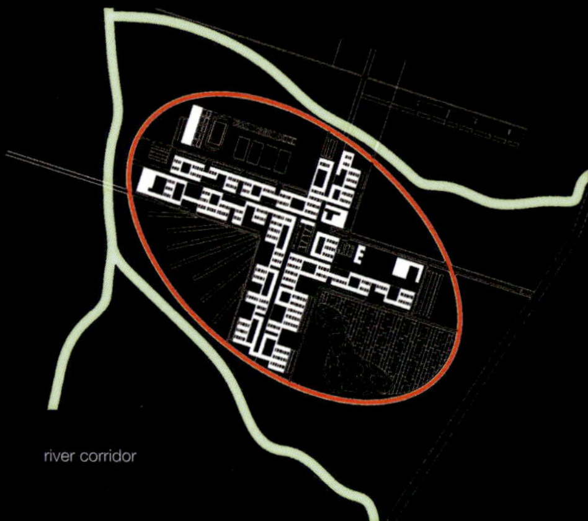

river corridor

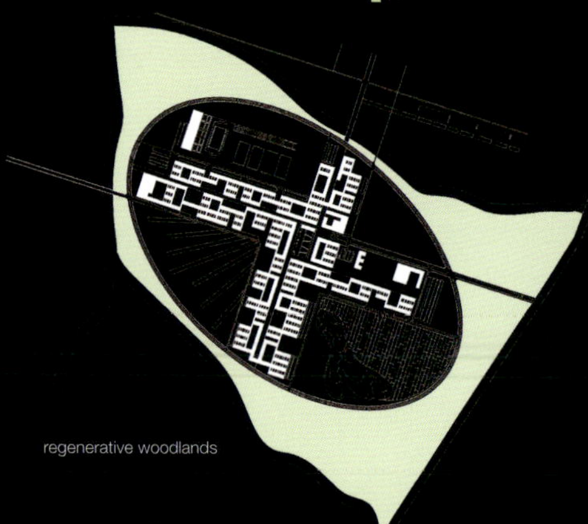

regenerative woodlands

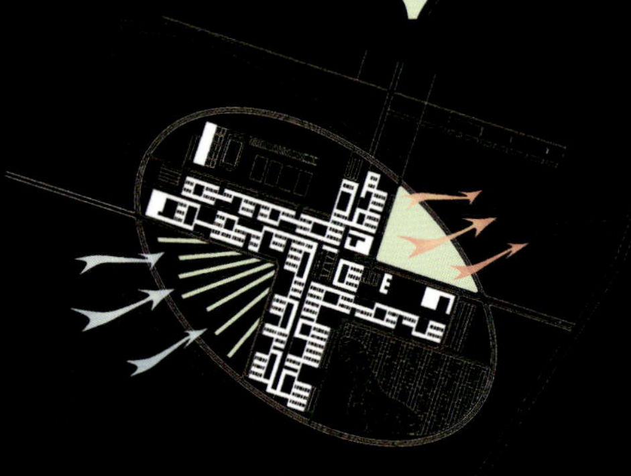

wind harvesting

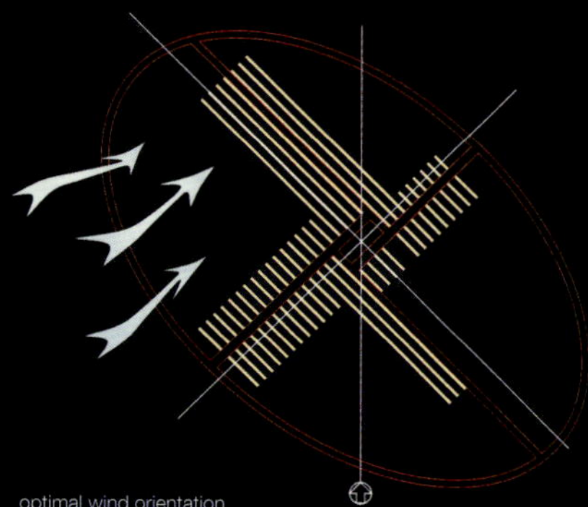

optimal wind orientation

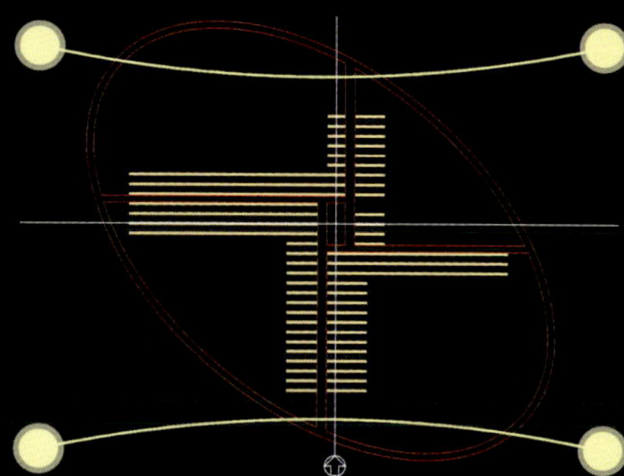

optimum sun orientation

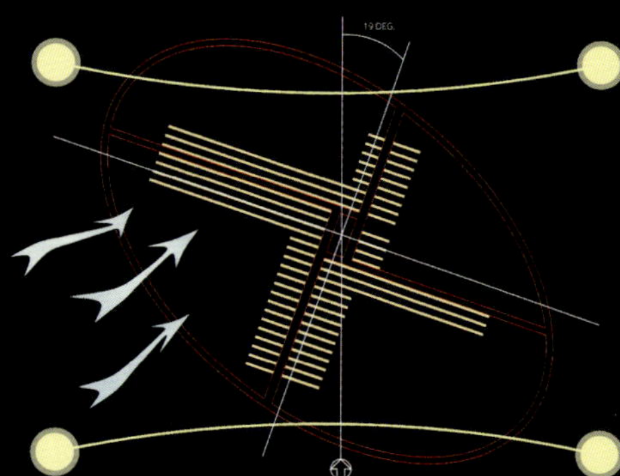

final campus orientation

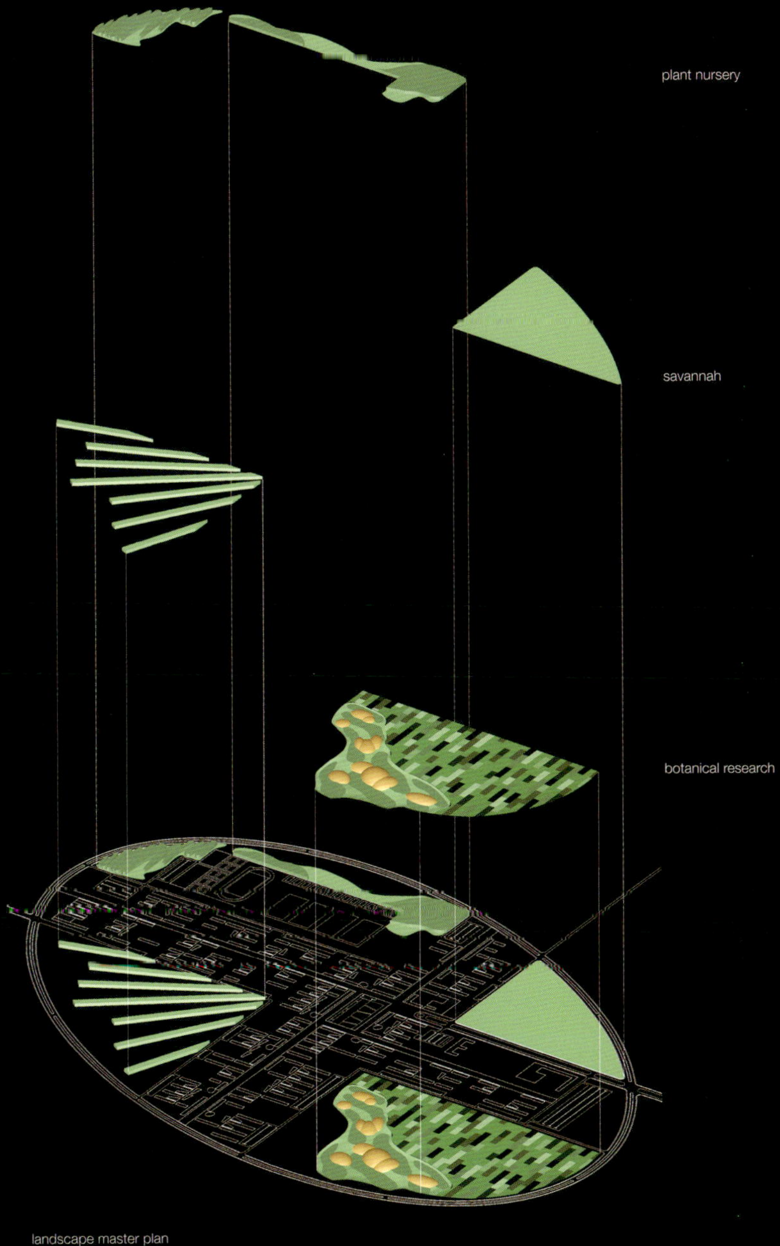
plant nursery
savannah
botanical research
landscape master plan

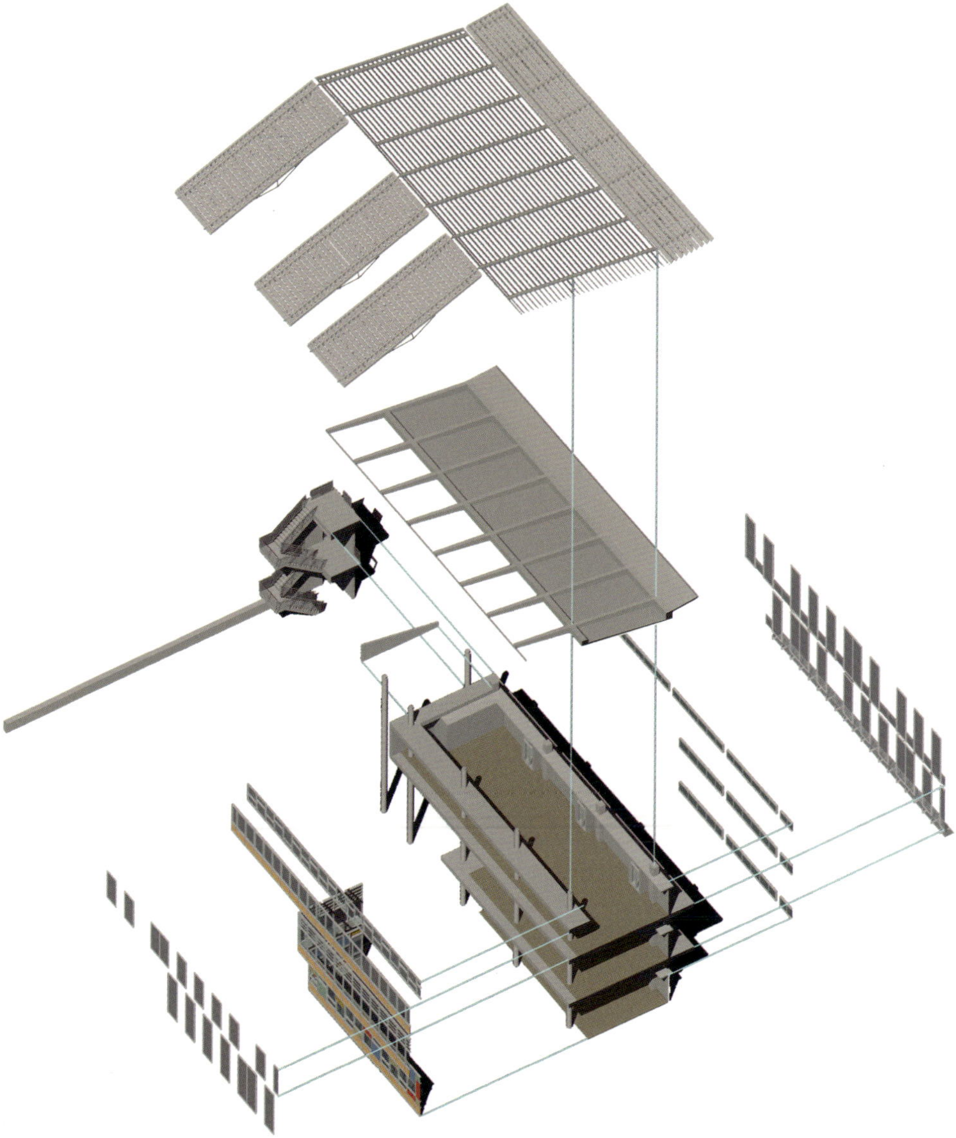

PREVIOUS SPREAD. Universidade Agostinho Neto, Angola: environmental logic of master plan

ABOVE. Universidade Agostinho Neto, Angola, typical classroom components

FROM FAÇADE TO INTERFACE

Johnson's particular take on sustainability, an approach that tackles material as well as cultural aspects of growing environmental issues, reaching for signification through performance, is exercised in several recent projects and at different scales of interventions.

It is clearly demonstrated in the master plan and design for the Universidade Agostinho Neto on the outskirts of Luanda, Angola. This is an academic campus for 17,000 students on 5,000 acres. It is circumscribed by a ring-road that looks perfectly circular in the aerial perspective. With rational underpinnings evidenced in the perfection of the geometry the plan recalls visionary schemes for ideal cities. The circle is actually distorted to adapt to the site. It is an ellipse that is designed to squeeze between river washes. Ideal form here yields to the particulars of context and strategic thinking supplants instrumental rationality.

Take, for instance, the distorted lines in the open fields. These landscape features are designed to channel the prevailing breezes to optimize the ventilation of buildings. The plan in its broadest outlines thus indexes an environmental sensitivity, especially in the orientation of the grid-pattern: at 19 degrees east of the north-south axis is a finely calibrated compromise between optimal sun and wind exposures.

With the notable exception of the library and the central quadrant where public spaces and amenities are orchestrated in complex overlapping patterns, most buildings on this campus have a straightforward loft-like quality. Simple domino-frame concrete construction and fairly shallow floor plates provide for adaptable plan configurations and flexible occupancy. The architectural rhetoric is concentrated in a shading canopy that protects buildings and open spaces in a gracefully undulating course that is designed to enhance shading and ventilation.

The canopy presents a continuous and finely articulated field in contrast to the more circumstantial distribution of Spartan structures below. Although detached and lifted above the buildings, we may say that it constitutes their main elevation or façade. The canopy carries the civic weight of the campus: it gives character and identity to what is otherwise deliberately muted and strategically generic. Not only does it ensure the sustainability of the campus by enhancing climatic conditions with passive shading and ventilation, it also presents these environmental control processes as an intelligible and memorable form. The finely calibrated features that enhance its performance are indeed what distinguish it as a remarkable architectural statement. Environmental performance is, in short, monumentalized in the canopy-façade. The iconic and functional monument is identified with the mission and values of the institution.

The Qatar Broadcasting Services Complex uses a similar strategy with a screening superstructure enveloping the entire complex as a shading and character-giving feature. The shading screen wraps around buildings, unifying roof planes and elevations with a continuous surface. The roof plane, usually invisible and relegated to mechanical equipment in modern commercial buildings is here rhetorically equated with the elevation, the face of the building. As the primary solar interface, the roof performs functions that are critical to the sustainability of the building. Johnson recognizes it as such and reinvests it with architectural content.

The rhetorical affirmation of the empowered roof is most evident—and perhaps most warranted—in buildings Johnson designed for warm sunny climates, where shading and energy collection are most critical and effective in aiding sustainability. Johnson acknowledges the roof's new status in more subtle ways in a number of important if not extreme statements.

In the headquarters for Crate & Barrel, an oversized trellis canopy and various accents to the roof-line fulfill more than compositional purposes. They do more than form a crown in a classical compositional sense and redefine the roof plane as an important environmental interface.The roof's capacity for daylighting is accordingly exploited and emphasized in the lobby with an array of skylights that resemble ribbon windows. Here again Johnson's design conflates roof and façade, establishing functional as well as symbolic parallels between a building's environmental performance and its public face.

This device is developed further in the Chevron building where a section of the roof that is punctuated with window-like openings is framed as an iconic feature above the portico-like entrance. This is Johnson's most literal—and rhetorical—statement of the roof-as-façade idea. It demonstrates and monumentalizes the environmental capacities of the roof and its role in interfacing with climate, in modulating light and in potentially gathering energy.

ABOVE. Qatar Broadcasting Services complex

BELOW. Al Shark Tower project

"For Johnson, architectural signification consists in shaping intelligible and memorable figures from the building's functional and constructional logic."

FROM BUILDING TO LANDSCAPE

The Haworth Headquarters overtly aims to represent the environmental ambitions of the client. The building achieves ambitions beyond the features that secured its LEED® Gold status. The green roof, for instance, absorbs storm water but also performs rhetorically as an extension of the landscape. This device facilitates a reading of the building as an open matrix that is continuous with the adjacent field: a landscape that provokes opportunities for social interaction.

The building-as-landscape scheme is a recurrent and increasingly formative theme in Johnson's work. It is developed and treated more or less literally in several recent projects where buildings are embedded in a web of lateral connections extending their presence and influence horizontally. Johnson's designs have consistently challenged the autonomy of the architectural object by attuning buildings to complex contextual conditions. The building-as-landscape scheme pushes this tendency further by blurring the distinction between architecture and landscape, and in extreme instances, dissolving buildings entirely into context.

The Musée de Louvain-la-Neuve radicalizes ideas that were tested in the Haworth Headquarters by further merging building with landscape. This project proposes a hybrid program combining cultural and natural amenities. Public facilities are tucked under undulating roofscapes that extend the field of a lake-side park above and into the building. Reading as both architecture and nature, the building embodies latent civic as well as environmental aspirations for the site: to sustain a park-like setting on the lakeshore and provide a gateway to the adjacent campus.

Heping Park, a centerpiece for a high-rise development in Tianjin, China, brings this mixture to a finer degree of resolution. It interweaves park and building in a series of programmed strips with accessible roofs that slope in alternating directions. The artificial topography with its ingeniously devised section is planned for effective storm-water management. It is also designed to allow for pedestrians access to public amenities continuously and directly from the planted roofscape. The innovative solution crystallizes the notion of a hybrid building/landscape in a novel type that is as rich in cultural association as it is effective in addressing environmental concerns.

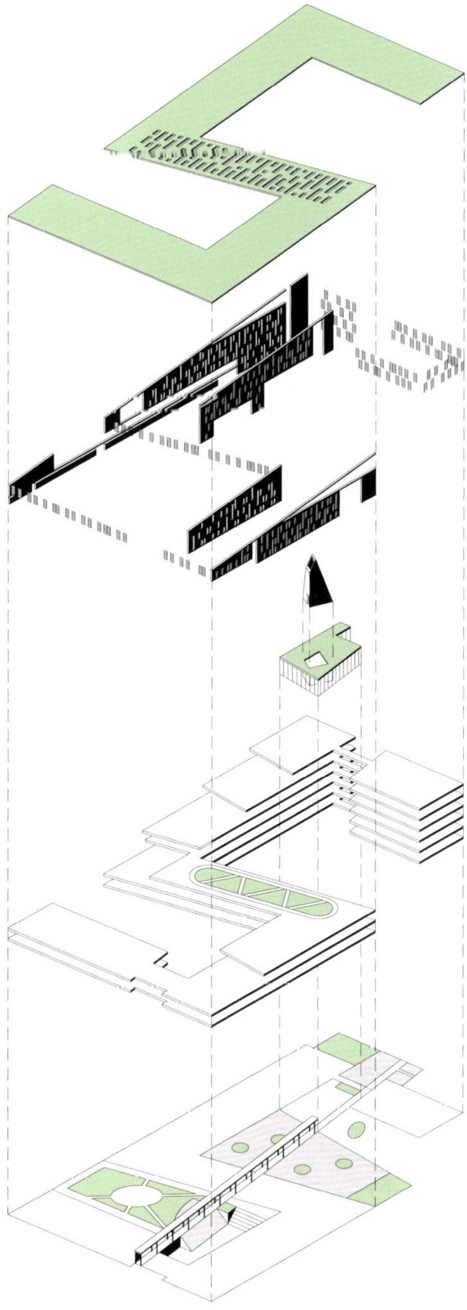

ABOVE. Chevron international Trading Company, diagram of constituent parts and landscape features

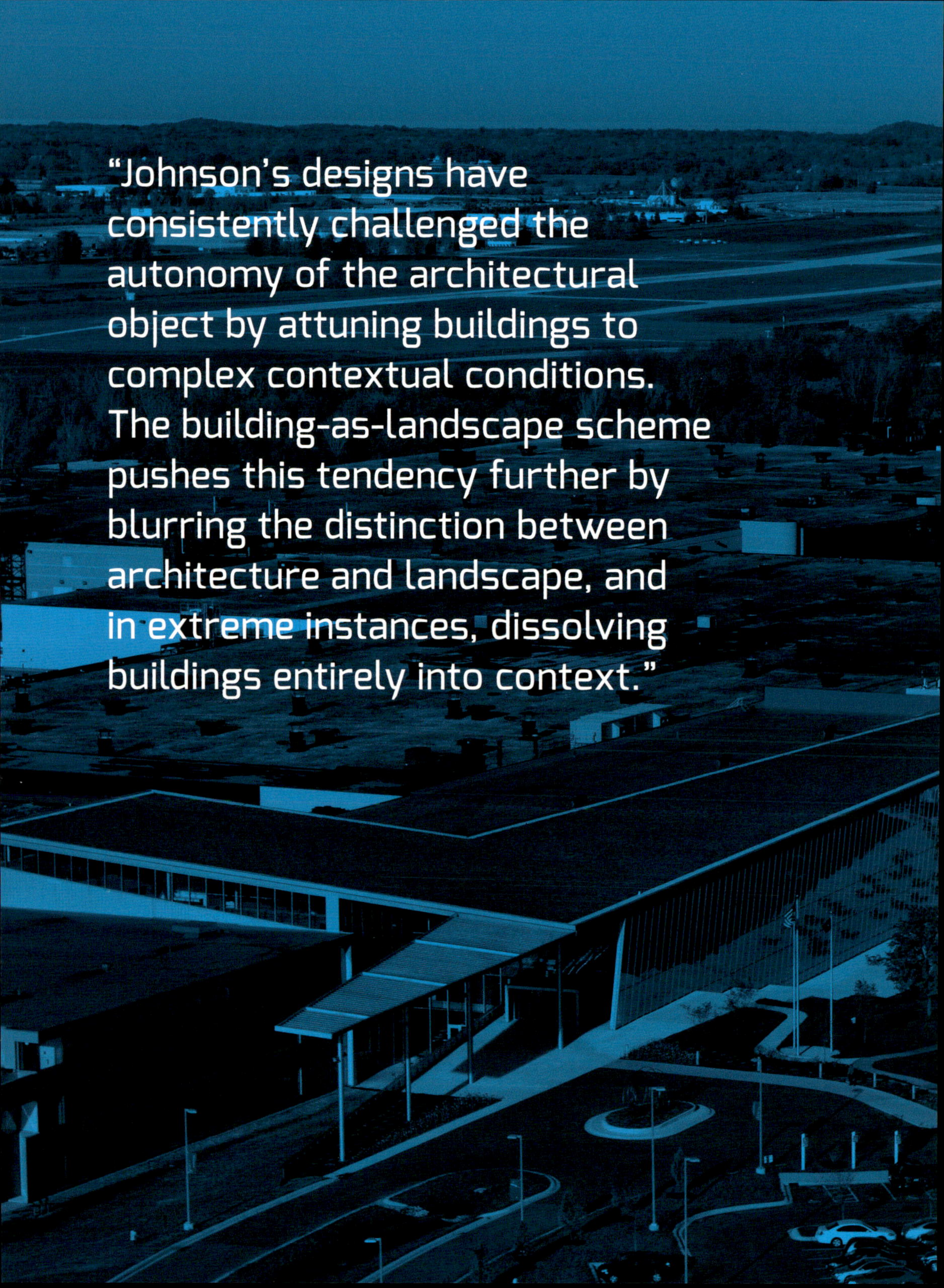

"Johnson's designs have consistently challenged the autonomy of the architectural object by attuning buildings to complex contextual conditions. The building-as-landscape scheme pushes this tendency further by blurring the distinction between architecture and landscape, and in extreme instances, dissolving buildings entirely into context."

The functional as well as symbolic integration of building and landscape is a primary dedication of the Shanghai Nature Museum. The project rehearses some of the recurrent themes just discussed, especially in recasting the seamless transition from ground to roof in a monumental sweep.

But unlike other projects that enacted an attitude toward nature solely by dramatizing the processes that mediate between building and environment, this building deploys, in addition to an array of environment-friendly features, compositional techniques that stage this rapport as an immersive experience. Nestled in a courtyard with a nautilus-inspired geometry, between walls that are tessellated in a cell-like pattern, is an architectural mise-en-scène with geological/organic references that delivers the convergence of nature and artifice as a multi-sensory experience. The immersive and mimetic figuration is new to Johnson's work. Whether this is an isolated experiment inspired by the didactic program or a precursor to a new chapter in Johnson's work remains to be seen.

ABOVE. Shanghai Nature Museum

RIGHT. Heping Park, Tianjin, diagram of landscape and building integration

GREEN SPACE

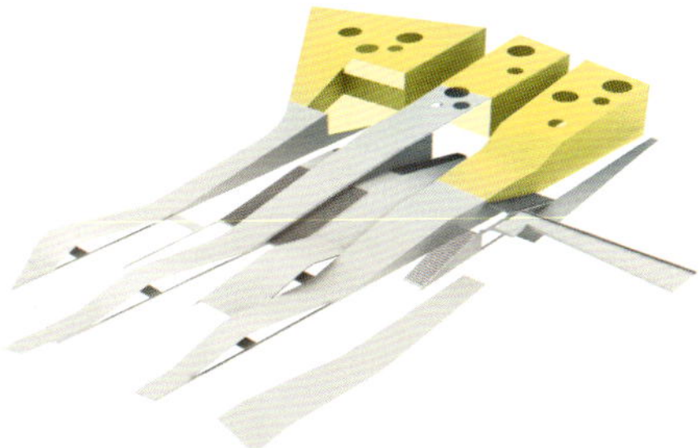

COMMUNITY SPACE

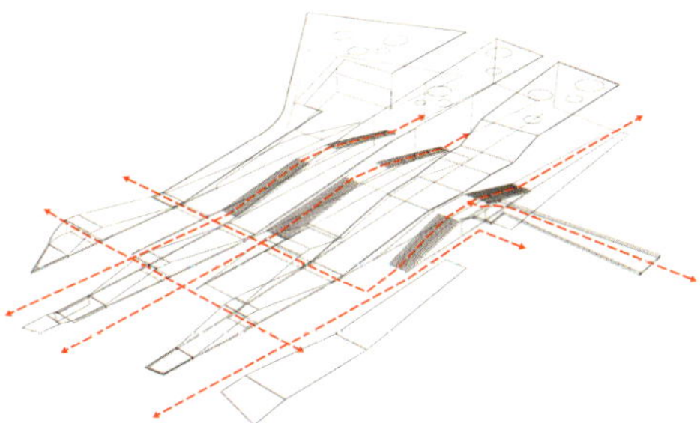

PEDESTRIAN CIRCULATION PATH

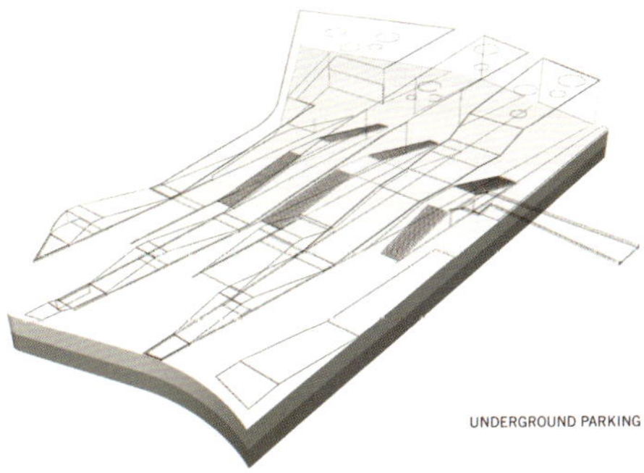

UNDERGROUND PARKING

- RE-IMAGINING PROPINQUITY: HÖWELER + YOON ARCHITECTURE

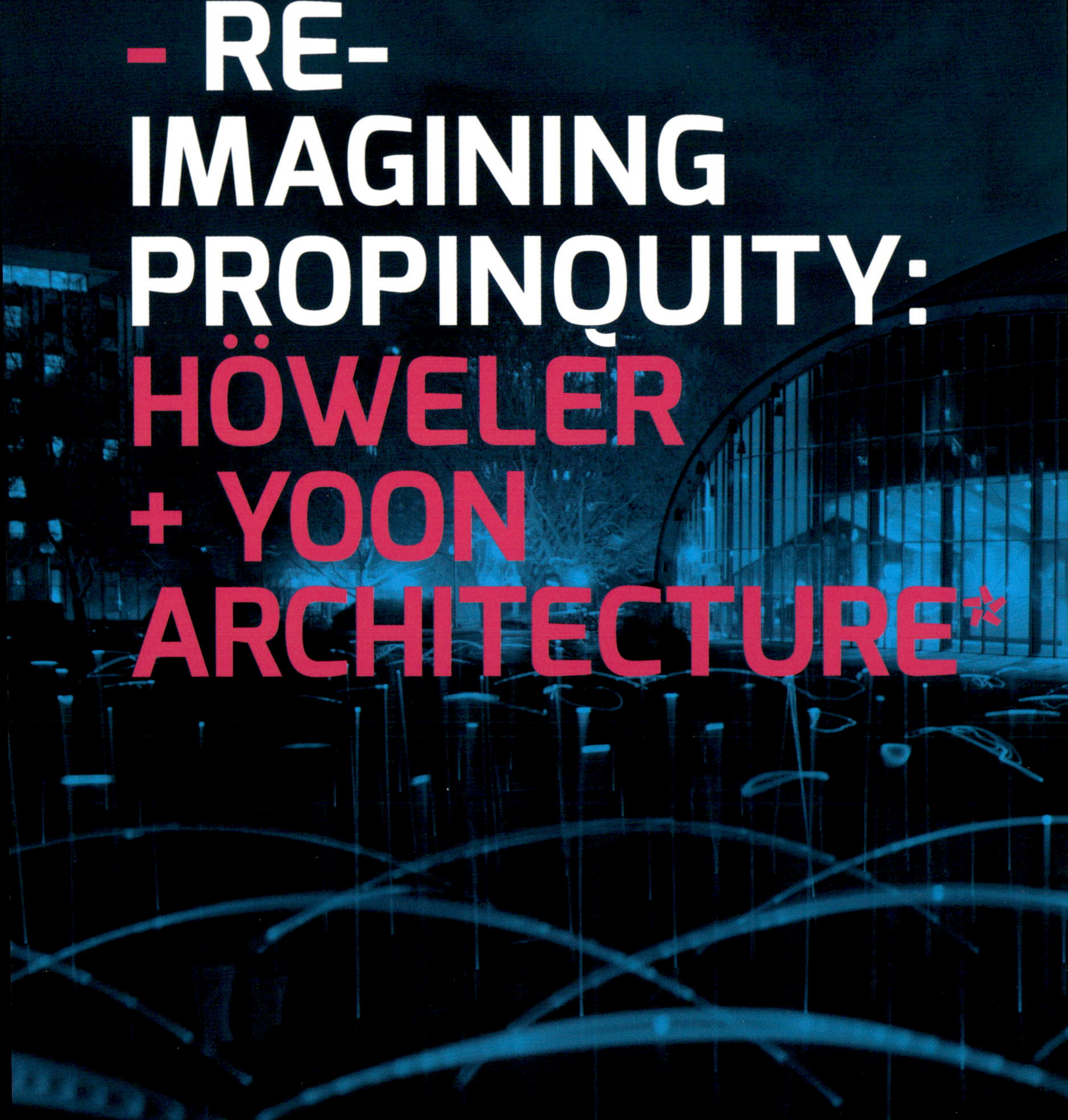

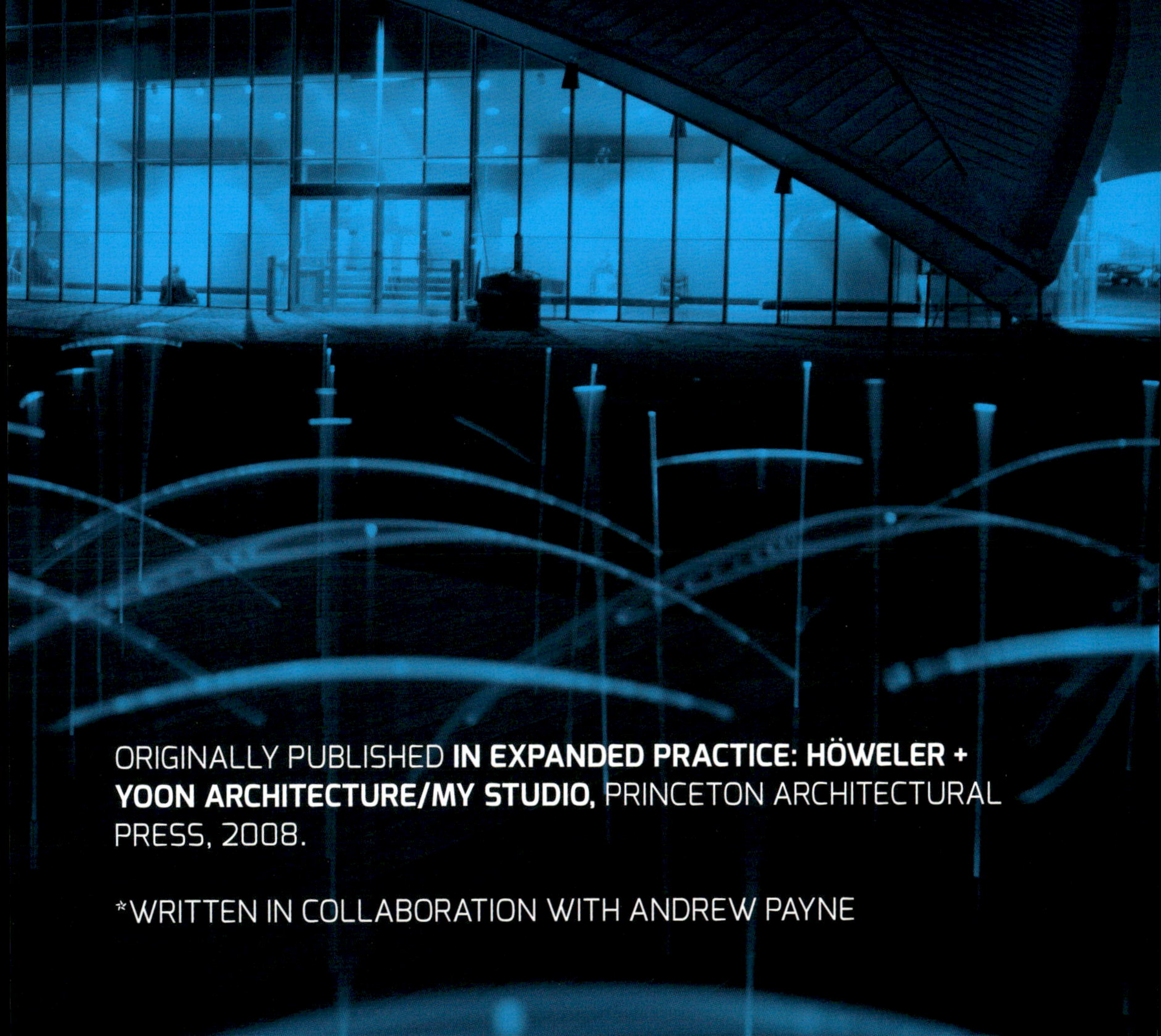

ORIGINALLY PUBLISHED **IN EXPANDED PRACTICE: HÖWELER + YOON ARCHITECTURE/MY STUDIO,** PRINCETON ARCHITECTURAL PRESS, 2008.

*WRITTEN IN COLLABORATION WITH ANDREW PAYNE

THE WORK OF HÖWELER + YOON ARCHITECTURE (hereafter HYA) is animated by a set of dedications and preoccupations familiar from contemporary discussions of architecture. Their pursuit of the new plastic freedom afforded by digitalization of the design process, their interest in the sensorial potentials opened up by the architectural deployment of intelligent surfaces, their preference for an atmospheric aesthetic organized around transitive phenomena, their understanding of architecture as working between the materiality of built form and the immateriality of the informational networks that traverse and inhabit it, their commitment to seeking out new reciprocities between artificial and living systems—all are in sympathy with a broadly shared conception of what the issues and opportunities facing the discipline are today. Similarly representative is their ambition to negotiate between professional realism and a view of architecture as a research practice that has affinities with both the experimental ambitions of the twentieth-century avant-gardes and the more ideologically circumspect trajectories of ecological, technological, and social/cultural investigation that today constellate under the rubric of product design semantics. What perhaps distinguishes the work of HYA from that of many of their contemporaries is the way in which these commitments are focused around a sustained attention to the role that built form has in shaping the experience of propinquity at the three scales that have stratified the architectural imagination since Vitruvius: that of the body, that of the building, that of the city. The experience of "being-with" as it unfolds at these three scales is the special concern of their research, and the enigmatic object of the experiments to which that research gives rise. In what follows, we will briefly discuss three projects that we imagine to be respectively representative of these three scales: Defensible Dress, LOOP, White Noise/White Light. First, however, a few words about the quality and substance of that propinquity that is the central stake of this work.

In order to both distinguish the sense of propinquity that is at work in these projects and to appreciate its contemporaneity, it is perhaps useful to briefly compare it to the conception of propinquity that was at play in the theorizations of "public space" that appear in postmodern theorists of the urban condition like George Baird, Kenneth Frampton, and Richard Sennett. The conception of propinquity that is developed in different ways by these three theorists is one that is aptly summarized in Hannah Arendt's description of the Greek agora—her model public sphere—as a space of reciprocal appearance, a space of dialogue, and a space of plural and co-implicated agency. According to Baird, Frampton, and Sennett, both the forms of collective appearance, speech, and action that were invented in ancient Athens and the built world connate with those forms is today threatened by the forces of capitalization and the erosion of democratic political traditions that these forces have instigated. In response to that erosion, Baird, Frampton, and Sennett call for both a reinvigoration of the forms of embodied appearance, speech, and action that have traditionally defined public life in the West and a reinvention of the architectural idioms designed to accommodate that life. By contrast, the conception of propinquity advanced by HYA, as by many of their contemporaries, is one in which the distinction between public and private modalities of social experience, so central to the conception of propinquity advanced by Arendt and her architectural avatars, gives way to an at once more pervasive and less determinate experience of being-with, an experience of irremissible self-differing constitutive of individual as much as of collective experience, and therefore operative at all scales and in all modalities of occupation. The collective experience to which HYA direct their attention is one in which the carnal co-presence of political agents so dear to the Arendtian conception of propinquity is vitiated by a plethora of communicative technologies designed to mediate, simulate, and increasingly to supplant it. The collective experience to which they direct their attention is also one in which the forms of critical reflection and responsible self-disclosure that the Arendtian conception of speech suggests, give way to the instrumental and largely anonymous modalities of communication associated with contemporary information culture. Finally, the collective experience to which they direct their attention is one in which the Arendtian emphasis on action is inflected by, on the one hand, a renewed interest in the role that our perceptual and affective faculties have in the construction of collective experience, and, on the other, an emphasis on the ludic or theatrical, as against the instrumental or practical, implications of the verb "to act." It is from the perspective of this transformed conception of the space of appearance and the forms of discourse and action that such a space affords that HYA's work at all scales must be understood. With these summary comments in mind, let us turn to the three projects mentioned above, in order to better appreciate how they respond to this transformed sense of collective experience and of architecture's role in shaping it.

DEFENSIBLE DRESS

In recent history, a lively exchange has transpired between clothing designers and architects. As more than one commentator has observed, this exchange has deep roots in the analogy between building and raiment that shaped the theory and practice of late nineteenth-century and early twentieth-century architecture. As in the first instance, the current pursuit of this analogy is organized not merely around shared structural and aesthetic concerns, but also around a shared curiosity about how individuals and communities of individuals negotiate the new modes of propinquity arising from new forms of metropolitanization.

One expression of the current intersection of clothing design and architecture is the emergence of a new order of urban artifact that is situated ambiguously between the status of a garment and that of a building, often with intelligent technologies of one sort or another serving as the mediator between these distinct artifactual realms. Thinking from the side of clothing design, Hussein Chalayan's Remote Control Dress (Spring/Summer Collection 2000), which integrates wireless technology, electrical circuitry, and automated commands after a fashion that recalls the intelligent architectures of our day; and Lucy Orta's various experiments in intimate architecture, which link communities of wearers by clothing them in a single collective garment that prescribes novel ratiocinations of collective organization and individual autonomy (Nexus Architecture), and whose scale

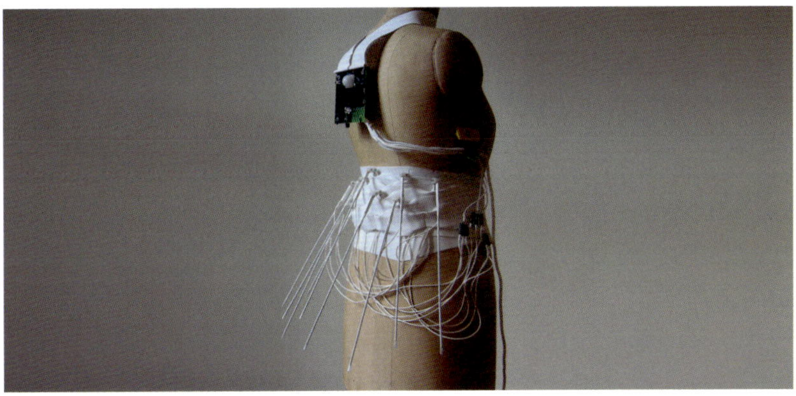

ABOVE. Defensible Dress, prototype

LEFT. Defensible Dress, prototype

and structure often suggests a complex of at once minimal and nomadic dwelling units (Connector Mobile Village), stand as distinguished examples of this rapprochement of architecture and clothing design. Thinking from the side of architecture, the role played by the "braincoat" in Diller Scofidio + Renfro's original proposal for their Blur Building is exemplary of the way in which architects are also engaging the full spectrum of membrane structures shaping our relationship to our surroundings in an effort to question and reorder the terms of contemporary social engagement.

HYA's Defensible Dress is an artifact entirely in this vein. Incorporating sensory technologies, a circuit board, and a series of actuated quills, the dress allows its wearer to program a microcontroller that, by sending an electronic current through flexinol ligaments embedded in each of the quills, operates the ligament like a lever, thereby prompting a horizontal extension of the quills and with that extension an aggressive expansion of the wearer's space of embodied occupation. We might say that the extension of the quills translates the ethical and social imperative to exercise tact in or dealings with others (*Noli me tangere*) into an implacable fact. As in the work of other artists and architects exploring the uncanny and at time even sinister underside of intelligent machines—the sculptural installations of Philip Beesley come immediately to mind—the Defensible Dress gives positive figure to unresolved ambiguities, tensions, and resistances arising from the current technological transformation of our socius. By concretizing the garment's charismatic aura, giving it literal form and material extent, the Defensible Dress underlines the contested nature of even the most intimate experiences of propinquity.

Another garment project, the Möbius Dress, represents a kindred material meditation on the negotiable thresholds that comprise intersubjective experience in the contemporary setting. Challenging "clothing's absolute adherence to conventions of interiority and exteriority" (Höweler + Yoon), the Möbius Dress represents a kind of sartorial synecdoche of Jean-Luc Nancy's re-conception of the social bond as a (k)not to be incessantly untied and retied: "The (k)not [of being-with] involves neither interiority nor exteriority, but ... in being tied, ceaselessly makes the inside pass outside, each into (or by way of) the other, the other inside, turning endlessly back on itself without returning to itself ... the tying of the (k)not is nothing but the putting into relation that presupposes at once proximity and distance, attachment and detachment, intricacy, intrigue and ambivalence."

LOOP

A similar ambiguity is sustained in LOOP. In this work, HYA distill the salient ideas of its practice in an installation proposal for the MoMa/PS1 Young Architects Program. Installation projects, especially as framed by this program, constitute an R&D genre for emerging practices. They have repeatedly offered HYA opportunities for aligning professional and practical interests with an experimental agenda.

Tightly filling its site with a continuous polycarbonate ribbon, Loop explores Voronoi Packing geometry to build an intricately variegated 3-D matrix in the museum's courtyard. The ribbon performs as both support and enclosure, continuously folding and twisting to densely occupy the courtyard with a variety of cellular configurations. Differing in size orientation, and position, the local surfaces produced by the ribbon's continuous extension suggest a variety of familiar functions (table, bench, etc etera), while at the same time remaining available for unprescribed forms of occupation and appropriation.

The installation is a tour de force of manufacturing and building innovation, aligning cutting-edge experimentation in geometry with new material and fabrication methods. This line o f research into packing and minimal surface geometry has already produced interesting

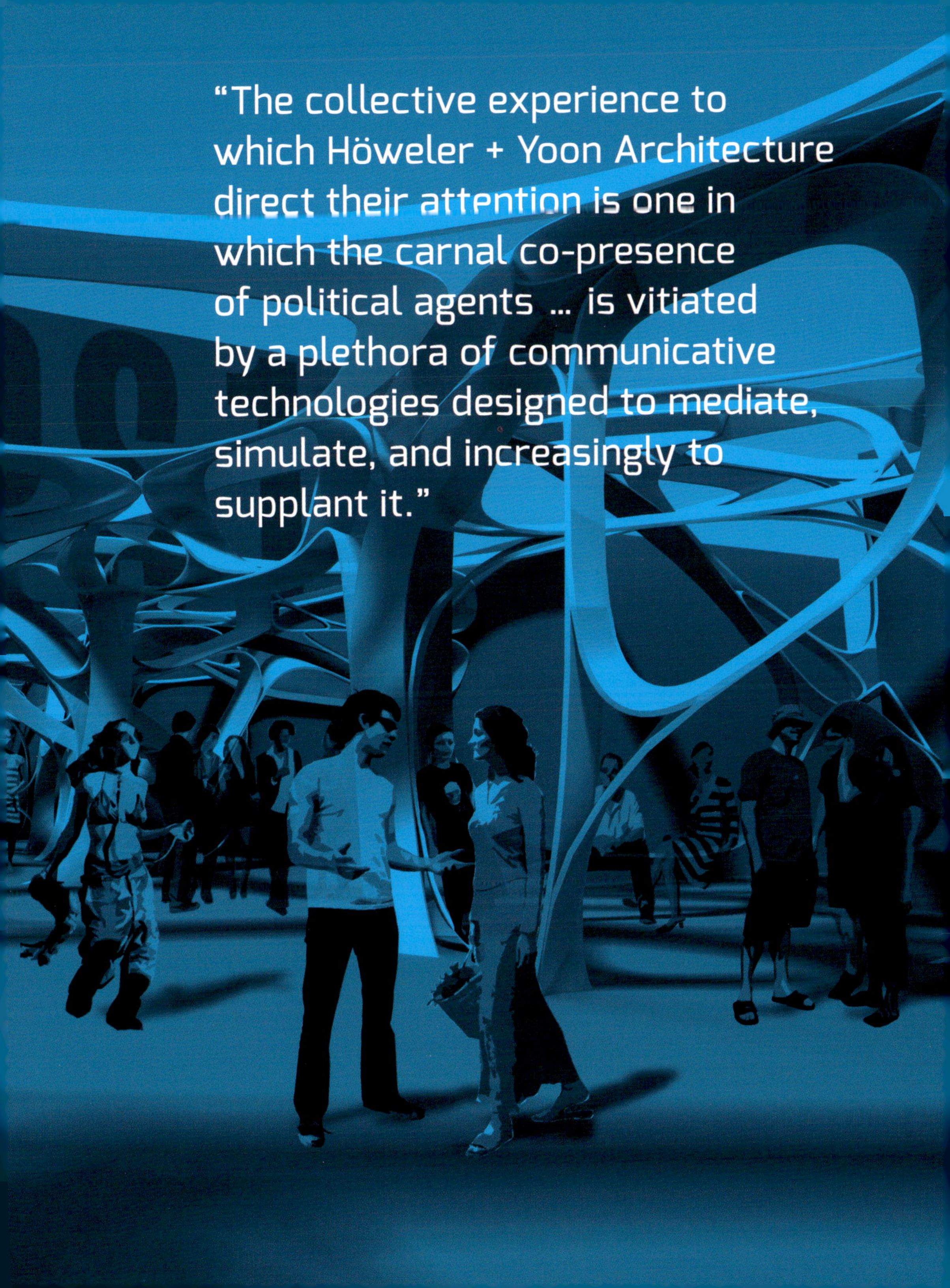

"The collective experience to which Höweler + Yoon Architecture direct their attention is one in which the carnal co-presence of political agents ... is vitiated by a plethora of communicative technologies designed to mediate, simulate, and increasingly to supplant it."

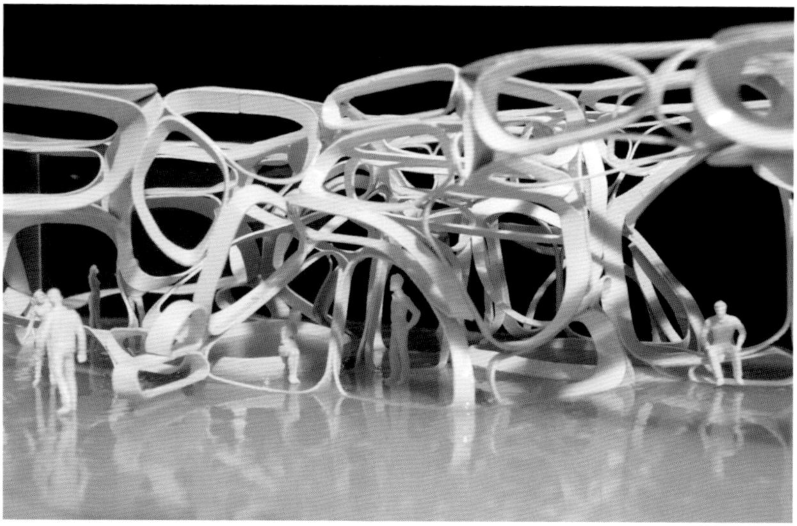

ABOVE. Loop, proposal for PS1 installation competition

buildings, such PTW Architects' Water Cube for the Beijing Olympics, and promises more important results in optimizing structure and reducing building mass in the pressing quest for lightness in architecture. HYA add a twist to such experiments with irregular geometry and structure by conflating surface and vector active components, building the entire structure with 888 wide plastic sheets.

The technique brings to mind experiments by Office dA such as Voromuro and Voroduo, where the material, structural, and surfacial qualities of thin polycarbonate strips are exploited in most ingenious and unexpected geometrical iterations. However while Office dA's intricately convoluted ribbons are deployed in configurations we still recognize in conventional architectural terms (wall, roof, dome) and serve to clearly demarcate enclosure, HYA's plastic loops transgress the defining limits—physical and conceptual—between space and enclosure to occupy the entire space with a foam-like architecture. At once volumetric and planar, full and empty, massive in its consistent and homogeneous materiality, and ultra fine in its constituent parts, this built foam subverts familiar distinctions between wall and space, solid and void. To enter LOOP is to become enmeshed in a latticework of pliant surfaces that promote a sense of collective occupation as dependent on our affective as on our intellectual responses.

WHITE NOISE/WHITE LIGHT

The preoccupations that we have observed to be at play in the work that HYA have produced at the scale of the body and the building are also apparent in their urban-scale interventions. These interventions often consist of temporary pavilions or event structures of one sort or another. Whether ephemeral or permanent, they invariably take the sensate body and its spatio-temporal envelope as the intimate locus of social connection. Having said that, this sensate body is treated as a body not merely susceptible to, but entirely traversed by and suffused with the informational networks that define contemporary social life. The White Noise/White Light project that HYA installed for the 2004 Athens Olympics is a case in point. Situated on the public plaza facing that most auspicious of sites in the history of urban spectacle, the Theatre of Dionysius, White Noise/White Light transformed the plaza into a visitor-activated synesthetic "sound and light scape" fed by a constellation of fiber optic strands, infrared sensors, and outdoor speakers. Movement of a visitor across the site would prompt the fiber optic outlets to transmit light from white LEDs, while at the same time prompting speakers situated below the installation's raised deck to emit Johnson Noise, a form of white noise produced from the thermal motions of electrons in a resistor carrying a current across an electronic circuit. The result of these transmissions was that each visitor's traversal of the site carried with it a spectral echo and afterglow, a physical and immediately collective memory that, after a fashion reminiscent of the Defensible Dress, amplifies the visitor's charismatic aura so as to expand his or her sphere of social influence. At the same time, the project gives positive figure to the otherwise invisible complex of movements that comprise the site's collective psychogeography.

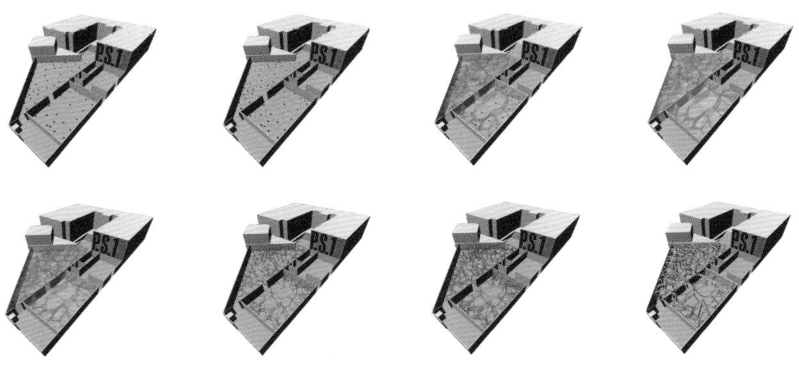

ABOVE. Diagram of constituent parts

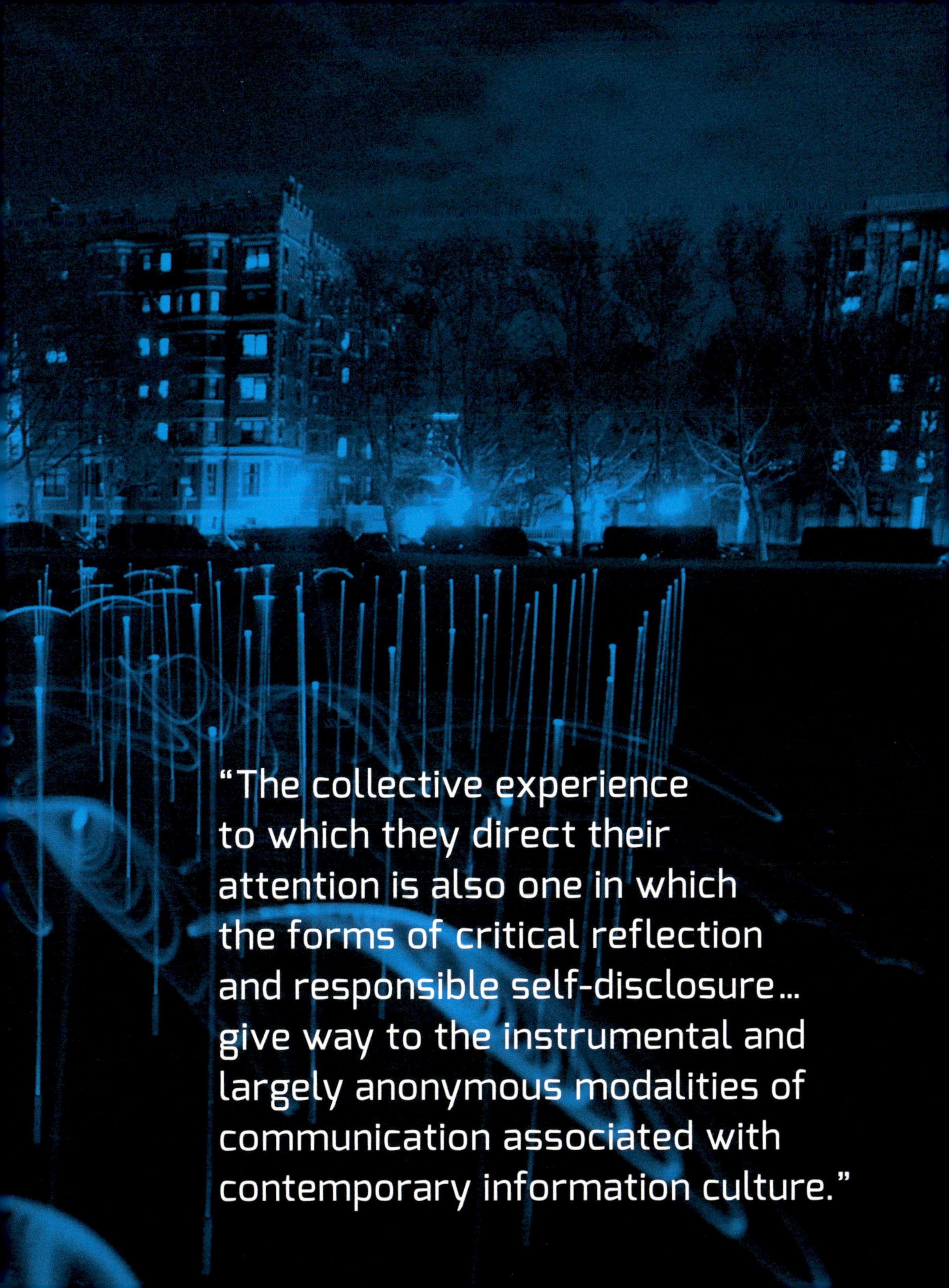

"The collective experience to which they direct their attention is also one in which the forms of critical reflection and responsible self-disclosure... give way to the instrumental and largely anonymous modalities of communication associated with contemporary information culture."

ABOVE. Roof plan

REIMAGINING PROPINQUITY

The interest of HYA's work lies not only in its timely exploration of a set of themes that currently hold the attention of the profession, but also in the persuasive way in which these themes (and the techniques, tactics, and stratagems they imply) are brought into communication with the more ethically and politically motivated dedications of the generation that preceded them. At once insisting on propinquity as the fundamental condition to which architecture is in response, and demanding that, in thinking on and responding to this condition, we give sober consideration to the massively changed circumstances under which we continue to differ together, HYA present a model of how professional circumspection and social commitment, technical adroitness and critical reflection, robust construction and sensitivity to phenomenological effects can coexist to produce an architecture in which aesthetic experience rediscovers its social context and reinvents its political vocation.

ABOVE. White Light/White Noise on the MIT campus

- COVERT DESIGNS: STEPHAN JAKLITSCH

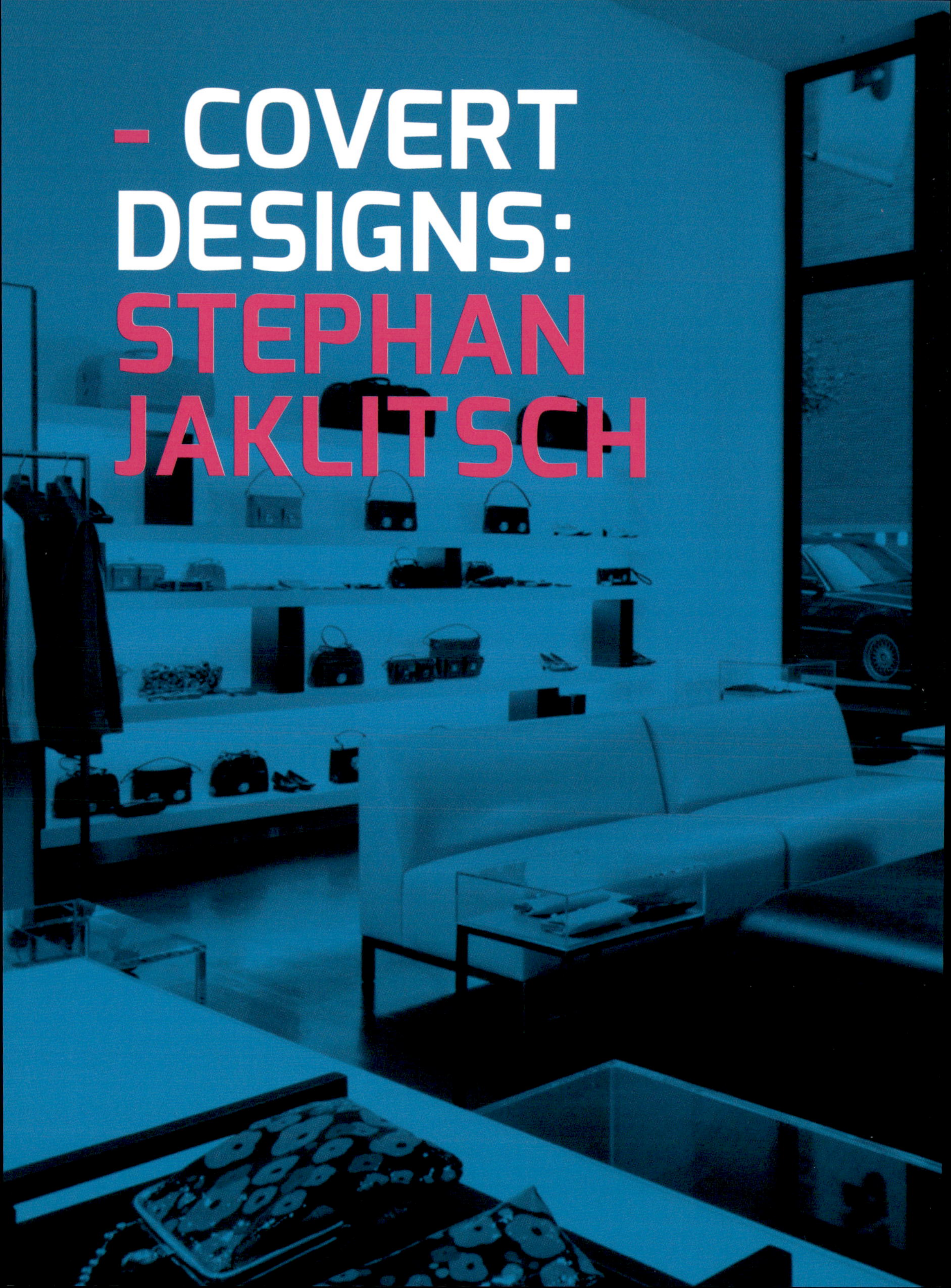

ORIGINALLY PUBLISHED IN **STEPHAN JAKLITSCH: HABITS, PATTERNS, ALGORITHMS**, ORO EDITIONS, 2008.

Let him who has something to say step forward and be silent!
—Karl Kraus

A small L shaped stainless steel bar sits on Stephan Jaklitsch's desk in his New York office. It is a flawless welding sample sent by a contractor in Japan. The architect proudly displays it; it is undeniably a persuasive demonstration of his attention to detail and the standards of execution that his firm is known for. But Jaklitsch's marked attachment to the shiny object suggests that there is more to this unlikely fetish than meets the eye. It is undeniably striking in its flawless smoothness: there is no evidence whatsoever of the welding, plating, and polishing processes that have produced it. It is as if it had been magically cast into the world *tel quel*, as a monolithic and finished artifact. This is an exquisitely crafted object that derives much of its value from—and commands a high premium for—the meticulous concealment of the craft.

A high level of precision in manufacturing is now actively sought by several of Jaklitsch's generation—especially in New York's commercial arena, where high profile boutiques have set equally high expectations with new standards of execution. But what is particularly evocative about this sample is the flawlessness with which it erases all traces of labor, almost transcending materiality with sheer perfection. What sets it apart and so endears it to the architect is its capacity to laconically encapsulate a whole aesthetic. Ostensibly, the sample is a demonstration of technical competence, but it actually holds much more: in its effortless flawlessness it stands for a whole design philosophy.

The aesthetic is not unique to Jaklitsch, but the stores that his firm has built for Marc Jacobs make one of the better cases for it. According to this aesthetic, design is most effective when it tends to disappear. Much like the impeccably crafted joint, design painstakingly covers its tracks in the Marc Jacobs stores. It strives to appear effortless. Jaklitsch doesn't seem to be trying too hard as he draws in and seduces you with the bare essentials of architecture. He won't recast the boutique environment in a totally new form, and deliberately chooses to re-work familiar elements: found objects ready to be re-invented by design.

Unlike the Prada stores, to name one example, where a panoply of design tricks is indiscriminately unleashed as part of a campaign that seeks cultural

ABOVE. Knize, Men's Apparel Store in Vienna

ABOVE. Calvin Klein Store in New York

status and legitimacy for the brand on all fronts, Jaklitsch's is an elitist strategy. It works by appealing to the designated patrons as "insiders." Jaklitsch's shops do not loudly state their design ambitions: they whisper to people "in the know," as if to forge a complicity between like- minded individuals who supposedly don't need design cues to recognize quality.

Paradoxically, Jaklitsch enhances the Marc Jacobs brand by resisting fashion. By maintaining a certain detachment from the immediate preoccupations of design culture, such as in avoiding the familiar cues that consumers have learned to recognize from popular magazines like *Wallpaper* or *Monocle*, Jaklitsch situates the Marc Jacobs stores in a seemingly timeless realm that is deaf to the clamor of the market. The fact that the denigration of fashion may be an ultra fashionable stance in its own perverse way does not detract from the efficacy of the design. The stores do not fail to gain in cachet as Jaklitsch reiterates his indifference to the latest trends, pursuing his own "less is more" philosophy in a consistent and understated look for Marc Jacobs.

Only a few gestures and furnishing suffice to set the stage and achieve the unmistakable effect. The frugal and judicious use of resources—now a staple of Jaklitsch's boutique design—still has to be distinguished from minimalism. Jaklitsch's economy of means has more to do with reserve than provocation. Unlike the minimalism of John Pawson- the designer behind the Calvin Klein boutiques of the late nineties Jaklitsch's restraint is not a statement in itself, the kind of extreme reduction that loudly announces its stylishness as an identifiable and commodifiable index of capital "D" design.

Adolf Loos famously described a best dressed man as someone whose formal attire doesn't get noticed at a party. The comment is consistent with his critique of Art Nouveau's design excesses in favor of an understated elegance. It also betrays a disdain for artifacts that vie for distinction by overtly stating their status as design objects.

The sartorial analogy is not accidental since Loos was seriously interested in fashion and had designed several shops for Knize, a men's apparel store that epitomized the tailored elegance that he favored. The simple and skillfully machined glass and steel vitrines in the Vienna shop wouldn't be out of place in the Marc Jacobs Paris flagship store at the Palais Royal. The Paris store is perhaps the most literally Loosian in its timeless elegance and opulent material palette. With its vaulted ceiling and symmetrical plan, it has an aristocratic air and faintly nostalgic flavor no doubt inspired by the decorous setting. But the Loosian ethos is discernable elsewhere, in other Marc Jacobs stores, where the defining principle is "good design is invisible design."

The San Francisco store designed by Jaklitsch in 2000 sets the tone for the many later examples. A few simple moves here establish the broad outlines of a distinct look that would be picked up and refined to consistently identify the brans and its various offshoots.

The main ingredient for the still- evolving formula are already in place: the loft- style sparseness and openness that references Marc Jacob's New York origins; the floor to-ceiling glazed façade, bringing the store and the articles on display in direct visual contact with the street; the simple and finely crafted cabinets, shelves and racks that have a distinct modernist flair; the art- gallery flavor in the sparseness of the displays, featuring a few carefully selected items in a manner more reminiscent of curated shows than retail space; the living- room- like arrangement of Christian Liaigre's comfortable but crisply contoured leather benches, couches, and armchairs that bring a domestic touch to the space of commerce, as if to allow regular patrons to casually appropriate the space as members of the Marc Jacobs family.

The same elements—with more or less adaptation to different context and sometimes benefiting from various enhancements from local craftsmanship and expertise—populate this expanding chain of stores with the usual sparseness. Of course, the danger with aiming for reserved elegance is ending up with the banal, especially when the means are too frugal or subtle. Because of repeated applications in multiple branches, the strategy also risks verging on boredom.

"Jaklitsch's shops do not loudly state their design ambitions: they whisper to people 'in the know,' as if to forge a complicity between like-minded individuals who supposedly don't need design cues to recognize quality."

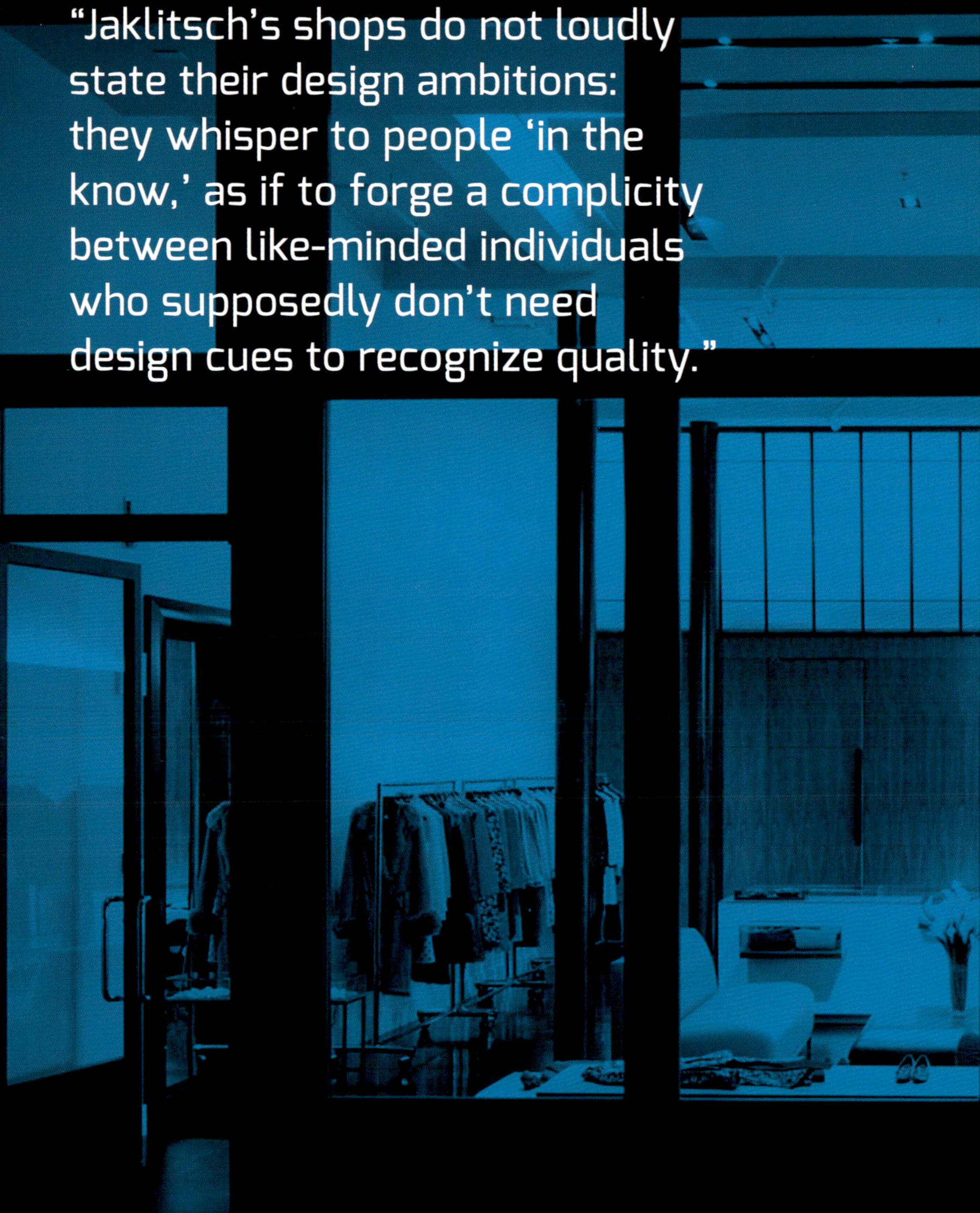

The fact that Jaklitsch succeeds in building an enduring and consistently engaging aesthetic with a rather reduced palette indicates that a sophisticated design philosophy is at work. It is perhaps best exemplified by some of the unbuilt projects that more explicitly express the architect's theoretical inclinations.

Studio X/Y was commissioned by a couple in North Carolina to accommodate a wood working workshop (for him) and a ceramic pottery studio (for her). The clients were interested in clearly differentiating and personalizing the two studios to convey programmatic and other distinctions such as gender and character. Jaklitsch wholeheartedly embraced the eccentric brief and delivered a tour de force of architectural characterization.

The two studios are contained within a single structure. The deceptively simple volume hardly deviates from the rectangular norm. A couple of inflections suffice to animate the prism with a subtle yet astonishing complexity. The strangeness of the ambiguous shape is heightened when, due to an optical illusion, it seems like it is L- shaped when viewed from certain angles. This is a compact prismatic structure, yet it stubbornly eludes a simple reading, as if resisting fully integrating its constituent parts into a unitary whole.

The building is chimera- like. Ostensibly, it presents a coherent body. Its contrasting constituent parts seem to neatly fit together. Although structurally and formally coherent, it remains divided by inherent contradiction, a monstrous heterogeneity. And much like the mythical beast, its uncanny oddity is exa cerbated by the neatness of its unlikely assembly.

The building sustains this paradoxical tension in different aspects of construction and representation. If the building's unity is affirmed in one register, it is also challenged in others, communicated by a choice of materials that underscores the autonomy and identity of its distinct parts. The impression is that of two individuals coming together in a dialogue that heightens their similarities and differences. Taken separately, the two interlocutors are hardly remarkable: they are almost literal translations of vernacular types that Jaklitsch deliberately chooses not to overtly transform. It is in the tense combination and resultant sharpening of their distinctness that these objects become extraordinary. The dialogue, especially in the interplay of reciprocal framing, is what defamiliarizes the quasi- vernacular sheds and repositions them

ABOVE. Marc Jacob store at the Palais Royal, Paris

as highly self- conscious design artifacts. Consider for instance the way the canopy of the pottery studio sets up—much in the manner of a theatrical proscenium—the stair leading to the upper level of the woodwork atelier behind.

I dwell on these aspects of this unbuilt project because they are more over expressions of the compositional strategies that Jaklitsch deploys with greater reserve in the boutique environment. Jaklitsch operates with a reduced palette in the Marc Jacobs stores, but achieves the same tension and drama in staging highly charged relationships between a few iconic pieces. Here, also, Jaklitsch resists that willful imposition of form and opts to reconfigure known types, which he treads like found objects. Design consists in an understated curatorial re-framing and exquisite fabrication of familiar artifacts. With a judiciously placed cabinet here and a shelf there, Jaklitsch manages to transform a rather sparsely populated stage into a gripping scene with an unmistakable look that has now come to identify Marc Jacobs.

If X/Y serves to illustrate Jaklitsch's capacity to build theatrical tension with modest means by staging (that is, designing) the relationship between objects, the private residence in Columbia County, New York, exemplifies another kind of theatricality. This kind has to do with Jaklitsch's keen sense of timing and dramatic delivery.

"The architecture is a theatrical device: it serves to set up, anticipate, and dramatize the discovery of the landscape."

Jaklitsch designs the approach to the site with a deliberate sense of pacing, deferring the prized view to a climactic unveiling in the living room. The architecture is a theatrical device: it serves to set up, anticipate, and dramatize the discovery of the landscape. Visitors arrive at a ridge in a heavily wooded landscape, a clearing where only low-lying retaining walls are in sight. They descend into the house, slipping between two stone walls only to discover the lakes at first on the side, and then in their full panoramic glory once within the main living space.

The previous house stood squarely at the highest elevation, towering over the landscape; this one is artfully sited below the ridge. It has an understated presence in the landscape, barely visible from the clearing beyond the bearing walls. The former delivers the "punch" predictably and rather prematurely. The latter draws the visitor in a protracted mise-en-scène that gradually yields its reward: a surprisingly generous interior and a spectacular view.

The spectacle is not limited to the view towards the lake. One of the most striking features of the house is the proscenium-like dining room that frames, in the opposite direction, the ruins of the old house in a sunken patio. The theatrical character of the dining room is reminiscent of Loos's interiors, where architectural devices rhetorically frame rituals of domestic life. While Loos preferred a rather claustrophobic setting, with all gazes focused inwardly on the private realm of civilized bourgeoisie, the main space of Jaklitsch's house is tellingly and very deliberately positioned halfway between the spectacle of nature and the precisely staged scenes of domestic rituals. In this axial arrangement, the sight of the untamed wilderness is even more sublime when viewed against the forms of everyday life, as shaped by design.

Looking at the Marc Jacobs boutiques, one cannot help but see the same recurrent arrangement of contrasting scenes: the urban jungle seen through the floor-to-ceiling windowpanes, and the opposing presentation of precisely framed artifacts. And while the stage may be set for an interesting dialogue, the lines are neither loud nor clear. The burden of meaning in Jaklitsch's architecture is placed on the user; the message is not neatly packaged and ready for consumption. It is for us to discover by interrogating the stubbornly laconic architecture in its covert operations.

ABOVE AND BELOW. XY Studio

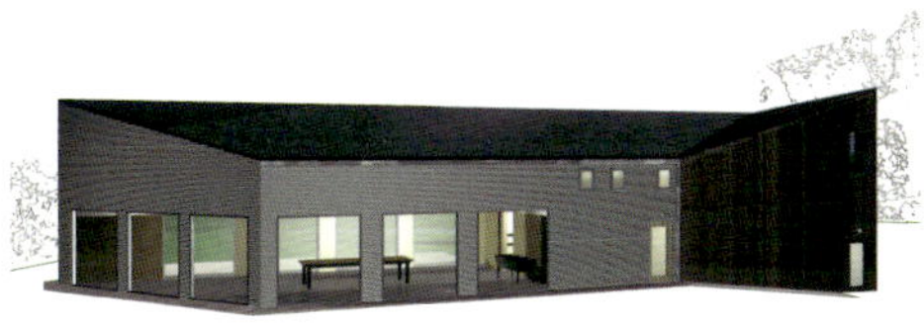

– SMART FIGURE/ SENSIBLE GROUND: ANDREW BROMBERG OF AEDAS

ORIGINALLY PUBLISHED IN **ARCHITECTURE AND SENSUALITY: ANDREW BROMBERG OF AEDAS, RECENT WORK**,
ORO EDITIONS, 2008.

ANDREW BROMBERG'S West Kowloon development, as a case study of his work, is an urban environment with multiple levels of commercial and public facilities that only metropolitan urban cores like Hong Kong's could sustain wit the vertical density and consistent intensity suggested in the renderings. The dominant architectural element is a colossal modular canopy supported on tree-like pillars and extended repetitively over 40 hectares. It shelters a densely packed cityscape arranged in an intricate pattern of interlocking building blocks and spaces. This urban scenario is presented among more or less familiar features: an archipelago of suspended gardens with unobstructed views of the city; a network of public walkways and shops stacked on several levels above a complex of performance venues; and, towering above the layered landscape, a collection of high-rise buildings of varying sizes and shapes.

From a bird's-eye view the whole development stands out as a distinct, branded artifact against the competing patterns of adjacent districts. The strong identity is due to a unique formal language that is consistent in plan and elevation. It would be instantly recognizable in the Hong Kong skyline, as easily as in the satellite imaging of a Google Earth search. In the close-up views we see a media-saturated environment with activities staged on every level. Throughout the project and at all scales the plans call for extraordinary architectural means to orchestrate shopping, entertainment, and leisure into a spectacle of urban life designed to stimulate the senses as much as commerce.

This is a phototelegenic architecture that is very much attuned to the demands of the market. The economics and spatial logic of retail, entertainment, and real-estate development have been assimilated into the design intelligence that guides every move. Ostensibly free-flowing lines and whimsically shaped volumes are informed by pro-forms, market analyses, and demographic studies. They are engineered for optimal views, optimal exposure, optimal accessibility, optimal capacity, and optimal variety.

The mercantile framework also accounts for the bold formal moves that seem to elude any overt utilitarian logic. They are valued for their capacity to reinforce the brand with distinctive features. Even the atmospherics are subjected to the demands of the market: colors, mood, and ambiance are mobilized in delivering the memorable experience that would give this development a competitive edge in the new economy.

Bromberg's architecture is conditioned under enormous financial pressure by market imperatives. But what sets it apart from the overwhelming majority of commercial-building projects is its unrelenting capacity to escape the commonplace. At every opportunity it reaches into the unknown with unprecedented propositions in lieu of the tried and tested solution that risk-avoiding speculation continues to favor.

And with every risky move comes a great deal of innovation and ingenuity. The new architectural forms are thrilling. But equally inventive—and rewarding—are the means, techniques, and processes that the architects devise to translate the bold new vision into a buildable and viable proposition.

Bromberg's is a commercial architecture that is motivated by private interests. It is, nevertheless, setting a new standard for what is possible in the field. Not only is it pushing the envelope in terms of form and building technology—it is also reshaping the public realm with a civic ambition that had been primarily reserved for buildings with more overt public mandates and institutional sponsorship.

For a critical establishment in architecture that is accustomed to valorizing artisanally crafted and highly customized building, for high profile clients and institutions, the notion that commercial architecture like Aedas' should be leading the field in design innovation may be a difficult, if not surprising, proposition. But few would doubt the innovative resourcefulness of market-driven practices in other fields. Compare, for instance, a consumer product such as a Ducati motorcycle to a masterfully customized chopper. I can safely assume that anyone who is remotely invested in design would favor the Ducati—we are not comparing performance, where the crushing superiority of a Ducati would be an objective and quantifiable fact. However seductive the originality of style, the artistry of construction, the impeccable finishes, and the exquisite craftsmanship, the chopper will be found lacking in the rigor and discipline that a precisely calibrated consumer product demonstrates. Granted, in the context of industrial design, the comparison is rather unfair given the disciplinary prejudice in favor of mass- produced products. But the analogy is relevant insofar as it exposes architecture's own prejudice. The fact that architectural critics tend to privilege the precisely tailored, thoroughly customized, exquisitely detailed, and lavishly produced one-off designs over the streamlined commercial products is a reality that begs further critical scrutiny. It is bound to reveal a reactionary, hard core within the architecture discipline.

RIGHT. Hong Kong, West Kowloon Cultural District

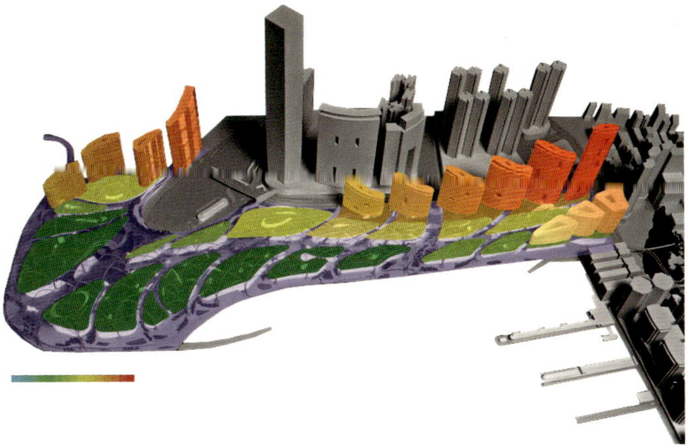

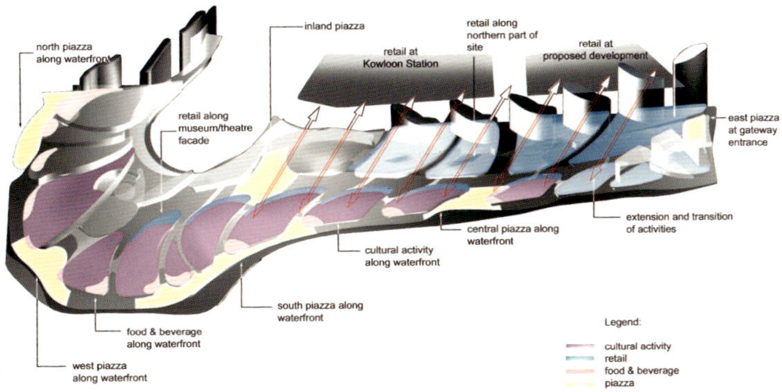

ACTIVITY LINKAGES

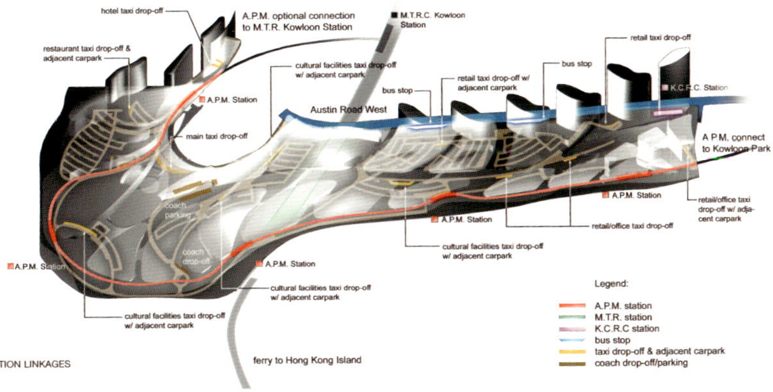

TRANSPORTATION LINKAGES

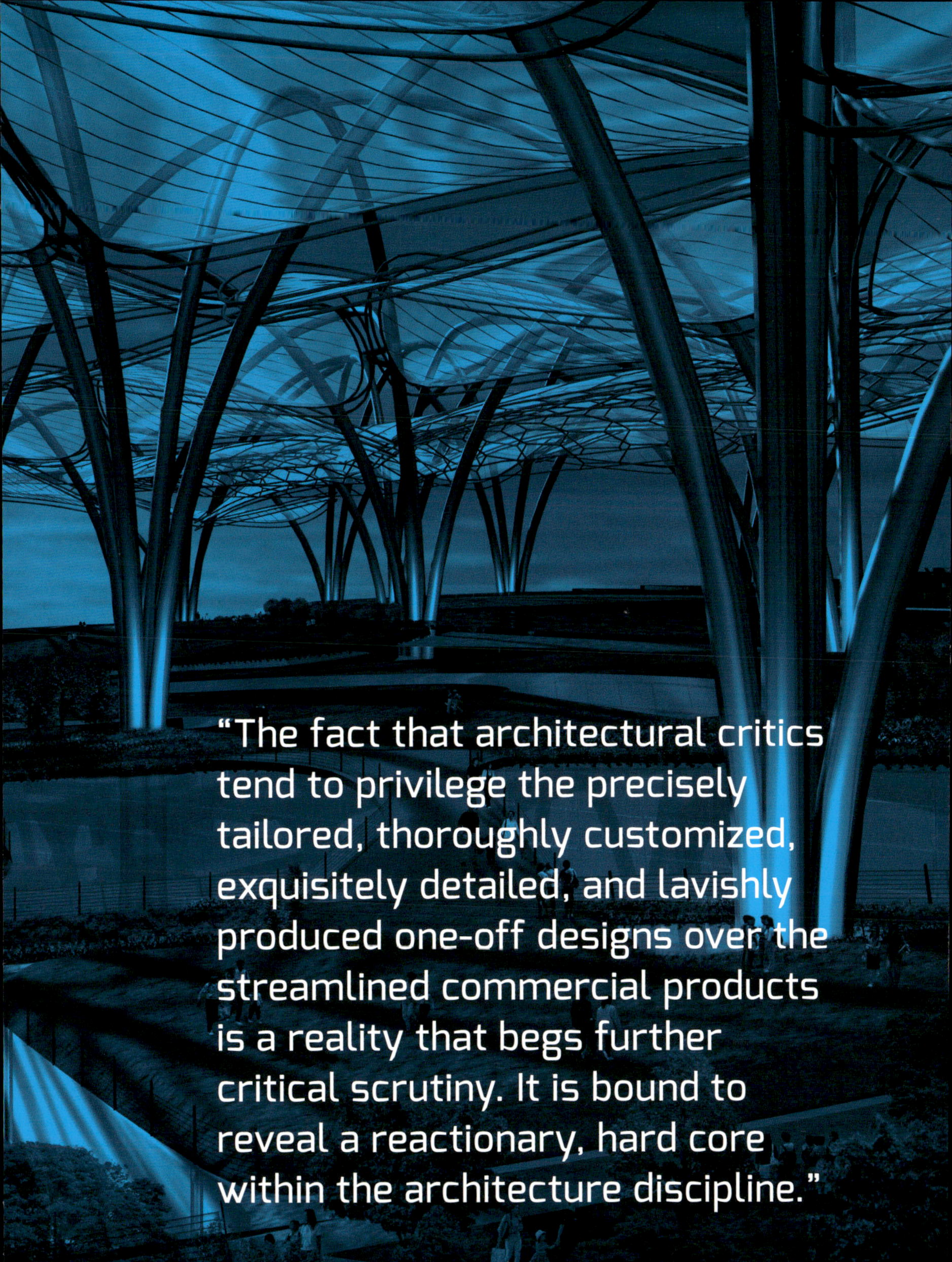

"The fact that architectural critics tend to privilege the precisely tailored, thoroughly customized, exquisitely detailed, and lavishly produced one-off designs over the streamlined commercial products is a reality that begs further critical scrutiny. It is bound to reveal a reactionary, hard core within the architecture discipline."

COMPLEX BEINGS

The search for the iconic form that would sell the project in a highly competitive global market is perhaps the most potent force that drives Bromberg's architecture. In a place like Dubai, where every building stridently proclaims its unique identity, superlatives—tallest building, largest units, highest ceilings—were all it took, only a few years ago, to sell property. Far more extraordinary attributes are now required in attracting increasingly sophisticated *Wallpaper* magazine-trained buyers. If there was one single critical quality that distinguished Bromberg among other talented designers in rival commercial offices, it would have to be the knack for nailing down the extraordinary form that never fails to sell his signature buildings.

His staple forms are vaguely figurative but not literal. They are strangely evocative of familiar yet unknown things. Occasionally, they approximate anthropomorphic or zoomorphic shapes while remaining somehow abstract. They are never reducible to a single reading, leaving the viewer guessing as to the intended meaning or references. Some acquire monikers that unfortunately tend to narrow down the interpretive options, fixing the semantic fluidity perhaps too prematurely.

Anthropomorphic references are common in journalistic accounts of Bromberg's architecture. The interplay of masses in Dancing Towers, a commercial development in Abu Dhabi featuring two high rise buildings, is, for instance, inevitably likened to the notion of a ballet. The slabs in question are strictly non figurative. The ballet connotation is entirely due to the complexity of the composition, to an intricacy in the interplay of actions and reactions between two responsive forms. The sense of responsiveness is what facilitates or even encourages the anthropocentric projection of effect. In Dancing Tower's form we see a dancer's posture; in another twin tower proposal we see legs and even a hint of eroticism.

How do Bromberg's strange forms provoke such empathy, allowing us to imagine a gesture or an embrace in place of objects in space? How does abstract geometry become virtually figurative? Bromberg states that he "looks for soul," this remark has to be taken more literally beyond the cliché that attributes to a spiritual character to architectural essences. The soul, or animus, is what animates objects—breathes life, so to speak, into form.

ABOVE. Abu Dhabi, Dancing Towers

Bromberg doesn't shape his buildings freely, as if from readily malleable clay. The masses he works with are always already buildings, complex organizational and material propositions that he works into new configuration by means of design. Every move he makes is considered with respect to the repercussions it would have on program, structure, material, and building cost. When he bends a line on the elevation, he is also devising ingenious ways to deform the curtain wall at no additional cost and anticipating how stacked building systems will be impacted. So when you look at the twisting geometry of Dancing Towers, you can actually see, literally, in the hinged deformation of the curtain wall, how the orthogonal steel frame has been engineered into a new form. The transformative process that pushed against the norm is laid bare for you to comprehend and appreciate, beyond the formal interest of the sculpted envelope.

Bromberg wrestles with the "stuff" of architecture to produce his forms. Commentators have called him an "artist" to account for the sculptural character of his architecture. But this is an artist who is heavily invested in the particulars of his medium, in what is unique about its material and craft, in the discipline and practice of architecture.

When we look at his buildings we see artfully sculpted form, but we also recognize how objects with complex constitutions and internal organizations have been reworked into these sculptural contours. It is the capacity to intuit the organizational and structural complexity that lie just beneath the surface, in the continuously adjusting trajectory of a studied curve that imparts intelligence, a soul, to Bromberg's architecture.

The curve is one of the persistent features in Bromberg's high-rise designs. It is pervasive in plan as much as in section, imparting the distinct kinetic quality that characterizes much of his work. The curve is not only about styling, although it is quite effective in branding the work with a characteristic figure. Beyond the gestural effect, it liberates the building from the normative orthogonal framework, providing opportunities for a more fluid and diversified occupation of the floor plates. In contradistinction to conventional high-rises, where a single extruded plan basically generates the entire building, Bromberg's curvilinear forms differentiate each floor, providing for slightly different unit layouts on each level. Curvature also helps in optimizing views for a maximum number

LEFT. Dubai, Ocean Heights One

"Emerging high-stakes real-estate markets with staggering financial interests invested in building have steadily elevated expectations for quality and innovation in design... In the last few years, innovation has migrated from academic research centers to the professional arena, from studios at Harvard or Columbia to the trenches at SOM, Arup, and Fosters."

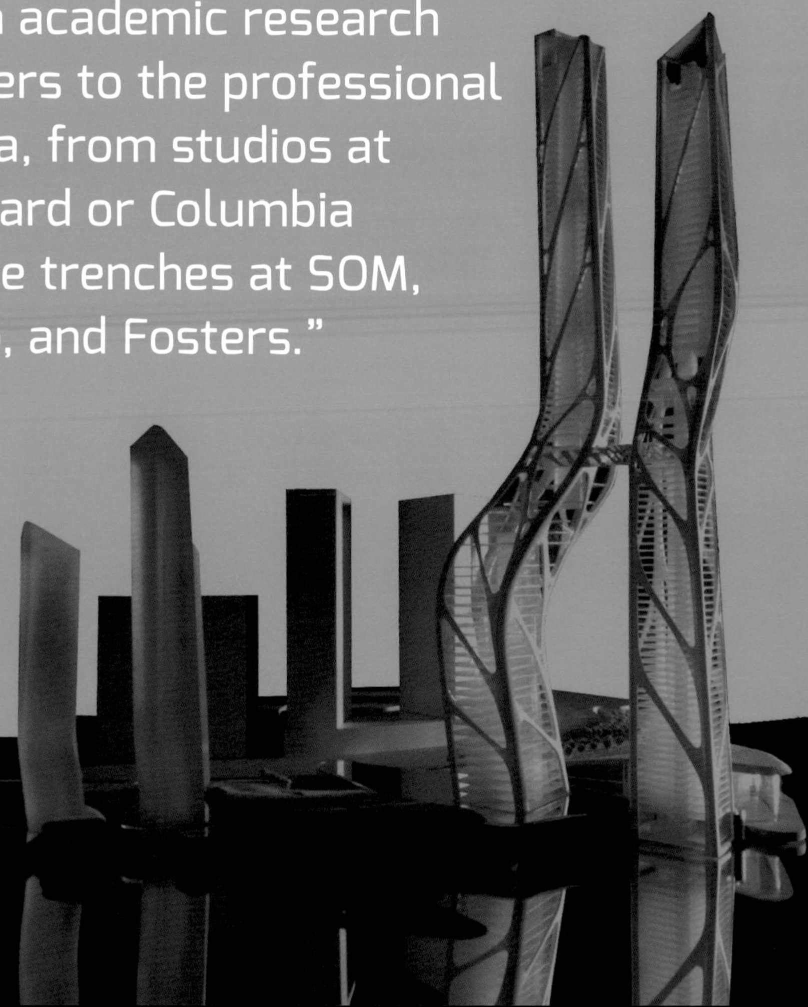

ABOVE. Empire Tower, Abu Dhabi One

of units so as to significantly enhance their value. For instance, in Ocean Heights One, the entire structure torques so as to expose all sides to a greater variety of views.

The curving geometry is not a superficial treatment It permeates the whole building to occasionally even refashion the structural frame and liberate the plan from the "orthopedic" restrictions of the vertical core. Empire Tower is a remarkable example of this structural tour de force. In this 230- meter- tall tower, the concrete piers gradually bend as the building mass splays wide open toward the base to maximize the occupancy of the lot. Unlike most other instances where curvilinear inflections are limited to the building envelope, the entire structure here is bent. Even at the scale of the individual unit, the eccentricity of the structure is made palpable in the slight but dramatic deviation of the load- bearing walls from the expected vertical. This organic relationship between the individual dwelling and the overall shape is furthermore articulated on the striated elevations. Vertical recesses here objectify the stacked housing units in distinct stripes. Their varying curvature exacerbates the deformation of the building shaft, translating the building's organizational diagram into an expressive form. The diagram aims for the most efficient exploitation of the site by means of a smooth transition from a large base to a slender tower, from maximum coverage and exposure at street level to maximum distance from property lines and clear views higher above. But the unprecedented architecture it serves to generate far exceeds the brute economics of the market conscious strategy. The building is unlike any other; it is made possible by means of considerable technical innovation, and a great deal of imagination. Once again it illustrates how Bromberg's designs elevate necessity into art and fashion, and transform banal objects to remarkable ones.

SOCIAL OBJECTS

The affirmation of the object in Bromberg's work must be read in light of a market logic that privileges or even demands individuality and imageability over the polite anonymity of contextually integrated buildings. The same logic drives the tendency for rapidly developing cities such as Dubai to sprawl into a collection of discrete objects, all gesticulating for attention in an undifferentiated metropolitan field.

Bromberg's objects are very much prone to such gesticulation. But the gestures, as I earlier stated, are of a sophisticated kind. Their language is clearly distinguishable from the more common variety. The temptation is to attribute the je ne sais quoi that sets them apart to the ineffable workings of a design intuition. There is a more tangible explanation: Bromberg's forms are not superficial effects that are gratuitously overplayed on indifferent structures. His bulges, twists, and sweeps are precisely and painstakingly negotiated with a building's normative constitution. They rub against the set of material, typological, and cultural predispositions that cosmetics treatment would leave unperturbed and that Bromberg chooses to engage in depth with the transformative power of form. In Bromberg's strangely shaped buildings, each curve manifests the outcome of an conceptual and material struggle through which type and structure are transformed by design.

In addition to the inner organizational turmoil, the object's contours also register the complex rapport they have with their surroundings. These are discrete objects but they are not entirely autonomous. They may stand as separate entities, but they have a keen sense of the context. Theirs is a complex personality that has a capacity for a nuanced and responsive attitude to the surroundings. They converse with their environment. They are urbane subjects.

Consider, for instance, Pentominium, one of the highest towers currently planned for Dubai. On the side facing an unusually close tall building, the building mass is clustered into a set of discrete five-story pods cantilevered from the core and separated by generously proportioned gardens. The crenellated side creates a memorable silhouette; it also serves to mitigate the proximity of the neighboring tower. It is an object with a very distinct image, but one that was fashioned in response to context. Pentominium's distinct figure against the adjacent building and the sky framed in between radicalizes a more or less latent tendency in Bromberg's design: the propensity for shaping space as much as the objects they inhabit.

This explains, perhaps, why Bromberg is particularly successful with building ensembles in which two or several structures are caught in a complex web of reciprocal influences. Dancing Towers is the prime example of a charged relationship between two objects, fraternal twins whose individual characteristics are heightened by mutual responsiveness. But what is also unique and equally effective is the way the two towers shape the surrounding space. In Dancing Towers, much like in most of Bromberg's ensemble compositions, positive building masses and negative residual spaces share a common pattern language, so much so that figure and ground become reversible, in a manner reminiscent of some of M.C. Escher's puzzles, where one pattern gradually morphs into another while figure and ground are reversed in their respective roles.

Let us translate Escher's Sky and Water One 1938 woodcut into an architectural language. Imagine the dark bottom of the picture to be a Nolli Plan-like diagram, with the fish representing a space that is shaped by the poché of building mass. In this analogy the duck on top would be a modern object-building freestanding in an open field. Space is figured below and residual at the top. It would be typical of traditional urban form below and of modern cities above.

RIGHT. Pentominium Tower, Dubai

In this diagram Bromberg's architecture would occupy the central band, where figure and ground are reversible, and where both fish and duck sustain their legibility in an interplay of mutually defining contours. In most urban projects designed by Bromberg, buildings consistently define the surrounding space as much as space shapes the enveloping buildings. Take a look at the North Star development, or Union Square: are the public corridors residual, leftover spaces between figured slabs? Or, is it the other way around? Are the buildings shaped by the figure of the public realm?

This ambiguity is one of the defining features of Bromberg's urbanism. It is evident, for instance, in the design for a residential district in historic Xian. The site is a former ammunitions-storage area that is crisscrossed with disused rail tracks. Bromberg here deploys an array of housing slabs in a pattern that negotiates the traces of the obsolete infrastructure as well as the city's orthogonal grid. The reversible figure ground—as well as the concomitant spatial ambiguity—is here applied persistently.

The design still features a dispersed field of atomized masses, the quasi-universal attribute of commercial developments. But there is no residual space in this field. The public realm is shaped with the same deliberate strokes that have fashioned the building blocks. The strategy allows for buildings to be individuated and tailored for optimal views and exposure, to effectively compete in the marketplace with subtle but effective inflections. It also provides for civic conformity, and a capacity for integration in a larger whole and with a common purpose.

The bird's-eye view is very telling, almost emblematic of Bromberg's urban sensibility: it shows his strange objects in a swarm-like pattern, as if locked in a synchronized movement. Each object has its own character,

ABOVE. Escher, Sky and Water One

implicit in a distinct bend or a kink. This character is mindful of others, though. It betrays a social aptitude in the virtual flocking behavior. It is unmistakably urban.

Perhaps the greatest virtue of Bromberg's strange objects is their not-so-strange relation to the ground. The Dancing Towers' eloquent ballet is very effective in selling the development with compelling images of graceful building silhouettes. It is also tremendously convincing in shaping and animating the surrounding urban field into an inviting public space.

The commitment to the city's public realm is most forcibly stated in the Union Square development for Dubai. This is a project that is primarily dedicated to the deliberate shaping of urban space and to fashioning a rich and sustainable urban realm. Much like in Bromberg's larger urban plans, the buildings here are discrete objects as much as containers, figures as much as ground. They maintain their status as independent objects but they are still coordinated in their primary dedication: shaping the space in between. We recognize Bromberg's staple urban strategy, but there is a new twist in this particular scenario. Beyond a figurative, symbolic subordination to a civic program, the buildings here also perform as public infrastructure. They provide structural support for a canopy that is designed to enhance the quality and sustainability of the public realm.

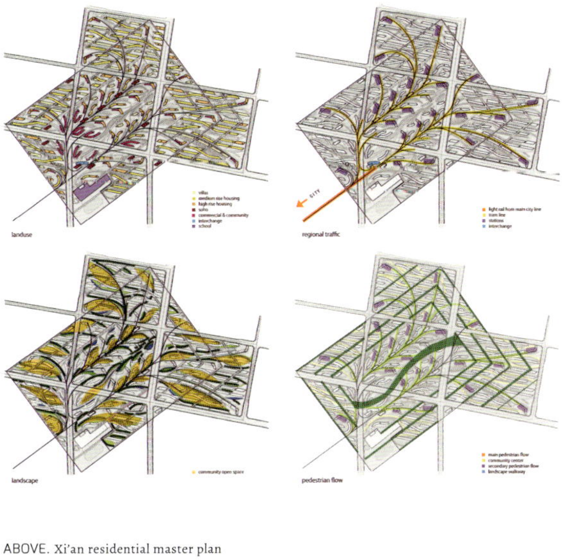

ABOVE. Xi'an residential master plan

CONCLUSION

Emerging high-stakes real-estate markets with staggering financial interests invested in building have steadily elevated expectations for quality and innovation in design. They have created a competitive environment in which large corporate offices are able to capitalize on formidable resources to project architecture forward, pushing the envelope of building science and design with every new unprecedented structure. In the last few years, innovation has migrated from academic research centers to the professional arena, from studios at Harvard or Columbia to the trenches at SOM, Arup, and Fosters.

The new design vanguard is now busy at work, as Bromberg's buildings clearly suggest, in offices such as Aedas Hong Kong. They now define what is possible and find ways to make it buildable. They give us the Ducatis of architecture when it comes to refinement and technological sophistication. At their best they also do more. Bromberg and his team have the quasi- utopian drive—architecture's defining ethical trait— that delivers socially and environmentally responsible environments for all.

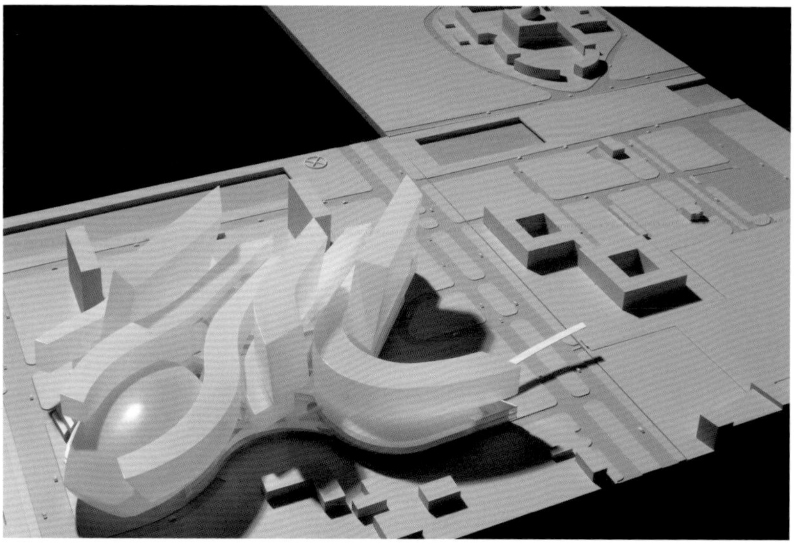

ABOVE. North Star Performing Arts Center, Singapore

RIGHT. Media Tower, Dubai

FOLLOWING SPREAD. Xi'an residential development

- BETWEEN AIR AND SPACE: AN TE LIU

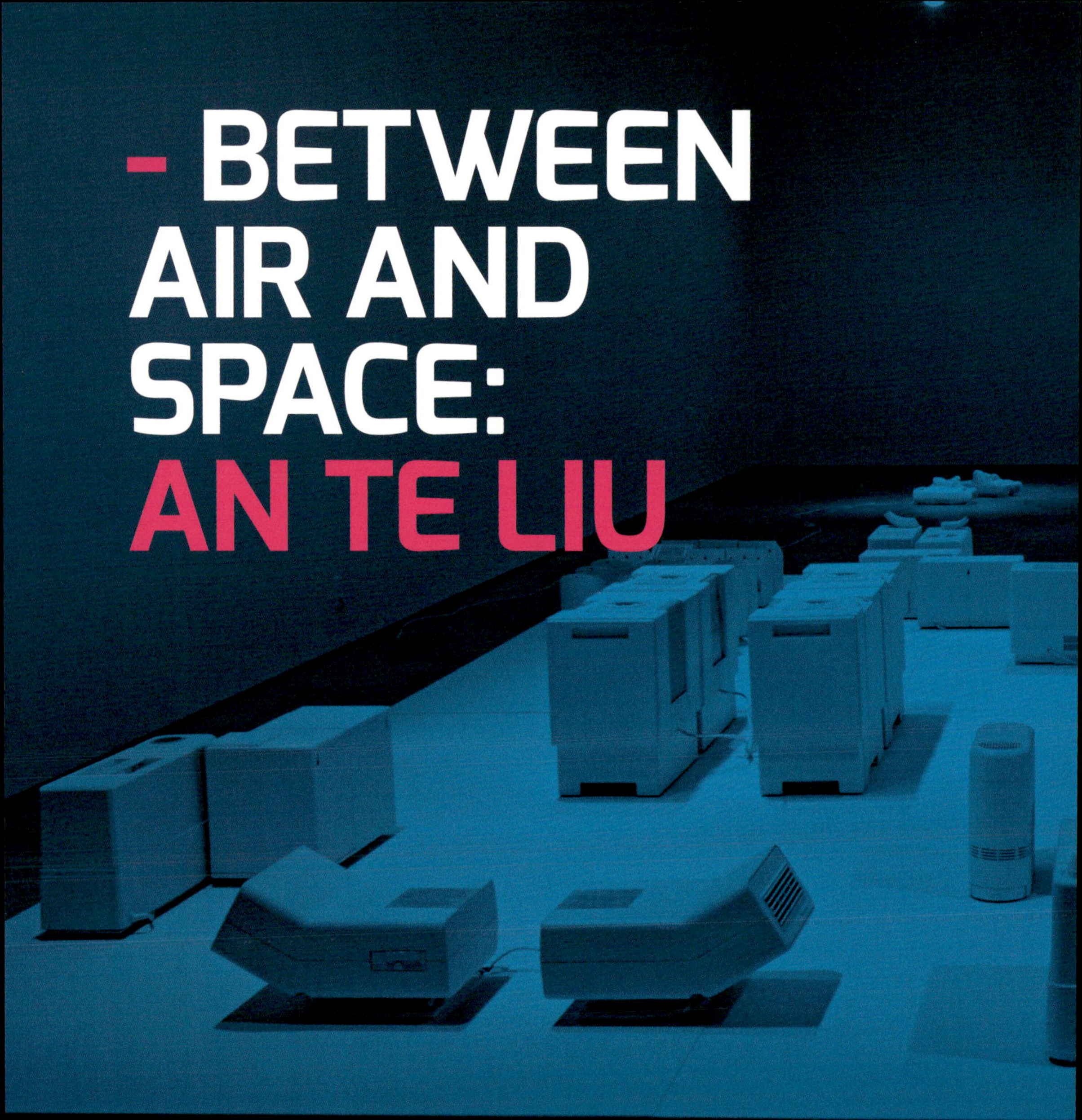

ORIGINALLY PUBLISHED IN **THRESHOLDS**, WINTER 2002.

THE WORK OF AN TE LIU is strategically situated between architecture and art. Unlike other works of architectural means and proportions that we are now accustomed to find comfortably installed in art galleries, some of Liu's more unsettling pieces are nowhere quite at home. They are designed for the gallery, yet they perform as architecture: "machines for living" seemingly designed to correct behavioral and environmental deviance. The fact that they perversely succeed in being totally useless does not detract from their pragmatic—architectural—logic.

Condition, Liu's recent show at the Henry Urbach Gallery, featured "Type/Need" and "Exchange," two new works elaborating themes initially tackled in the Sclerotic (1998) and Soft Load (1999) series.[2] Much like its precursor Sclerotic III—a pair of safety grab bars flanking an electric outlet "Type/Need" contrives strange but uncannily plausible artifacts from a dystopian universe where a hygienic re-construction of the body is played out to perverse extremes (Fig 2).[3] Flesh-colored contraptions are assembled from salvaged exercise equipment in unlikely yet seamless configurations. The purpose and origin of the machine parts are still legible in the new assemblage, much like the latent bicycle in Picasso's "Bull's Head" (Fig 3). The fragments here are not reconstituted into an organic figure; they are merely reshuffled to produce a different machine. A deviant machine. The perversion is latent: "Type/Need" is not so much an iconic conflation of the mechanical and the organic—the familiar topos of the historical avant-garde—but more of a catalytic platform for potentially grotesque rituals and obscene hybridizations.

"Exchange," the pièce de résistance of the *Condition* show, aligns with the Soft Load series—household sponges arranged into architectural and artistic parodies (Fig 4)—in staging the uneasy convergence of the aesthetic and the hygienic. "Exchange" presents fifty-six HEPA air cleaners in seven column-like stacks (Fig 5). Together they are claimed to recycle the air of

[2] An Te Liu speaks of the appliance's placebo effect in an interview with Aaron Betsky: "My college roommate and I had two Bionaire purifiers/ionizers in our apartment. We would sit around drinking scotch in a smoky haze with the machines running full blast in case our parents showed up unexpectedly. After a few hours, the air seemed to tingle with clean, negatively charged ions, and we were sure we could feel it. Or was it the single malt? In any case, the indicator light was on, and we were assured that something good was happening, even if we didn't understand the mysteries of negative-air ionization. 'Placebo' comes from the Latin 'to please,' and we were damn happy with our new devices." Aaron Betsky, "Safe Haven," interview with An Te Liu, *Surface* 25 (Fall 2000), 155.

[3] An Te Liu, Sclerotic III, 2000 (Fig 14).

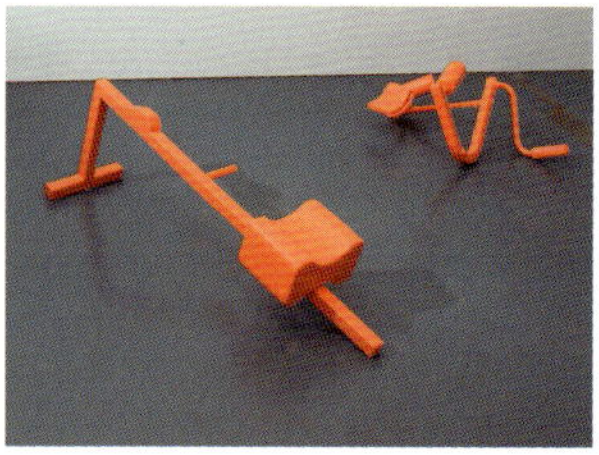

ABOVE. An Te Liu, "Type/Need," 2001. Exhibited at the Condition show at the Henry Urbach Architecture Gallery, New York, 2001.

ABOVE. Untitled (Complex II)

the gallery every twenty-one seconds. They also generate a considerably high level of white noise and a distinct odor akin to that of freshly opened plastic packages. The installation mobilizes all the senses to dramatize the discourse of hygiene in an assault on imperceptible air pollutants.

"Exchange" is consistent with Liu's earlier parodies of hygienic practice, contriving a "pathological" performance from "normal" domestic rituals. What is unusual here—and certainly not typical of contemporary art practice—is the empirical preoccupation with air, the air of the gallery. "Exchange" operates on the air of the gallery as much as in the space of the gallery. Ostensibly because of its hygienic mandate, modern architecture is known in particular to have occasionally equated air with space. Liu's work overlays a haptic experience of air on the abstract intuition of space—the ubiquitous medium of art.

Although equally fixated on space, architecture has had a more sustained dialogue with air. The notion that air has a critical role to play in the precarious equilibrium of health and is therefore subject to architectural speculation has been a commonplace since antiquity. Hence Vitruvius's instructions for the optimal orientation of the streets: "They will be properly laid out if foresight is employed to exclude the winds from the alleys. Cold winds are disagreeable, hot winds enervating, moist winds unhealthy."[4] The mechanical and physiological intricacies of pneumatic processes remained confused and controversial until the dissemination of Antoine-Laurent Lavoisier's (1743-1794) research on respiration and Jan Ingenhousz's (1730-1799) on photo synthesis. Still, the beneficial effects of "fresh air"—i.e., freely circulating air—and the hazards of stagnation were never in doubt. The sight of laboratory animals promptly dying in hermetically sealed vessels was ample proof.

[4] Vitruvius, *The Ten Books of Architecture* (1960) 24-31.

ABOVE. An Te Liu, "Soft Load," 1999. Exhibited at the *Luster* show at the Henry Urbach Architecture Gallery, New York, 1999.

Air became a focus of scientific research after 1750, thanks mainly to Stephen Hales (1677-1761), whose work turned air, hitherto understood as an elementary fluid, into a heterogeneous mixture of chemical components.[5] Research into its unknown and threatening composition was followed with particular urgency in the second half of the eighteenth century, when it was obsessively fueled by the anxieties of pre-Pasteurian mythologies.

The interest in air pathology was not limited to the scientific academies. By the end of the century, the trend spread toward the bottom of the social pyramid to become a staple of popular culture. Public opinion was repeatedly mobilized to protest the degradation of the urban atmosphere. The writer Louis-Sébastien Mercier's (1740-1814) invective is characteristic of the collective hyper-sensitivity to aerial pollution in eighteenth-century Paris:

The moment that air ceases to contribute to the preservation of good health, it becomes lethal. But health is that attribute which man treats with utmost indifference. Streets that are narrow and poorly accessed, houses that are too small and that impede the free circulation of air, butcher shops, fish stalls, sewers, cemeteries—all these corrupt the atmosphere. And the enclosed air becomes laden with impure particles, heavy and malignant.[6]

[5] Air, formerly an elementary medium of generation and vitality, was hence recast as a suspicious brew: "... a frightening mixture of the smoke, sulfurs and aqueous, volatile explosive, oily and saline vapors that the earth gave off, and occasionally, the explosive material that it emitted, the stinking exhalations that emerged from swamps, minute insects and their eggs, spermatic animalcules and far worse, the contagious miasma that rose from decomposed bodies." Alain Corbin, The Foul and the Fragrant: Odor and the French Social Imagination (1986), 13.

[6] L. S. Mercier, *Tableau de Paris*, vol. 1 (1994), 114.

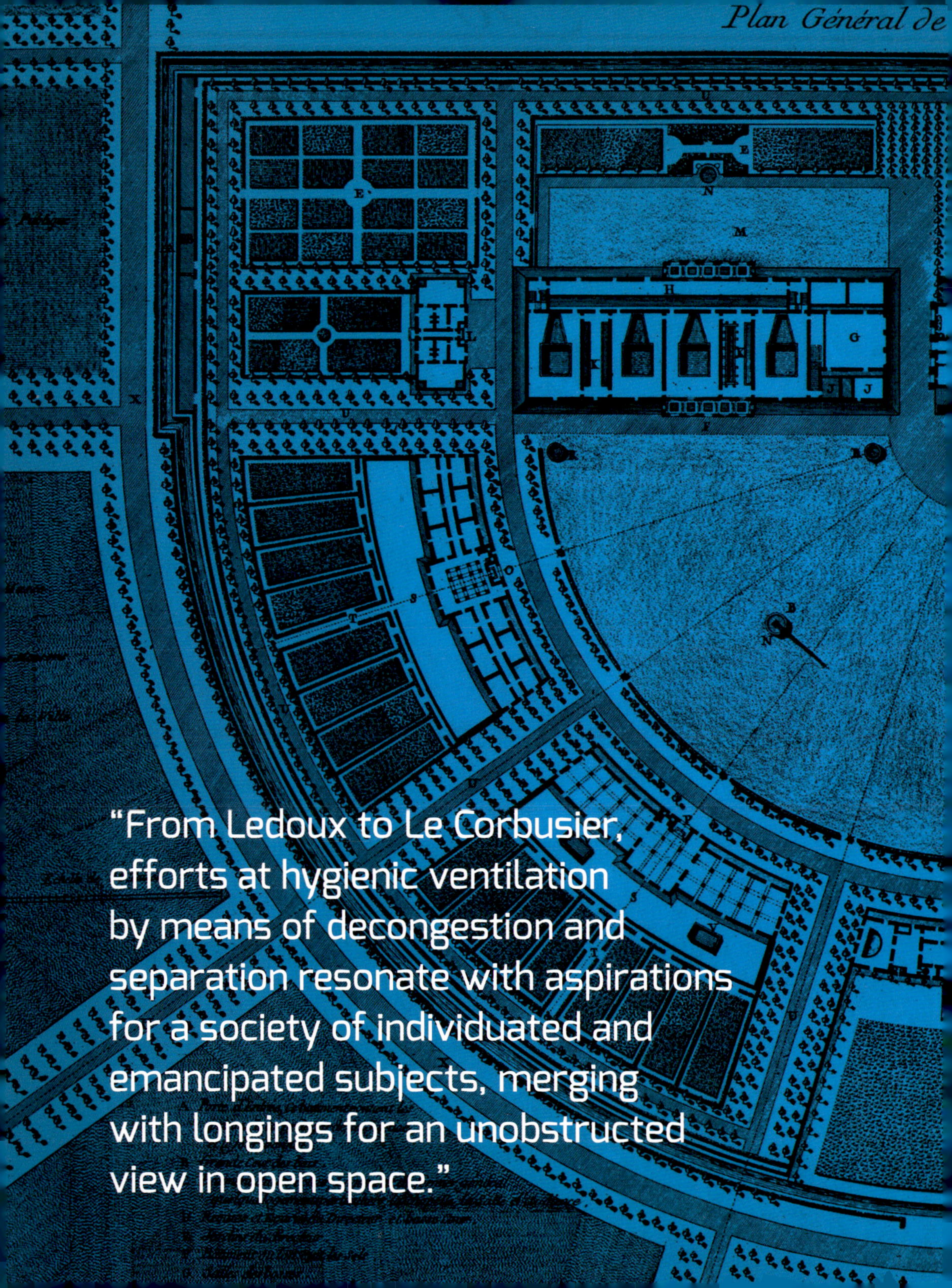

"From Ledoux to Le Corbusier, efforts at hygienic ventilation by means of decongestion and separation resonate with aspirations for a society of individuated and emancipated subjects, merging with longings for an unobstructed view in open space."

line de Chaux
Masse
des Maisons
de la Ville
N Abreuvoir
O Bâtiment des Ouvriers avec leur cheminée commune
dans le milieu dudit bâtiment
P Bâtiment des Tonneliers avec les magasins
Q Bâtiment des Maréchaux avec les magasins de fers
R Puits
S Cour des ouvriers
T Jardins des ouvriers
U Allées

The city is consistently incriminated in this discourse: by virtue of its sheer mass, it is an obstacle to the movement of the air. Hence, a general tendency toward looser and more permeable urban fabrics, advocated in many treatises and partially tested in the "openness" of the Place Louis XV.

Nicolas Ledoux's (1736-1806) ideal city of Chaux is a radical departure from the norm and yet is entirely consistent with the "decongestive" trend (Fig 6). The traditional—and pathological—urban fabric is here entirely relinquished in favor of an open and expanded field where detached and individuated structures are bathed in unhindered airflow.

For Emil Kaufmann, whose formalist reading was largely responsible for the postwar revival of Ledoux as a "visionary architect," *the jeu de masses* of detached pavilions anticipates the freestanding blocks of Le Corbusier and Gropius's combinatory of discrete spatial units. The free-standing structures, Kaufmann claims, are the concrete manifestation of the principle of autonomy in which the architectural object is released from all external contingencies to realize its own material, formal, and tectonic volition. [7]

For Kaufmann, architectural autonomy is indicative of a paradigm shift that is registered in other spheres of cultural production. It is recognized in the emphasis on line and contour leading to the formal detachment of the figure in late-eighteenth-century painting. It is also relevant to the formal structure of the political order theorized by Rousseau: "a form ... by which each may be united to all but nonetheless retains command over himself and remains as free as he had beforehand. Such is the fundamental problem that is resolved by the social contract."[8]

That the ideal city of Chaux should reflect the political philosophy of The Social Contract comes as no surprise, considering Ledoux's explicit allegiance to Rousseau. Still, beyond denoted affinities, the freestanding building represents the confluence of deeper structures converging on the transformation of the environment since the late eighteenth century.

LEFT. An Te Liu, "Exchange," New York, 2001

[7] In Kaufmann's words: "The new combination of parts is the free assembly of individual elements that do not have to sacrifice their particular existence and whose form is subordinated only to their own finality. It is their particular laws that determine their form." E. Kaufmann, De Ledoux à Le Corbusier (1990), 79.

[8] Ibid. 77.

ABOVE. An Te Liu, "Sclerotic III," 2000. Exhibited at the *Pathology* show at the Contemporary Art Gallery, Vancouver, 2000.

From Ledoux to Le Corbusier, efforts at hygienic ventilation by means of decongestion and separation resonate with aspirations for a society of individuated and emancipated subjects, merging with longings for an unobstructed view in open space.

Hygienic arguments for thoroughly ventilated and separated dwellings may have driven the discourse of "decongestive" urbanism. Yet, the longing and struggle for open space is largely visual: an aesthetic impulse that was enacted and legitimized in various ideological registers—political, economical, and social.

The hygienic/aesthetic impulse is manifested in the great optical utopias of Fourier, Bentham, and Rousseau: imaginary worlds built on varying measures of transparency and visibility. While some strove primarily toward the transparency of the subject in a naturally crystalline nature, others had less faith in the purity of human nature; they sought the transparency of the environment only to precipitate the hopelessly opaque subject into greater visibility.

Hence the contradictions of the modernist city. The city mass is reorganized to benefit from greater exposure and permeability to its natural milieu: air—an empirical medium. The city is also reconstituted rationally in space—a theoretical abstraction. The hygienic building is subject to external processes; it must be permeable to clean air. While the rational building is to be an object developed plastically in absolute space, it must simultaneously be made to go away, because it is an obstacle to the epiphany of transparency in open space: "Great blocks of dwellings run through the town. What does it matter they are behind the screen of trees."[9]

Similar contradictions are effectively rehearsed in Liu's "Airborne," exhibited at the Contemporary Art Gallery in Vancouver in 2000 (Figs 1, 7, 9, 10). In this direct precursor to "Exchange," sixty household humidifiers, air purifiers, and negative-air ionizers are painted a uniform gray and distributed on a white platform in a composition strangely reminiscent of a modernist city. A scale-model of a modernist city, to be more precise, the kind we are accustomed to see photographed along with the disembodied hand of the architect ominously hovering above (Fig 8).

The modernist city is most promising—and convincing—in model form, ideally photographed from above as a rational and total artifact. Ironically, the realized version is typically found lacking in the bird's-eye view: it looks too much like a model—the cliché reaction to aerial photographs of Brasília! (Fig 11) The model satisfies the demand for the rational materialization of the object; the bird's-eye view frustrates the concomitant fantasy of its dematerialization in space.[10]

"Airborne" operates on several levels and scales, equally gratifying and frustrating in its oscillation between model and machine, between symbolic representation and indexical process, and between a position in space and a situation in air. It is at once a scale-model for an imaginary modernist city; a dizzying mise en abîme of the Ville Radieuse—imagine the same appliances plausibly deployed in Corbusian housing blocks, stubbornly filtering the air that was supposed to ventilate the same building; a Van Doesburg-inspired composition of solids in space; a sardonic display of mass-produced consumer goods—Hannes Meyer comes to mind (Fig 12); a show room for Honeywell; a dystopian domestic setting; a minimalist sculpture; a new-age wellness center in downtown Vancouver.

[9] Le Corbusier, *The Home of Man* [1942] 1948) 91.

[10] Brasília and Chandigarh are most photogenic in wide-angle shots at eye level when the dwarfed monumental architecture defines negatively—the far more sublime immensity of open space (Fig 15).

"Just like the air-cleaning appliance, which is promoted against all sorts of domestic pathologies from allergy to furniture damage, modern urbanism requires a leap of faith in its hygienic claim. Its short-lived success may have been due to the 'placebo' effect rather than the 'science' of the Unité d'Habitation. It delivered the promise of a liberated and lucid environment as an aesthetic experience rather than a material and social fact."

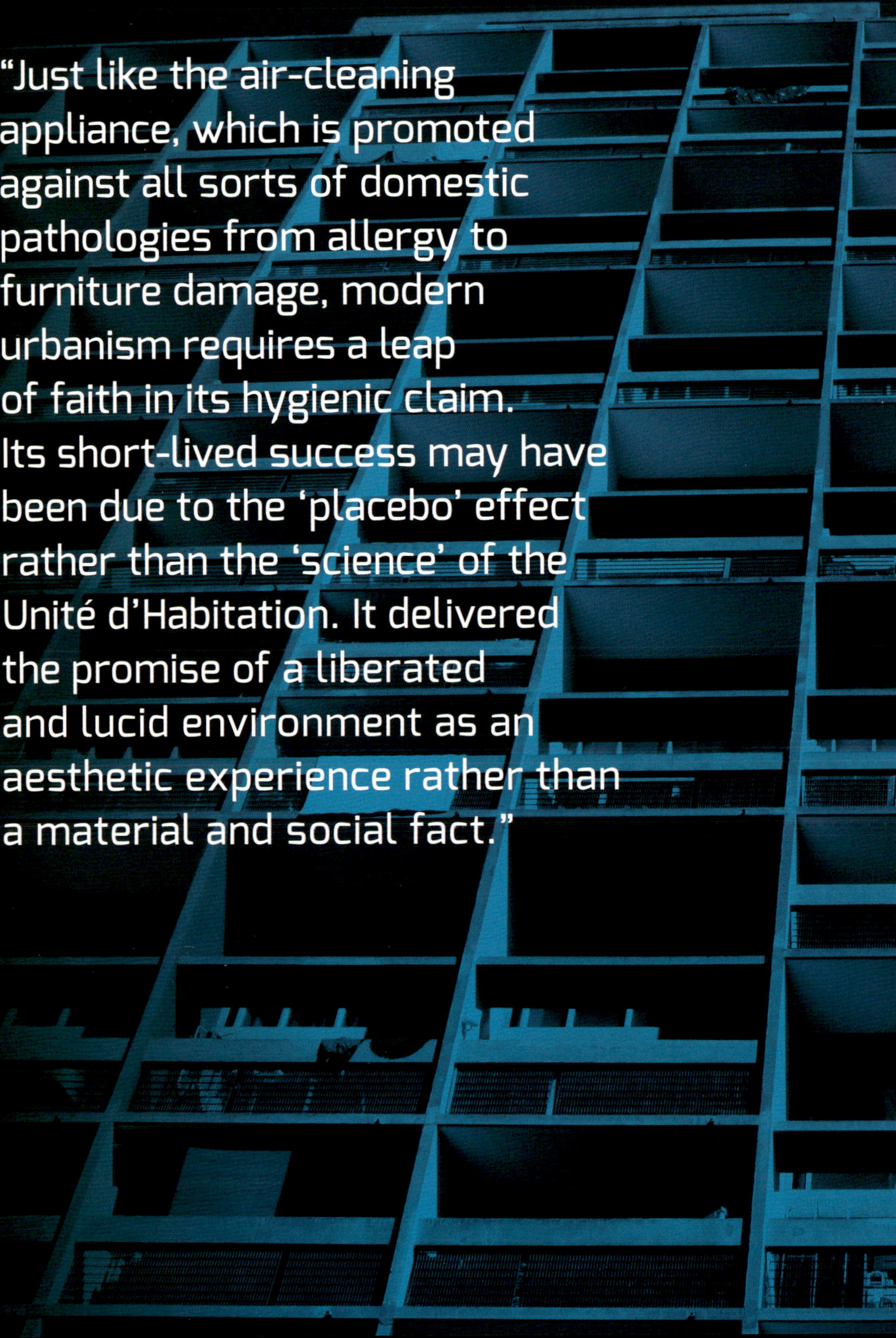

The multiple readings and registers capture the predicament of the modernist city—and that of its legacy in today's urbanized world. Just like the air-cleaning appliance, which is promoted against all sorts of domestic pathologies from allergy to furniture damage, modern urbanism requires a leap of faith in its hygienic claims. Its short-lived success may have been due to the "placebo" effect rather than the "science" of the Unité d'Habitation.[11] It delivered the promise of a liberated and lucid environment as an aesthetic experience rather than a material and social fact.[12]

The placebo appliance is most effective in its conspicuousness, as a physical presence in domestic space—the only tangible evidence of its remedial but imperceptible operation. As demonstrated in "Exchange" and "Airborne," the cumulative effect of the residual but critical physicality – the noise-polluting, energy-consuming object—is psychologically counterproductive. An isolated HEPA machine may suggest the possibility of healthier air, but its relentless deployment is indeed more alarming than therapeutic. The air may be actually cleaner in the Henry Urbach Gallery—it is recycled and filtered every twenty-one seconds! Its hygienic virtues are hardly more credible.

In Liu's installations, the effect of the placebo—dare we say "the aesthetic"—falters against the overpowering effect of the real. And vice versa. May we say the same of the Ville Radieuse?

The pragmatic and aesthetic agendas of modern urbanism are ostensibly consistent. Yet, they may not completely overlap: there is a gap between space and air in the world they project. This is where Liu's work is uncomfortably at home.

[11] An Te Liu speaks of the appliance's placebo effect in an interview with Aaron Betsky: "My college roommate and I had two Bionaire purifiers/ionizers in our apartment. We would sit around drinking scotch in a smoky haze with the machines running full blast in case our parents showed up unexpectedly. After a few hours, the air seemed to tingle with clean, negatively charged ions, and we were sure we could feel it. Or was it the single malt? In any case, the indicator light was on, and we were assured that something good was happening, even if we didn't understand the mysteries of negative-air ionization. 'Placebo' comes from the Latin 'to please,' and we were damn happy with our new devices." A. Betsky, "Safe Haven," interview with An Te Liu, *Surface* 25 (Fall 2000), 155.

[12] The social and political critique of the modernist city that fueled the postmodern return to a traditional configuration of block, street, and public space is beyond the scope of this essay but not foreign to Liu's work: that a display of consumer goods should so readily evoke a modernist cityscape is a striking but familiar demonstration of the affinities between capitalist and utopian logic.

RIGHT. Le Corbusier, Unité d'Habitation, Marseilles

FOLLOWING SPREAD. Pattern Language: Levititown (brown/seafoam)

– HOUSE DRESSING: OFFICE DA

ORIGINALLY PUBLISHED IN **OFFICE DA**,
ROCKPORT PUBLISHERS, 1999.

Cutler: It's about the skin, an old idea that is cleverly done.

Jimenez: We're seduced by surface manipulation. There is a joy in the fabrication of the surfaces.

Hadid: It's a prop. The skin is like a temporary structure. It's like a house wearing an inexpensive dress. You can take it off and on, change it in time. The architect puts too much emphasis on the skin; it is disposable.
Hanganu: It's a trick, but a nice trick, to take the undulated metal and perforate it, which changes the materiality and makes it transparent.

Kennedy: I think the project is about image and iconography. I wish the details they showed were actually crucial for making the project. It purports to be about tectonic issues and materials, and I'm not sure it really is. It's about image. My second concern is the back of the house. I would be enthusiastic about this project if it was all about skin and how it moves from the inside to the outside—a body wrap. But there's a loose arbitrary addition. This is a highly sophisticated project aesthetically. But the house itself, in terms of rooms, is completely conventional. Architecture, *April 1998.*

Office dA received a Progressive Architecture Award in 1998 for the Weston House. The jury's comments above give a fair idea of the standard reception of the work. It is typically ambivalent. The work's power is acknowledged, but not without some reservation: the jurors bestow the award but are compelled to express a concomitant disapproval or justify their choice in quasi-apologetic terms. When the skepticism is not overt, words like "sophisticated," "clever," "seduced," or "trick" hint at the architecture's deceitful charm, the critics' unwholesome indulgence.

The ambivalence is symptomatic of a pervasive attitude: an equal dissatisfaction with the drab iconoclasm of orthodox modernism and the frivolous rhetoric of postmodernism. Office dA's projects suggest an intermediate course of action, "between language and matter," to use Graham Owen's formulation. The stock reactions to these proposals, whether in guilty approbation or reluctant condemnation, distill the tendencies of the current architectural debate and thus compel me to offer additional commentary. My aim is to define the general terms of the debate as much as to clarify Office dA's particular position. If my remarks seem biased, it is because I was a former member of the Office dA team; my interest in the work, its familiar past, and its promising future is more than academic.

The architect puts too much emphasis on the skin; it is disposable. The polemics of the surface have kept two generations of critics busy since postmodernism's jubilant experiments in semiotics and later, through the postmodern infatuation with surface effects. Robert Venturi and Mark Wigley may have their differences but they concur in their profound appreciation of the superficial.

Theories of the surface have indeed been treated extensively and may very well be the most significant contribution to recent architectural criticism. There is no point in rehearsing here the lessons of Las Vegas and Nietzsche except to point out Office dA's own contribution to this line of research and reopen, at least momentarily, a debate that has apparently been closed, perhaps prematurely.

Judging from the *Architecture* jury's comments, it would seem that the proverbial pendulum of history has gone full swing and that the surface is again suspect, its legitimacy as a privileged site of architectural value questioned. It is in short "disposable." The accusations are familiar; they have effectively served the modernist denigration of ornament with customary references to fashion, to the accessory and the feminine. Dejàvu? Are we dealing here with some curious cultural amnesia or perhaps a full-fledged modernist backlash?

ABOVE AND NEXT PAGE. Weston House, model

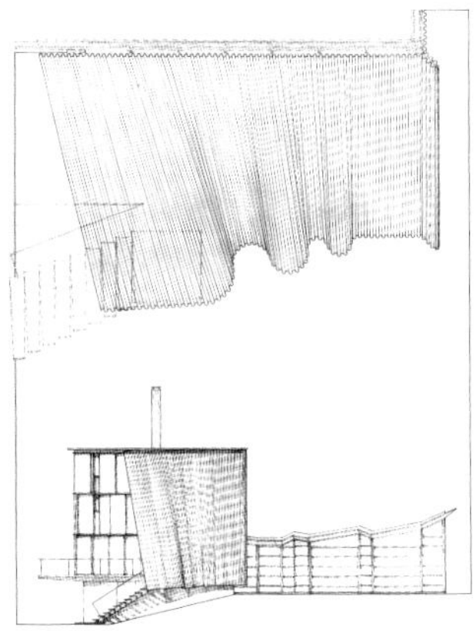

ABOVE. Weston House, elevation drawing and detail of undulating wall

ABOVE. "Fabricating Coincidences"; Installation at MoMA commissioned for Fabrications show

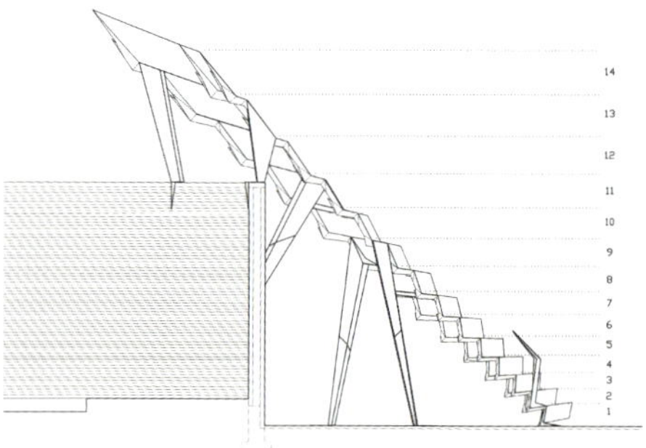

ABOVE. "Fabricating Coincidences"; anamorphic projection

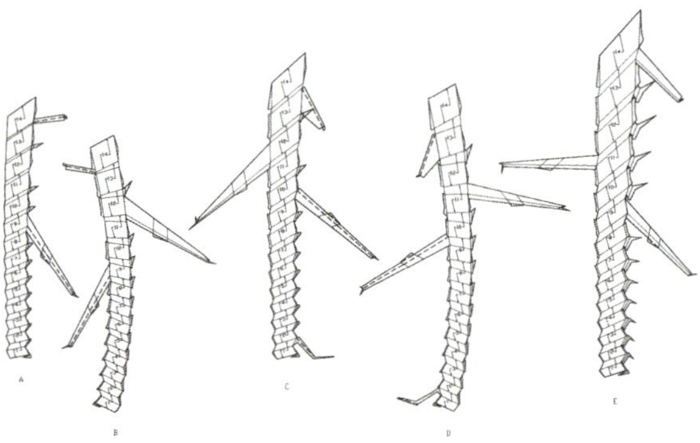

ABOVE. "Fabricating Coincidences"; detail of structural spine

Populist investments in surface may simply have been too vulgar and the post-structuralist kind too arcane to merit serious and lasting attention. Granted, the mere existence of the Piazza d'Italia is reason enough to justify the moratorium on "façade." But what about Herzog and de Meuron? They have built an entire career on ingenious and skillful surface treatments; they seldom fail to seduce traditionalists and avant-gardists alike, and have yet to exhaust their creative potential in reinventing the elevation.

And whatever happened to the feminist/post-structuralist critique of the ornament? Already forgotten or never heard in the first place? Wigley recently demonstrated how white paint, the most immaterial of building revetments, was indispensable to the project of modern architecture. He may argue how whiteness, while representing the erasure of ornament, still functioned as a necessary ornamental substitute, but none of this will keep the Zaha Hadids from dismissing a whole building envelope as "disposable" accessory.

Hadid's disdain for accessory cladding is all the more intriguing when provoked by a renovation project such as Office dA's Weston House: a project that by definition consists in supplementing an existing structure with new features, a design that is ostensibly most successful in integrating the new features into the existing framework. In fact, the consistency and coherence of the reclad house is such that an unsuspecting viewer would be hard-pressed to ever distinguish the skeletal ghost of the original.

The project in question is a renovation and addition to a suburban house in Weston, Massachusetts, a wood-frame building from the nineteen-fifties conforming to conventional typology, both in matters of construction and iconography. The new design calls for a strategic redistribution of the room layout and circulation with intent on maximizing the programmatic potentials of the building with minimal alterations to the structural frame. A garage, which also functions as a greenhouse, is an important new feature. Its glass-clad facets are coordinated with the "draped metal forms of the house itself," in a composition of contrasting effects.

The new garage is furthermore integrated planimetrically: its crystalline geometry extends into the house to reorganize the central hall and the vertical circulation into a smooth sequence of perspectival effects. But the pièce de résistance in this renovation is a new envelope, which transforms the external appearance of the house as much as the nature and quality of the living spaces within.

Short of total demolition and reconstruction, any renovation project has to deal—more or less self-consciously—with its accessory nature, with the fact that it is an add-on to an autonomous building. In the Weston House, no external traces are left of the old structure and no discernable seams lay bare the devices of the architectural "makeover." There are no attempts to represent the former autonomy (structural and formal) of the building, say by orchestrating a dialogue between old and new components. The original structure may still be supporting the roof but it is totally masked—and subsumed—by the new features.

And this is precisely why the design is an offense to modernist orthodoxy: because it allows the supplement to overwhelm the structure and make reality a function of appearance. Far from being disposable, the new cladding represents the very essence of this house. Office dA may have designed only a "dress," to use the jury's term, but this dress substantiates the clothed body; there is no body, no architecture independent of the dress.

To invest so much in the superficial accessory, to give it a structural role in defining architectural character and identity, to therefore suggest that architecture is, in a major way, a function of cladding is typical of Office dA's work but also characteristic of a wide range of postmodern practices. The distinguishing factor in Office dA's work is the investigation of the surface as a primary field of construction: building as a function of cladding. In this capacity Office dA is more in tune with Gottfried Semper's theories than Venturi's. The surface is not applied to a pre-existing solid wall as a symbolic or linguistic veneer. It is understood and designed as a constitutive spatial element as much as a vehicle to architectural and cultural signification. For Office dA, both space and language are an effect of surface constructions.

"It purports to be about tectonic issues and materials, and I'm not sure it really is. It's about image." "Tectonics" is one of those catch-all terms that can evoke a wide range of ideas and align with different, if not contradictory ideologies. Perhaps because of this resilient ambiguity and a convoluted—if not confusing—genealogy in architectural theory, tectonics can be now found at the core of a building mythology that is keen on anchoring architectural value in the "pure presence" of building matter.

Largely in reaction to the structuralist/post-structuralist infatuation with the free-floating signifier and the indeterminacy of meaning,

ABOVE. Inter-Faith Chapel, Northeastern University

BELOW. Inter-Faith Chapel, Northeastern University: diagram showing the three cladding systems

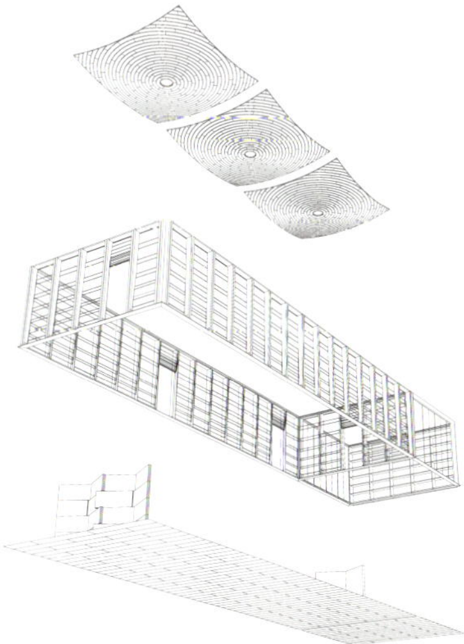

"The surface is not applied to a pre-existing solid wall as a symbolic or linguistic veneer. It is understood and designed as a constitutive spatial element as much as a vehicle to architectural and cultural signification. For Office dA, both space and language are an effect of surface constructions."

ABOVE. Miami Overpass Project

the cult of architectural authenticity undermines "representation" in the pursuit of some onto- mystico- metaphysical presence or "presentation." Its rhetoric is fueled by Heideggerian clichés that architects have found particularly resonant in their allegorical reference to building and dwelling. What results is an iconoclastic brand of architectural criticism that persists on building a whole theoretical edifice on the precarious distinction between what is apparent and what is real—among other binary oppositions that phenomenology, ironically, had set to undermine.

According to the gospel of authenticity, issues of iconography, of language and rhetoric, are secondary—if not inconsequential—to essential matters of materiality and fabrication. Hence, the current profusion of statements, that all too readily contrast "image" and "tectonics," as if their mutual antipathy is a self-evident truth.

Yet one of the most productive themes in Office dA's work is the intersection of rhetoric and fabrication. Consistently, the detail is the field where the actual and the visible are reinvented in unexpected alliances that push both the material and method of construction to unprecedented limits.

Consider for instance "Fabricating Coincidences," an installation commissioned by New York's Museum of Modern Art for an exhibition showcasing issues of fabrication. It was constructed—with indispensable assistance from CAD/CAM technology—from sheets of steel that were creased, pleated, and folded into an elaborate sculptural form. The detail here speaks eloquently of the method of construction. Like a genetic code, it encapsulates the artifact's morphological structure and demonstrates the process of its realization. "'Tell-tale details" of the sort are sanctioned by tectonicism, never mind the fact that overall image of the artifact hyperbolizes the process of fabrication in a quasi-rococo composition of pleated facets that puts Issey Miyaki to shame. Things get a bit thorny when the anamorphic feature of the piece is considered, when an optical agenda displaces the work to the "suspect" realm of the image.

Viewed from a designated station across MoMA's sculpture garden, the installation momentarily collapses into a flat plane. This singular optical event is an integral component of the piece and in many ways a generative factor in the design. The geometry and tectonics of the artifact were elaborated in the anticipation of this visual illusion, which simultaneously contradicts and reinforces the material and constructional principle of the detail. Here, image, geometry, material, and fabrication process are coordinated into a tense hybrid of tactile and optical effects. Does the optical rhetoric of the piece—which proves to be constitutive—and its dematerialized representation of flatness compromise the soundness of its so-called tectonics? Or, on the contrary, does the particular tectonic quality of the piece emerge from the contrived tension between fact and illusion, between what is represented and what is presented, between the image and the material structure?

Another fact will complicate the picture even more: the rigidity of the steel facets is not entirely due to the fold; a camouflaged conventional beam provides additional support and stiffness. Camouflage consists here in a staggered contour that allows the beam to be "smuggled" in the fold. In a true camouflage manner, the artifice is simultaneously revealed and concealed: The beam is visible and the logic of stealth intelligible. The architects draw you into the tectonic representation of the fold with a complex and ambivalent visual device. They count on the visual to complement rather than merely present the actual performance of the detail. What things look as though they are doing is as important as what they are actually doing.

Such artifice, whether entirely concealed or deliberately laid bare, is bound to put off the mainstream tectonicists; their purism will tolerate neither sham nor rhetoric. Yet any experienced practitioner will recognize the artifice for what it really is: a mere trick of the trade.

Germain Soufflot had much use for it in Sainte Geneviéve—one of the first self-consciously modern monuments where issues of tectonics were paramount. Hidden arches and elaborate steel reinforcement here assist, covertly, in demonstrating the tectonic verity of the freestanding column and the simple rectilinear beam, the constitutive elements of Soufflot's Gothic-inspired architecture. The building is most valued as a quintessential illustration of Rationalist structural principles; never mind that despite its copious provision of stealth supports, the building would have long collapsed without a battery of additional tricks.

Speaking of the Gothic, what would the tectonicist make of flying buttresses? They are ostensibly designed to sustain a structural illusion within the nave, an image of lightness and effortlessness that is contradictory to their prodigious display of structural gymnastics outside. Epitome of tectonic expression or shameless visual deception? Consider the possibility, daringly suggested by Erwin Panofsky, that the stone vaults did not always require additional bracing, that the flying buttress was a matter of rhetoric as much as statics. The flying buttress—so dear to a Violet Leduc—would be tricking us into thinking that it is performing a structural trick. Two-fold illusion; double heresy?

This much is clear: image and tectonics are far from enemies, and Office dA capitalizes on their complicity. Instances where the optical logic of the image permeates the haptic principles of construction are indeed a staple of Office dA; they are perhaps the firm's most consistent and original contribution to the poetics of building. The curtain wall of the Weston House performs accordingly and accounts for much of the building's appeal. Consider also the garden wall of Casa La Roca: the undulating filigree of bricks is designed to provide a thin freestanding wall with structural integrity, but the visual impression is one of fragility and dramatic instability. And, as if the contradiction between structural material and visual effect were not enough of a heresy, the overall image of a drawn curtain adds a quasi-surrealist touch of dematerialization.

"This is a highly sophisticated project aesthetically. But the house itself, in terms of rooms, is completely conventional." Most of Office dA's buildings have conventional plans. They are conventional in their predominantly orthogonal geometry and in their conformity to established types. This is evidently the case in renovation/appropriation projects in which the architects had to operate within pre-existing frameworks, but also true of new structures where ostensibly benign plans seldom convey the flagrant inventiveness of the spaces they create.

There is no accident in Office dA's interest in transforming existing structures: They allow the architects to rely exclusively on sectional and elevational strategies as a means to complement and transcend the pragmatic contingencies of the plan. The Inter-Faith Chapel is a case in point: the cladding strategy (including floor, wall, and ceiling revetments) transforms a standard windowless room that is accessed from an institutional corridor into an otherworldly luminescent space—totally unexpected and far from conventional as a spatial phenomenon; still your run-of-the-mill rectangular room in plan. The design for the Murr Tower performs analogous operations on a concrete monolith, this time with exterior cladding and virtually no alterations to the plan.

The Miami Overpass project also exemplifies Office dA's mode of operation: the new surfaces transform a merely functional piece of equipment into a public space that presents a convincing potential for the revitalization of a whole district. Once again, the design strategy overlays a whole new dimension to the structure without ever disturbing its planimetric and functional logic. Barely recognizable in its reinvented section, the new hybrid structure speaks, perhaps most eloquently, of the transformative—and redemptive—power of the surface.

ABOVE. Suchart House

Hence the design ambition behind the cladding strategy of the Weston House: "While the corrugated metal is wrapped around the existing house as a thin drape, it is also called on to re-formulate the idea, perception and space of the house." But in situations in which Office dA is not presented with existing structures for its redemptive process, the tendency is to rely on types or straightforward planimetric configurations to set up conventional frameworks for highly unusual phenomena. The device is tactical: the "ready-made" plan embodies the conventional and pragmatic aspects of building-for-everyday-life that are challenged by the unorthodox surface. The tension between planimetric expectations and sectional inventions yields a highly defamiliarized spatial experience, which accommodates and exceeds the commonplace.

What I have described is a general tendency and certainly not a constant in Office dA's work. There are instances where the transformative tension is played out differently, among other conflicting features of the project. For instance, the Suchart House confronts typological abstraction with symbolic figuration "by allowing the figure to infiltrate and occasionally subvert the frame." What is consistent is the (transformative) redemptive process that is built into the structure of the design: a conventional platform accommodates the mundane aspects of dwelling and provides a springboard for their transfiguration in design.

ABOVE. Casa La Roca, model

ABOVE. Casa La Roca, model

ABOVE. Casa La Roca, detail of patio wall

There is a pragmatic logic—and an implicit political agenda—in Office dA's design strategy, which merits some attention. The pragmatism is most evident in domestic programs where conventional room layouts are streamlined for customization through inhabitation. The "weak form" of the generic plan can accommodate standard furnishings and is most amenable to individuated lifestyles and decorative whims. Of the political, suffice it now to mention that when CAD/CAM technology makes "total design" an economically competitive option, Office dA's insistence on setting the particular within the generic is a function of ideology as much as of practicality.

A colleague related to me an incident that took place while he was serving on a jury for a prestigious architectural award. About to enter one of the buildings, that was short-listed for the first prize, he was stopped by an attendant who denied him access because of his shoes. This evidently brings to mind Adolf Loos's parody of jugendstile,"The Famous Story of the Poor Rich Man" where an overzealous architect tyrannically controlled every aspect of his total design, down to the slippers of his intimidated client. In the case at hand, however, the footwear was delinquent in matters of security rather than style. Apparently, the ramping floors of the building, designed to demonstrate the aesthetic and programmatic virtues of folded space, have proven to be treacherously slippery. After several mishaps with unsuspecting visitors, the insurance company dictated the use

"The 'ready-made' plan embodies the conventional and pragmatic aspects of building-for-everyday-life that are challenged by the unorthodox surface. The tension between planimetric expectations and sectional inventions yields a highly defamiliarized spatial experience, which accommodates and exceeds the commonplace."

of rubber-soled shoes within the premises. The building evidently did not fare well with the juror who, after exchanging his fine English shoes for the courtesy to—visitors—Adidas, was ill disposed for the leap of faith that avant-garde architecture so stubbornly demands. The virtues of the warped field and the architect's theories of emancipatory space—or was it the critique of capitalist flows?—left him cold.

Clearly no such challenges, intellectual or physical, are posed by the Weston House—or any other house by Office dA, for that matter. No ban on stiletto- heeled pumps; no claims for the deconstruction of ideological closure. The Weston House may be "a highly sophisticated project aesthetically," but it is still a house. Obviously, this is not a "completely conventional" house because the architects, while knowing where to tactically—and tactfully—conform to certain norms of building and habitation, also exploit the many opportunities for invention that do not impose tyrannical demands (financial, practical, or experiential) on the users. The demonstration of formal and technological ingenuity is unmistakable and far from conventional, say in the corner treatment, but that will not keep the living spaces from agreeing with IKEA furniture.

Office dA's tactics are clearly demonstrated in Casa La Roca: innovation is most radical in the sculptural garden wall extending from the main body of the house. When architecture is here released, physically and symbolically, from its more mundane domestic duties, it can assume more aesthetically ambitious aims, ones that are rightfully held within the reach of art.

So when Mónica Ponce de León and Nader Tehrani are commissioned to create an installation for an exhibition at MoMA—a bona fide work of art—they are not shy of theoretical and formal exuberance. And even rubber soles will not protect museum-goers from razor-sharp edges and treacherous trompe l'oeil should they foolishly brave the bizarre stairs the two concocted for the occasion.

The term convenance, inadequately translated as "decorum," comes loaded with wearisome allusions to stuffy Ancien-Regime codes of propriety and may be hopelessly antiquated. Yet, with some measure of adaptation, it may very well be suited to describe Office dA's ability to tactically calibrate the tone and intensity of their designs to suit particular cultural and material circumstances and I am obviously not talking about iconography nor contextualism.

This ostensibly rudimentary faculty, which requires some measure of judgment—and a great deal of restraint—currently seems to be blunted, especially in avant-garde practices. Office dA's work eloquently demonstrates how a keener sense of convenance can do much to sharpen the wit and poignancy of architectural invention.

ABOVE. Casa La Roca, detail of patio wall

- PARADOXICAL SEAMS: MACHADO AND SILVETTI ARCHITECTS

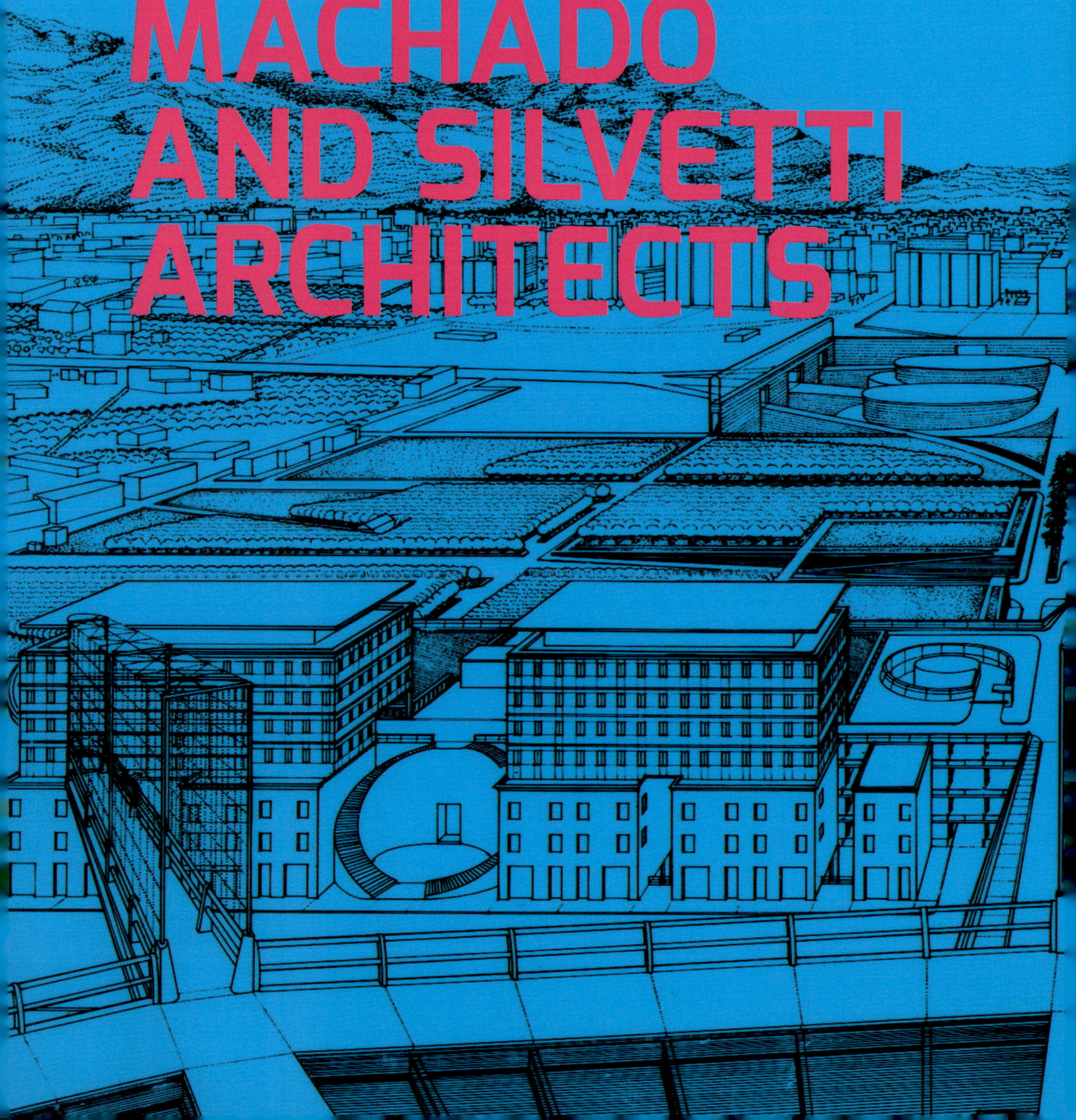

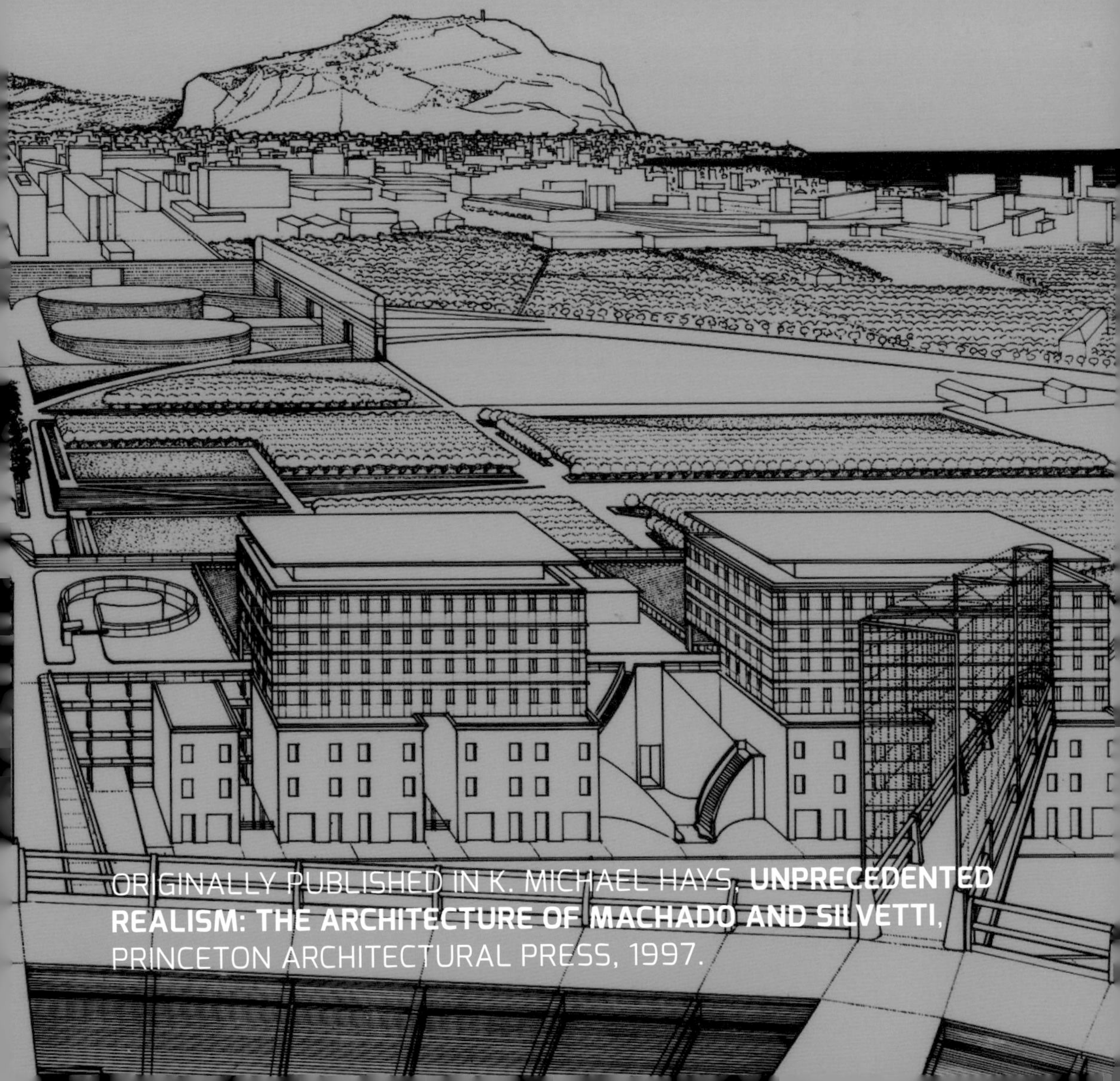

ORIGINALLY PUBLISHED IN K. MICHAEL HAYS, **UNPRECEDENTED REALISM: THE ARCHITECTURE OF MACHADO AND SILVETTI**, PRINCETON ARCHITECTURAL PRESS, 1997.

THE PRESENCE OF THE PAST (Fig I), a drawing for the 1980 Venice Biennale by Jorge Silvetti, summarizes the trajectory of Machado and Silvetti's practice up to that point.[1] In the manner of a potpourri, the drawing is composed of various fragments from previous projects. However incompatible in their mode of representation, scale, and order

ABOVE. Jorge Silvetti, "The Presence of the Past," 1980.

[1] The drawing was conceived, assembled, and originally drawn by Jorge Silvetti. There are three rendered versions of it: an ink on mylar drawings executed by James Favaro, a colored pencil on card stock by Daniel Wheeler (exhibited at the Venice Biennale), and a pencil on Strathmore paper executed by Peter Lofgren (exhibited at the American Drawings show in Helsinki).

of existence, the fragments are reconciled in a composition that gives an illusion of homogeneity. The illusion is fragile and momentary; it is fabricated with simple adjustments and alignments that integrate each fragment into the formal pattern of the immediate context, with total disregard to structural, spatial, and notational discrepancies. A line, for instance, continues uninterrupted across a series of differently scaled elements; abstract geometrical figures emerge, then change into plans or elevations; a small fragment is fitted within the pattern of a larger one. Occasionally, a layering of elements creates an effect of depth with the persuasive logic of representational verisimilitude; the drawing flickers with perspectival windows where disparate elements coalesce in naturalistic space. The sporadic flashes of naturalism, however, are undermined by contradictory representations in neighboring elements and the illusory homogeneity unravels paradoxically: seemingly continuous lines are fractured by discontinuous spatial and tectonic constructions while patterns extended across different registers are pulverized into a patchwork of incommensurable orders. Much like mannerist paintings, which elaborate spatial puzzles through the juxtaposition of contradictory perspectival frameworks or smuggle anamorphic monsters in through cloud formations, the drawing pushes conventional means of representation to paradoxical extremes so as to foreground the artifice of its realist posture. It breaks through the naturalized appearance of reality by calling attention to its paradoxical seams, to the fact that it has been sewn up from incompatible fragments and irreconcilable orders. The seams of this flawed mimesis in a graphic survey of the architects' oeuvre might be taken to problematize historical continuity. The drawing could then read as an allegorical commentary on "the presence of the past," the theme of the Venice Biennale.

More directly, the paradoxical seams convey a different kind of critical attitude about architecture. They demonstrate a formal strategy for assembling heterogeneous fragments that is distinguishable from the critical technique of collage. Collage starts from a formalist bias with the belief that certain constructions—the nonorganic work, also reformulated as "text"—hold a potential for deconstructing ideological closure. It proceeds to transgress the sphere of ideological representations through the unmediated heterogeneity of its constituent fragments. Silvetti's composite drawing reappropriates ideologically tainted languages and media not with the intent to destroy meaning but to produce a new meaning, allowing them to become instruments of criticism from within. Strategically speaking, the collage, with its direct and explicit attack on hegemonic formations, belongs to the avant-garde of traditional warfare, while the biennale drawing, in its covert operation, resembles the mythological Trojan horse. Only after being admitted within the walls of the city does the uncanny artifact reveal a subversive content behind a fascinating monumentality. Similarly, the recipient is seduced by Silvetti's figurative drawing into a familiar yet strange field of representation, only to experience the destabilizing effect of its fault lines and fissures.

The Trojan horse tactic has made sporadic appearances in the course of this century, mainly within the ranks of Dadaism and Surrealism. Among its polymorphic manifestations, John Hartfield's photomontages are paradigmatic. Max Ernst's "La femme 100 têtes" series (1929) and Rene Magritte's "Paris, Opéra" (1929) are also pertinent examples. All reorganize, if not undermine, the material differences of the assembled fragments so as to produce alternative realities within the limits and conventions of realist representation. The realism is strategic: "It is the marvelous faculty of attaining two widely separate realities without departing from the realm of our experience, of bringing them together and drawing a spark from their contact."[2]

Silvetti's drawing belongs to this lineage of montaged artifacts; the architecture it seeks to translate in a graphic montage also owes much of its critical power to the tension created in the paradoxical intersection of the commonplace and the unexpected, the marriage of a benignly coherent, "realist" mode of representation with an explosive content.

COLLAGE AND NEGATION

Critical theory assigns a positive function to art only when it stands in contradiction to social hegemony. According to Theodor Adorno, only art that stubbornly affirms its autonomy and noncommunicative function in the face of a reefed culture and severs all ties with the ideologically tainted language and iconography of the society in which it is produced can be considered "authentic." The nonorganic work produced by collage methods thus demonstrates its critical power through its "nonidentity" with the dominant ideology and through the increased opacity of its representation.

[2] A. Breton, quoted in *Dawn Ades, Photomontage* (1976), I.

Theories of the avant-garde accordingly have emphasized the explicit heterogeneity and destructured character of the assembled work of art. They have focused on the "emphatic gaps between one shard of reality and another,"[3] in which the contradictions of reality are registered. In *Theory of the Avant-Garde*, Peter Burger thus neglects John Heartfield's photomontage, where "the insertion of reality fragments ... is obscured or at least made difficult to spot,"[4] so as to privilege the collage as a paradigm of nonorganic representation in avant-gardist art. Inflected by Adorno's aesthetic theory, such readings still maintain the negation of synthesis as a compositional principle: the naturalized artifice of the realist or organic work is thought to project the illusion of a reconciliation of culture and nature, whereas the nonorganic collage registers the heterogeneity of reality and no longer creates even the semblance of reconciliation.

Something akin to Adorno's theory of the nonorganic work of art and its entailed rejection of synthesis have also informed recent architectural projects, loosely labeled "deconstructivist"—such as Bernard Tschumi's Parc de Ia Villette—that recycle modernist avant-gardist collage techniques for a poststructuralist critique of representation in architecture. Tschumi argues that today's cultural circumstances, with their disruptions, disjunctions, and characteristic fragmentation, demand discarding established categories of meaning. His architecture is presented as one "that would stress not only the dispersion of the subject and the force of social regulation, but also the effect of such decenterings on the entire notion of unified, coherent, architectural form."[6]

Tschumi's park is conceived in terms of independent compositional and programmatic systems, collided and superimposed, that "avoided all

[3] R. Krauss, *L'Amour Fou: Photography and Surrealism* (1985), 27.

[4] P. Burger, *Theory of the Avant-Garde* (1984), 76.

[5] While many other examples come to mind, Bernard Tschumi's work is here selected as a paradigmatic illustration of the use of collage in recent architectural practices because of its didactic clarity. The passage from two-dimensional collage to architecture might seem too abrupt and even unjustified, considering the complex political, economical, and material processes at work in the implementation of an architectural project. Nevertheless, the comparison holds true at the level of the aesthetic intent and especially when dealing with architectural drawings and models. Throughout this essay emphasis will be placed on such models of architectural representation because they most effectively—and reductively—articulate and disseminate the formal characteristics of the works.

[6] B. Tschumi, "Back to La Villette, Paris," AD, vol. 58 no. 3/4 (1988), 33.

attempts to homogenize the project into a totality."[7] This architectural collage, like Adorno's modern art, claims to make explicit in its disrupted syntax the cultural contradictions that are always reconciled in the nostalgic pursuit of coherence. The practice of collage in Parc de la Villette dislocates and deregulates meaning, rejecting the symbolic repertory of architecture as a refuge of "outmoded humanist thought." La Villette thus aims at an architecture that "means nothing, an architecture of the signifier rather than the signified."[8] La Villette means nothing in the sense that it lacks a synthetic intent that would override or sublimate divergent and often contradictory impressions. Rather, it presents a set of floating signifiers that frustrate the quest of traditional modes of reception for transcendent signification.

The individual parts and the whole form a dialectical unity in an organic work of art; the comprehension of the whole guides, and is simultaneously inflected by, the comprehension of the parts. A necessary condition for this hermeneutic process, therefore, is some form of congruence between the meaning of the individual parts and the meaning of the whole. As Peter Burger argues, this precondition is rejected by collage, or the nonorganic work, "and this fact defines its decisive difference from the organic work of art."[9] For example, in a typical Dadaist collage or a Surrealist automatic text, the parts are autonomous and lack necessity with respect to the whole. One could eliminate one of the pasted objets trouvés or "accidental" images from the composition· without disrupting the composition or altering the meaning of the work in any significant way.

The same holds for the Parc de la Villette, which could gain or loose some elements without disturbing the overall conception of the design. [10]

Because the reader's mode of reception has been formed by reading organic works of art and is, therefore, inappropriate to reading collage, the reader must suspend the hermeneutic process to direct attention back to

[7] Ibid. 36.

[8] Ibid. 36.

[9] P. Burger, *Theory of Avant-Garde*, 80 (1985), 147.

[10] The open-ended nature of Tschumi's design for La Villette has justified substantial cuts from the initial conception and a number of additional objets trouves that the Parisian municipality and capitalist development have "collaged" on this conveniently malleable site.

the principles of construction. In Tschumi's structuralist parlance, we might say that the reader abandons the signified to dwell on the signifier.[11]

In a provocative conflation, the eclipse of the signified also characterizes the schizophrenic breakdown of language analyzed by Jacques Lacan and reinterpreted by Fredric Jameson as a symptom of the "neurosis" of late-capitalist society. According to Lacan, schizophrenia entails a failure to accede fully to the realm of speech and language, resulting in the collapse of temporality-the experience of time as an "effect" of language: Schizophrenic experience is an experience of isolated, disconnected, discontinuous material signifiers which fail to link up into a coherent sequence. The schizophrenic thus does not know personal identity in our sense, since our feeling of identity depends on our sense of the persistence of the "I" and the "me" over time.[12]

With the breakdown of language in schizophrenic experience, only the material signifier as an image remains accessible in a perpetually present world. According to Jameson's analysis, the transformation of reality into images and the fragmentation of time into a series of perpetual presents are consequences of both late-capitalist alienation and the released play of the signifier in textuality and pastiche. In short, the fetishization of the signifier in postmodern art may be the very symptom of the schizophrenic collapse of the subject and historical narration in late-capitalist society. Hence a skepticism emerges regarding the critical efficacy of the postmodernist collage and its correlate, *architecture écriture*.[13]

Reformulated as text and emphasizing "the gap between the signifier and the signified, the lapse in meaning, the syncope in the experience

[11] The suspension of referential meaning in avant-gardist art aims at shock "as a stimulus to change one's conduct of life; it is the means to break through aesthetic immanence and to usher in (initiate) a change in the recipient's life praxis." (P. Burger, *Theory of Avant-Garde,* 80) However, the history of the avant-garde demonstrates the gradual neutralization and inevitable institutionalization of shock in a radically malleable culture. The radicality of late capitalism should allow little if any room for shock in La Villette since "more than any avant-garde, capital is the agent of transgression and shock- which is one reason why such strategies in art now seem as redundant as resistance seems futile." H. Foster, *Recodings: Art, Spectacle, Cultural Politics* (1985), 147.

[12] F. Jameson, "Postmodernism and Consumer Society" in *The AntiAesthetic: Essays on Postmodern Culture,* Hal Foster, ed. (1983), 119.

[13] On the collage character of *architecture écriture,* see G. Ulmer, "The Object of Post Criticism," in *The Anti-Aesthetic: Essays on Postmodern Culture,* Hal Foster, ed. (1983), 83-110. Ulmer argues that collage is the discursive manifestation of the gram principle and a privileged stylistic device in Jacques Derrida's deconstruction of mimesis.

ABOVE. Hannah Höch,"Cut with the Kitchen Knife," 1919. Reproduced from Dawn Ades, *Photomontage* (New York: Pantheon, 1976).

of the subject,"[14] it could only exacerbate the schizophrenic condition of consumer capitalist society, thus rendering even more difficult any attempt to think the present. Jameson states:

There is some agreement that the older modernism functioned against its society in ways which are variously described as critical, negative, contestatory, subversive, oppositional and the like. Can anything of the sort be affirmed about postmodernism and its social moment? We have seen that there is a way in which postmodernism replicates or reproduces- reinforces- the logic of consumer capitalism; the more significant question is whether there is also a way in which it resists that logic. [15]

COLLAGE VERSUS MONTAGE

Some composite works, assembled by modernists and postmodernists alike, incorporate fragments that remain semantically incompatible if not contradictory, and yet do not exhibit the characteristic formal disjunctions of collage but rather demonstrate the persistence of (a sort of) mimesis. This

[14] F. Jameson, *Fables of Aggression: Wyndham Lewis, the Modernist as Fascist* (1979), 20.

[15] F. Jameson, "Postmodernism and Consumer Society," 125.

ABOVE. Raoul Hausman, "Tatlin at Home," 1920. Photo by Moderna Museet, Stockholm. Reproduced from Dawn Ades, *Photomontage* (New York: Pantheon, 1976).

ABOVE Raoul Hausman, "Spirit of Our Time," 1920. Photo by Musees Natinaux. Reproduced from Dawn Ades, *Photomontage* (New York: Pantheon, 1976).

category of works is loosely labeled "montage" (which I will maintain for lack of a better term), and is distinguishable from collage in its formal qualities, historical manifestations, and modes of production and reception.[16]

The term montage was coined by the Dadaists as a substitute for "composition" to express a negational attitude toward bourgeois artistic hierarchies.[17] Dadaists also intended to reframe the artistic process in contradistinction to romantic notions of creativity and originality: montage denotes a kind of bricolage, a reorganization of existing material and codes. Dada photomontage thus sought an alternative to the hermetic rhetoric of expressionism and the semantic atrophy of nonobjective art by allowing the artifact to engage the world directly and more effectively. As Rosalind Krauss has observed, the photographic component of photomontage "is an imprint or transfer of the real; it is a photochemically processed trace causally connected to that thing in the world to which it refers."[18]

[16] The reformulation of "montage" in contradistinction to "collage" does not strictly coincide with the common or historical usage of the term. However artificial and anachronistic, this revision is necessary when dealing with seemingly seamless representations, such as the architecture of Machado and Silvetti. While this architecture has little formal resemblance to the more explicitly destructured assemblages of disparate elements characteristic of collage, it shares its fundamental heterogeneity.

[17] See K. Michael Hays, "Photomontage and its Audiences: Berlin, Circa 1922," in Harvard Architectural Review, 6 (1987), 18-31. As Raoul Hausmann states: "This term translates our aversion at playing the artist, and, thinking of ourselves as engineers, (Hence our preference for workmen's overalls) we meant to construct, to assemble [montieren] our works." Raoul Hausmann, Courier Dada (Paris, 1958), 42, quoted in Ades, Photomontage, 12.

ABOVE. John Heartfield, *"Rationalization is on the March!,"* 1927. Reproduced from Peter Pachnicke and Klaus Honnef, eds., *John Heartfield* (New York: Harry N. Abrams, 1992), 131.

The initial Dadaist experiments with montage, such as Hannah Hoch's "Cut with the Kitchen Knife of 1919" (Fig 2), thus used to advantage the indexical character of the photographic material to bypass mimesis and directly capture the heterogeneity of the real. Photographic fragments isolated against a white background in a collage fashion yielded a registration of the gaps, the fissures, the tensions—the contradictions—of that very reality of which they were merely the faithful trace.

A genuine mutation in the conception and practice of Dada photomontage is discernible, however, in Raoul Hausmann's "Tatlin at Home" of 1920 (Fig 3). In this work, the juxtaposed reality fragments are no longer isolated in their alterity by "rivers of white paper." On the contrary, the typically haphazard arrangement gives way to a more structured and mimetic assemblage of parts, and the negational silence is disrupted by faint but ideologically articulate messages. Hausmann's "Spirit of Our Time" of 1920 (Fig 4) repeats the experiment of Tatlin at Home in a three-dimensional object. The indexical moment of photography is translated here into mass-produced objects or objets trouvés, unmediated fragments of reality itself. A wallet, tape measure, collapsible drinking cup, and numbered card (among other things) are assembled onto a wooden head in order to "express the petty bourgeois spirit of the times, unthinking, without individuality, reduced to a cipher and progressively dehumanized."[19]

[18] R. Krauss, L'Amour Fou, 31.

ABOVE.Sherrie Levine (after Walker Evans), 1981. Reproduced from Hal Foster, *Recodings* (Seattle: Bay Press), 167)

Just like *Tatlin at Home, Spirit of Our Time* seizes reality and restructures it in order to allegorically communicate "not simply the fact which it shows but also the special tendency expressed by the facts."[20] Here lies, in this insistence upon meaning, the decisive break with collage. The aesthetic and political implications of this transformation were soon to be exploited in John Heartfield's photomontages.[21]

What differentiates Heartfield's work from the more random or undirected expressions achieved through similar means and media in collage is, indeed, the possibility of meaningful interpretation: "our gaining of new information, our receiving of a specific semiotically controlled message, through reading his precise layering of metaphorical devices."[22] Consider, for example, *Rationalization* is on the March! of 1927 (Fig 5). A human figure is constructed of machine parts. The structuring influence of the anthropomorphic layout channels the connotative fields of the assembled elements so as to elaborate an allegory of mechanization and modernity from emblematic industrial debris. The composition goes beyond Cubist portraiture to read almost narratively as a succession of metaphors converging on the anatomy of a technological body.[23]

[19] Ades, Photomontage, 30.

[20] J. Heartfield, Photomontages of the Nazi Period (1977), 26

[21] Louis Aragon noted the break in Heartfield's work when he wrote that "the scraps of photographs that he formerly maneuvered for the pleasure of stupefaction, under his fingers began to signify." Louis Aragon, Les Collages (1965), 29; quoted in Ades, Photomontage, 42.

[22] B. Johns, "Visual Metaphor: Lost and Found," in Semiotica, vol. 52, no. 3/4 (1984), 306.

[23] See Ibid. 305-06.

Heartfield's photomontage is primarily allegorical.[24] It is conceived as a semantically saturated image, condensing its information in visual discourse; its principle of construction is entirely subordinated to the necessary legibility and intelligibility of the message. The compositional treatment of the image thus overrides the incommensurability of the constituent elements so as to ensure the legibility of the restructured signs. It does not, however, achieve a complete synthesis of parts since the fragments remain internally separated by their semantic differences. Montage thus constantly oscillates between a resolved whole and a fragmented assemblage of suspended differences.

Work by certain contemporary artists elaborates this legacy of montage. Mark Tansey absorbs both the photographic and textual impulses of photomontage back into painting and produces allegories of contemporary cultural production itself (Fig 6). Sherrie Levine's work is a radicalized, contemporary instance of montage (Fig 7). Levine rephotographs photographs, robing them for the second time "in a true allegorical fashion,"[25] from their historical function and authenticity. Levine does not alter the appearance of the appropriated material or physically tear it out from a larger cohesive whole to reassemble it with different fragments (material or textual) in a new configuration. There is no figurative, collage like collision of incongruous parts. Her intervention- the degree-zero of montage- is strictly limited to allegorical confiscation, which nevertheless radically transforms the artifact in its semantic dimension. Levine's montaged photograph is thus a paradigm- and cas extrême -of the montaged allegorical work, simultaneously total and coherent, heterogeneous and fragmented. As Benjamin Buchloh has written, "Levine's notion of fragmentation differs from the phallocratic tendency which associates fragmentation with broken saucers, burnt wood, and crumpled straw. In her seemingly random selectionof imagery from the history of modernism, representations are literally fragmented,

[24] Allegory allowed Heartfield's images "to speak publicly with hidden meaning." Georges Grosz is explicit about the original circumstances, political context, and strategic intentions of his and Heartfield's invented technique: In 1916, when Johnny Heartfield and I invented photomontage in my studio at the south end of town at five o'clock one May morning, we had no idea of the immense possibilities, or of the thorny but successful career, that awaited the new invention. On one piece of cardboard we pasted a mishmash of advertisements for hernia belts, a student song book and dog food, labels from schnapps and wine bottles, and photographs from picture papers, cut up at will in such a way to say, in pictures, what would have been banned by the censors if we had said it in words. Georges Grosz, quoted in Ades, Photomontage, 19.

[25] See B. Buchloh, "Allegorical Procedures: Appropriation and Montage in Contemporary Art," Artforum 21 (1982), 43-56.

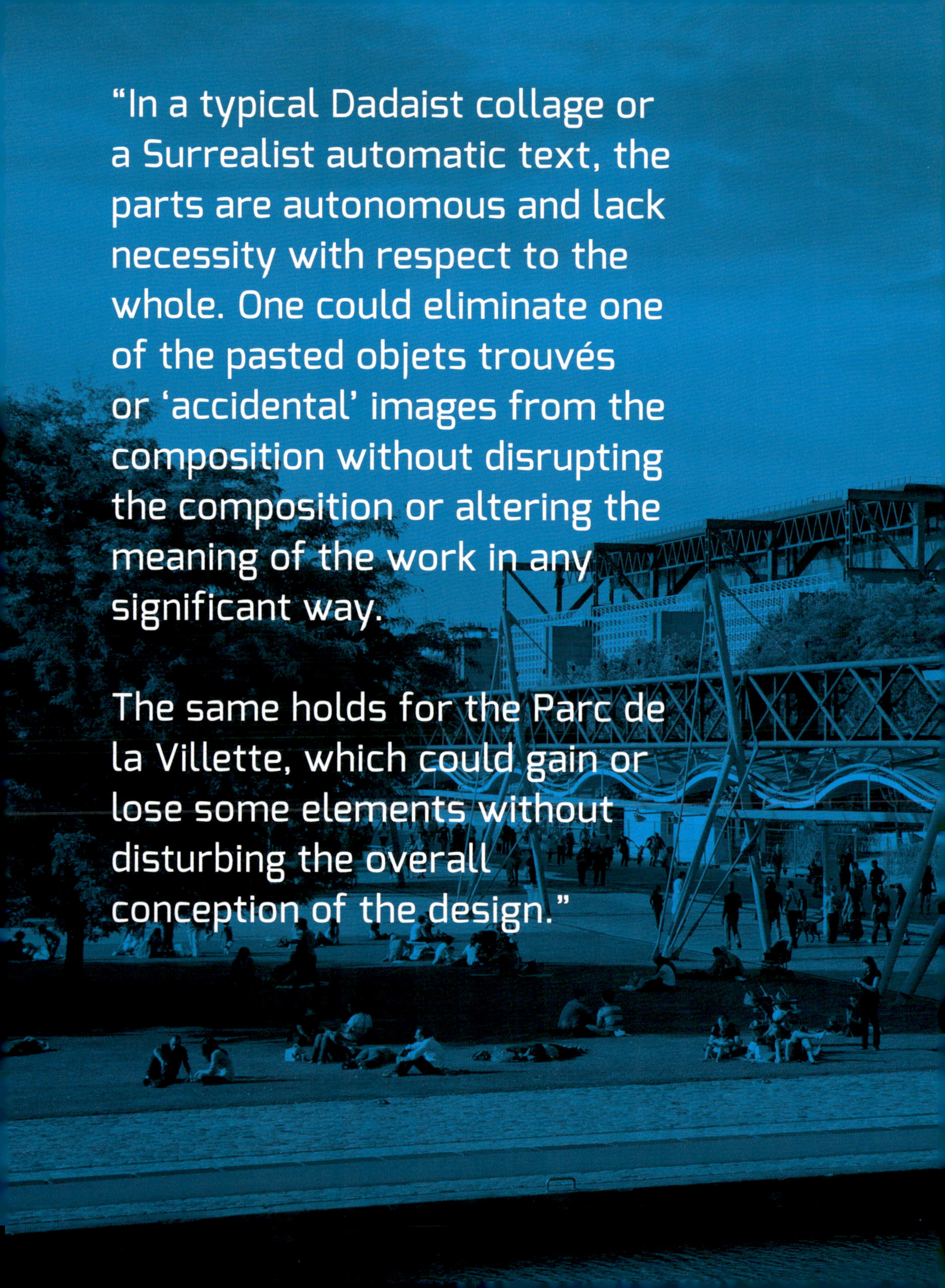

"In a typical Dadaist collage or a Surrealist automatic text, the parts are autonomous and lack necessity with respect to the whole. One could eliminate one of the pasted objets trouvés or 'accidental' images from the composition without disrupting the composition or altering the meaning of the work in any significant way.

The same holds for the Parc de la Villette, which could gain or lose some elements without disturbing the overall conception of the design."

torn from the hermetic totality of the ideological discourse within which they currently exist. Thus as [Walter] Benjamin described the allegorical procedure, Levine devaluates the objects of representation for the second time. She depletes the current commodity status of photography by Walker Evans, Edward Weston, Elliot Porter, and Andreas Feininger for the second time by her willful act of re-photography, by restating their essential status as multiplied, technically reproduced imagery."[26]

In their respective efforts to yield concrete and translucent representations of the dynamic tendencies of historical development, both collage and montage undermine a "reflection theory" of mimesis, which sees the vocation of the work of art to be to push beyond the world of surface appearance to capture, crystallize, and reflect some ostensible "essence of things." Collage professes the end of mimesis altogether with the logic of symbolic representation: the collaged work does not designate a referent beyond itself but rather expresses, in its very destructured form, an essentially heterogeneous reality. Montage, by contrast, is allegorical: it does not bracket off the referent but rather problematizes the very activity of reference by allowing supplemental signifieds to infiltrate the interstitial spaces of recycled signs.[27] In the allegorical montage, "any person, any object, any relationship can mean absolutely anything else."[28] The montaged work thus ruptures the supposedly indissoluble unity of form and content that is placed on history by ideology. But the montaged work also rejects the critical modernist (formalist) retreat into the opacity of the medium as a necessary step in countering the distortions of ideology. Instead, it recognizes and embraces the ideological contamination of its figurative and hermeneutically accessible representations as an instrument and a precondition for critical engagement in the cultural arena.

As a distinct category of assembled works, montage opens an alternative field of operation for interpretive strategies confronting the appropriation and recombination procedures in recent artistic/architectural practice as well as in the historical avant-garde.

RIGHT. L.A. Borghese

[26] B. Buchloh, "Allegorical Procedures," 52.

[27] Craig Owens has noted the supplemental character of allegory to account for its gradual marginalization in modern aesthetics: "The allegorical meaning supplants an antecedent one; it is a supplement. This is why allegory is condemned, but is also the source of its theoretical significance." Craig Owens, "The Allegorical Impulse: Toward a Theory of Postmodernism," Part 2, October 13 (1980), 69.

[28] W. Benjamin, *The Origin of German Tragic Drama* (1977), 175.

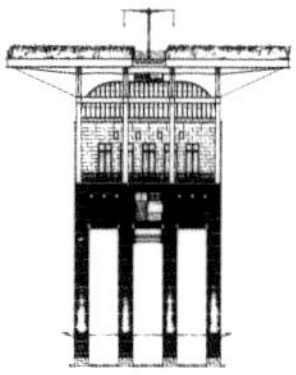

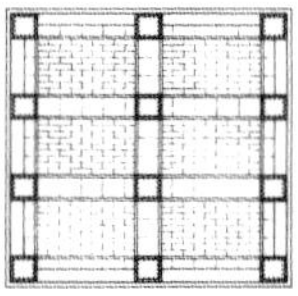

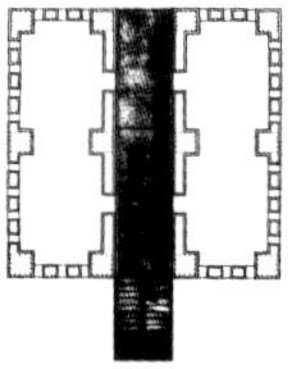

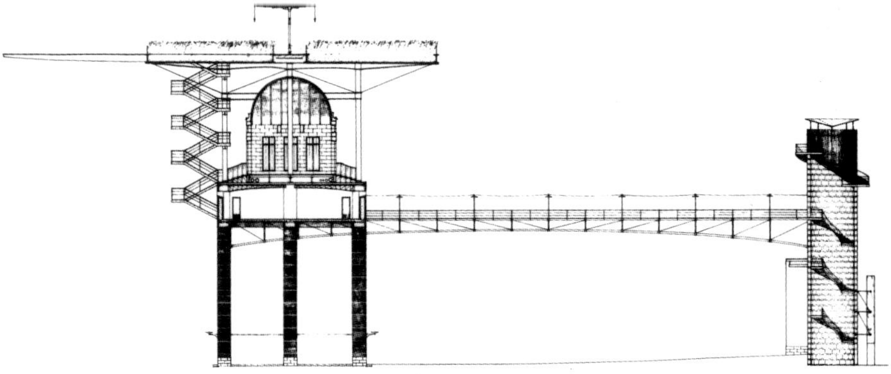

SECTION

ABOVE. Project for the city of Este

Montage allows the reconsideration of mimetic-yet-composite works outside the traditional dichotomy of organic versus nonorganic and its entailed separation of formal and hermeneutic procedures of interpretation. Earlier identified with the Trojan-horse tactics of the architectural drawing "The Presence of the Past," montaged works do not present the characteristic formal disjunctions and abstractions of nonorganic works, nor do they assume the transparent discourse of traditional realist, or reflection-theory modes of representation. Rather, they contrive a paradoxical congruence of fragments—the necessary condition in gaining access to content in the traditional hermeneutic manner—in order to exacerbate, in the reading performance, the contradictions between the various layers of the represented reality. Behind the realist imagery of these works, the reader encounters a decentered text that requires active participation in deconstructing its ideological closure.[29]

MONTAGE AND REALISM

Machado and Silvetti's architecture is assembled from different fragments, "bits and pieces from various heterogeneous systems of objects and buildings."[30] The fragments, however, are not collided or haphazardly collaged in order to exacerbate the heterogeneous character of the composition. On the contrary, while thriving on unprecedented configurations of elements, the architecture abolishes the material gaps between seemingly irreconcilable fragments by resolving their incompatibilities along carefully designed seams.

Consider as an example the chaise lounge, L.A. Borghese, one of Machado's early furniture designs that has the advantage of simplicity. As demonstrated in the pun of the title, the piece constructs a paradoxical congruence between radically different if not antithetical sensibilities: the cultural excesses of Los Angeles and the aristocratic classicism of Napoleonic Rome made fashionable in Paris of the nineteen-twenties. No gaps can be discerned between the juxtaposed fragments; no formal tension can belie the alterity of two contradictory derivations here united in a rather balanced composition and stable construction. The "properly" crafted and composed connection

[29] Hence the ambivalent nature of the montaged work: in order to problematize representation and resist mythifying it must represent and signify. In Craig Owens words, "we thus encounter once again the unavoidable necessity of participating in the very activity that is being denounced precisely in order to denounce it." C. Owens, "Allegorical Impulse," 79.

[30] Rodolfo Machado, course syllabus given at the Rhode Island School of Design, 1985.

between the metallic fragment of high-tech, pop character and the more traditional and noble affiliations of the chaise lounge momentarily abolishes the heterogeneity of the artifact with the persuasive logic of a tectonic assembly and the convincing elegance of the design.[31]

A similar resolution on a larger scale can be observed in Machado's Project for the City of Este.[32] Juxtaposed here are building fragments seemingly irreconcilable in their fundamental typological differences: loggia, basilica, belvedere, garden, and aqueduct. Their formal and material incompatibility seems, however, to be resolved in the cohesive syntagms of the structure. Indeed, the appropriated elements are readjusted so as to properly fit in their new context without, however, loosing their formal autonomy. For instance, while the transition between the underscaled basilica and the distorted loggia is totally resolved, the two elements remain clearly distinct in their separate morphological identities. The tense connection between the basilican roof and the garden convincingly, if somewhat painfully, resolves an inherent geometrical and constructional incompatibility between the pitched copper roof and the flat garden surface. An excessive precision in realistically detailed surfaces and structure furthermore argues, with the rhetoric of sound construction and concrete materiality, for the tectonic resolution of the syntagms.

In the L.A. Borghese montage, differentiated syntagms—the figural sycamore podium, the glossy black lacquered leg, the bolted stainless-steel table top, and the ivory-finished rustication—perturb the tenuous tectonic serenity of the design and impose a double reading: that of the fragment perceived in relation to its context of origin, and that of the same fragment incorporated into a new cohesive whole, a different totality. When the two readings are superimposed, the apparent coherence of the fabricated reality crumbles, along with the naturalized, truthlike authenticity of the original contexts—Los Angeles and Napoleonic Rome.

[31] A marriage of silk and leather cushions furthermore justifies th is bricolage with an appeal to the parodic irreverence of "camp."

[32] The project for Este was designed by Rodolfo Machado and a team of students from the Rhode Island School of Design as a submission to the Biennale di Venezia of 1985.

[33] Devaluated, mass-reproduced icons of cultural history are subjected to confiscation, alteration, and inscription within a new context. Here montage allegorically protests the devaluation of objects into commodities by reproducing the devaluation process in its very own practice: "The allegorist subjects the sign to the same division of function that the object has undergone in its transformation into a commodity. The repetition of the original act of depletion and the new attribution of meaning redeems the object." Buchloh, "Allegorical Procedures," 44.

ABOVE. Marcel Duchamp. Bicycle Wheel. Reproduced from Jean Christophe Bailly, *Duchamp* (New York: Universe Books, 1986), 48

ABOVE. John Heartfield, "A Pan German," 1933, Reproduced from Peter Pachnicke and Klaus Honnef, eds., *John Heartfield* (New York: Harry N. Abrams, 1992)

L.A Borghese is thus reminiscent of Dadaist and Surrealist artifacts that compose uncanny combinations of found objects.[33] Duchamp's Bicycle Wheel (Fig 8) is an obvious example: the wheel and the stool form in their juxtaposition an integrated and plausible whole; however, the stability of the : syntagms foregrounds, sharpens, and confronts opposing connotations generated from original contexts (sitting/traveling; rest/ movement; furniture/vehicle; etc.). L.A Borghese and the Project for the City of Este likewise remain heterogeneous, realizing the organic congruence of part and whole, form and content, only to shatter again into a multiplicity of irreducible elements. They are like the allegorical fragments described by Walter Benjamin and rehabilitated in recent criticism to characterize a particular trend of postmodern art.[34]

[34] Benjamin developed a theory of allegory in relation to the literature of the German baroque. Yet it is in montaged work that his theory finds its most pertinent object (Benjamin's interpretation of the baroque allegory was no doubt informed by his experience of the avant-garde ist montage, in particular that of Heartfield, whom he praises in "The Author as Producer"). His analysis construes the allegorical practice as a consequence of the "worldly orientation" of baroque culture, which undermines the anticipatory utopian dimension of historical time thus giving way for melancholic contemplation. Benjamin's reading of the baroque allegory elaborates a critique of the romantic symbol as it came to dominate the theories of representation since the late-eighteenth century. He rejects Goethe's canonical formulation whereby allegory and symbol are distinguished in the ways they relate the particular to the general. For Benjamin, the decisive difference lies in the category of time. In allegory, history appears as a petrified nature in decay, i.e., a ruin; the symbol is part of an organic nature that is "fluid and changing," it captures time as an instantaneous present, "in which the empirical and the transcendent appear momentarily fused within a fleeting, natural moment." S. Buck Morss, *The Dialectics of Seeing: Walter Benjamin and the Arcades Project* (1989), 168.

They "proffer and differ a promise of meaning; they both solicit and frustrate our desire that the image be directly transparent to its signification. As a result, they appear strangely incomplete—fragments or ruins which must be deciphered."[35]

This deliberate attempt to smooth out all gaps or discrepancies in the assembly can be compared to a *photomonteur's* efforts to hide all material evidence of the subversive operations and their characteristic disjunctions. For the effectiveness of montage greatly depends on the plausible integrity and verisimilitude of the alternative reality it seeks to construct: "The descriptive, realistic, technically minded, and believable drawings are intended to convince the viewer of the fact that what we have imagined is possible."[36] In other words, the effectiveness of montage depends upon an imitation of the seamlessness of reality itself.

Heartfield's "A Pan German" of 1933 (Fig 9) analogously demonstrates how the montage technique can effectively conceal the composite nature of the work by stitching together the seams that connect its different elements. Montage is therefore ambiguously related to photographic falsification where all artifice, all evidence of incompatibility between reassembled elements, is systematically erased. What separates the montage from the falsified image is not inherent to the formal properties of the work. The difference, rather, is between myth and allegory; it depends on "whether the construction makes visible the gap between sign and referent, or fuses them in a deceptive totality so that the caption merely duplicates the semiotic content of the image instead of setting it into question."[37]

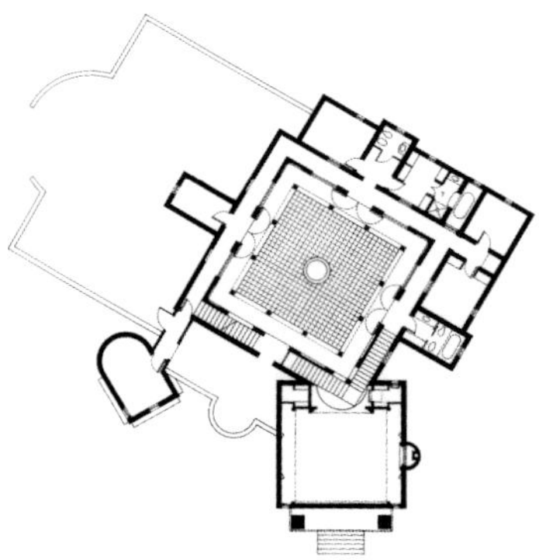

RIGHT. Jorge Silvetti, Villa on Lake Pergusa, 1982, second floor plan

[35] C. Owens, "Allegorical Impulse," 70.

[36] Rodolfo Machado, project description for A Project for the City of Este in this monograph, 65.

[37] B. Morss, *Dialeaics of Seeing*, 68.

Where the falsified image naturalizes its referent in uncritical affirmation, the allegorical supplement of the montaged work encodes two or more contents within one form and ultimately unravels the bond that forms between sign and referent.[38]

The montaged work is erected upon a paradox: while its effectiveness depends on the minimization of artifice, a strategic masking of its constructional seams, it becomes critically impotent as soon as the mask is no longer strategic but absolute. The montaged work strives to blur the traces of artifice; yet it fails when this task is totally fulfilled, when montage becomes ideological falsification, which is to say, pastiche. Herein lies the paradox: the montaged work should look "real," but faintly or ambivalently so; a trace of its seams should remain legible. Like Frankenstein's monster, the montaged work is an inorganic imitation of life that is perfected in the erasure of all visible artifice. Yet it is characterized or defined in the seam, the by-product of the technique, the trace of the artifice.

Literally discernible in the tailored stitches of the assemblage, or virtually intelligible within each fractured sign, the paradoxical seams of Machado and Silvetti's architecture are the locus of its meaning. Silvetti's Villa on Lake Pergusa (Fig IO), for instance, orchestrates a series of meaningful events along the seams of colliding orders: the classical and the vernacular, the private and the public. The site of collision is described as "the most important and memorable motif in the experience of the building. It represents the locus of convergence of most of the architectural, spatial, symbolic, and programmatic themes of the house."[39] The seams indeed provide "an opportunity to investigate and operate a system of composition other than the traditional 'poché' or the 'Cubist transparency' which seem to be today the two mutually exclusive techniques for dealing with such collisions."[40]

[38] As argued by Craig Owens, the dangerous-allegorical-supplement separates the confiscated material of montage from the mythifying quotations of historical precedents that have come to characterize postmodern architecture: "The appropriations of montage have to be clearly distinguished from the postmodernist predilection for historical quotation which leaves the original meaning of the quoted material unaltered and serves to further naturalize (mythifying) its innate authenticity and historical function-its social 'truth.' " the monteur-allegorist "does not restore an original meaning that may have been lost or obscured ... rather, he adds another meaning to the image." Owens, "Allegorical Impulse," 69.

[39] J. Silvetti, "Houseat Lake Pergusa, Enna, Siciy" in Landscape, Princeton Journal, vol. 2 (1985), 146.

[40] Ibid. 145-146.

[41] Ibid. 146.

ABOVE AND NEXT PAGE. Gateway for the city of Venice

Cubist transparency belongs to the pulverized space of avant-gardist collage. It seeks to be reconciled with a heterogeneous reality even as it portrays that reality as disintegrated in the unmediated collision of fragments. The traditional poché is the privileged device of pastiche: it reproduces the apparent seamlessness of reality in a flawless integration of different and potentially incompatible figurative spaces. Both formal attitudes—negational collage and conciliatory pastiche—are rejected in the Villa on Lake Pergusa. "Unlike the poché which hides the collision in favor of figural rooms, or the transparency which favors the flowing of space, sacrificing intelligibility," its eventful seams fabricate the characteristic illusion of montage from the figurative material of the collision. The seams represent an order that is plausible and figurative enough to be hermeneutically accessible, yet ephemeral and fragile enough to lay bare the artifice of its own making and signal its immanent breakdown into separate utterances. Silvetti describes the technique as one of " 'perspectival collision' (one-point perspective/two-point perspective), which recalls the scenographic techniques of the baroque theater, where the contradiction between the two systems is left in suspense by the frame of the proscenium."[41] A similar perspectival collision is evident in the projects for a garden folly and for the urban scenography of Vienna.

In other projects by Machado and Silvetti, the collision or superimposition of elements is not only treated allegorically or scenographically, but also functionally, as a practical solution to a programmatic problem. The crease on the bottom edge of the wall in the Gateway for Venice project, for example, creates a convenient bench for bus travelers while imitating the folds of hanging drapery. In the Municipal Cemetery of Polizzi-Generosa, a terraced lawn is connected to the confraternity and the columbaria in the floor below by a set of stairs that are disposed and designed in the imitation of tombstones. In both cases, the site of contact between the montaged elements takes on a functional role to resolve architecturally the virtual seams between different orders of representation: the emblematic and the pragmatic, the metaphorical and the literal, the ornamental and the structural. The practical ingenuity of the bench/crease thus compensates for the figurative excess of the curtain wall, while the functional necessity of the stair/tombstone reconciles the emblematic graveyard of individual tombs with the pragmatic columbaria of communal cells.

[41] Ibid, 146.

ABOVE. Municipal Cemetery, Polizzi-Generosa

Allegorical, scenographic, or functional, the tailored stitches of Machado and Silvetti's architecture reflect the inadequacy of a seamless simulation of organic coherence and reject the more disjunctive prosthetics of collage. The architects fabricate, instead, a scarred imitation of life, a pseudo-organic whole that registers the artifice of its own making in the persistent alterity of its parts.

MONTAGE AND MIMESIS

In contradistinction to collage's dislocated and often random compositions that resist any recognizable or naturalized order, montage borrows a functional syntax from the reality it seeks to imitate or analogically reproduce. This ordering system, however momentary or tenuous its hold, is a necessary condition for deciphering montage's allegorical ruins. The reality of montage can be entirely fabricated and unprecedented, as long as it is coherent and plausible, which is to say as long as it is possible within

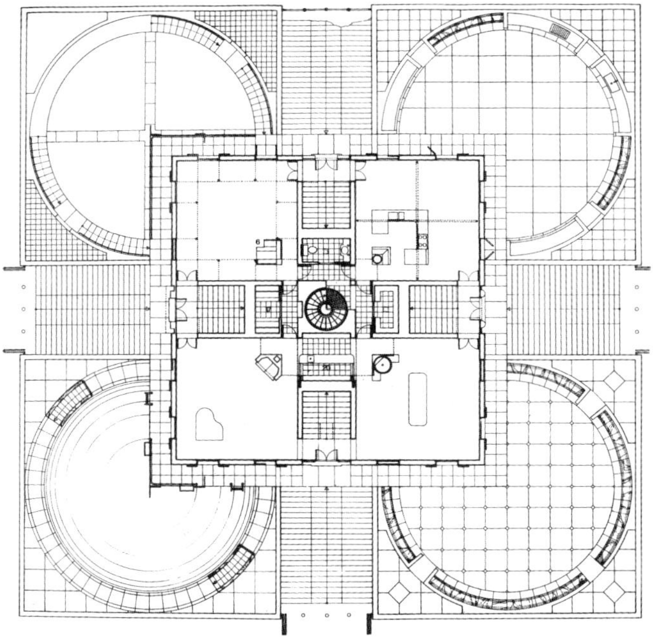

ABOVE. Country House, plan

ABOVE. Country House, perspective drawing of central hall

the defining parameters of a particular genre and a collective imagination. For montage does not seek truth but rather verisimilitude. Francis Picabia's machine-like objects and Man Ray's assemblages do not imitate nature or any known models. Like Duchamp's "Bicycle Wheel" they assemble heterogeneous fragments into plausible and even vaguely familiar objects, evocative of arcane or esoteric machinery. They gain their verisimilitude by imitating unprecedented but possible realities.

Whether conceived in terms of culturally encoded icons, ready-made morphologies, or conventional modes of discourse, a logic of types defines the plausible, intelligible, verisimilar reality of Machado and Silvetti's montaged mimeses.[42] Typology sets generic rules and references that loosely guide their architectural bricolage or more narrowly structure the composition of fragments according to a precisely articulated syntax. Although entirely unprecedented, Machado's Project for the City of Este exhibits some typological affiliation in its formal attributes, functional/symbolic programs, and particular position on the site. The intelligibility of this unprecedented building could hence be articulated by reference to the generic features of a familiar type: the monumental tower or belvedere, the basilica, the cultivated field.

Machado's Country House in Piedmont, Virginia, is rigorously composed within specific typological guidelines. Its origin can be traced to the

[42] As the abstract and figuratively hermetic propositions of modern architecture failed to communicate their revolutionary program for reorganizing the praxis of life, the traditional idea of verisimilitude was restored in the late fifties with a return to the logic of persuasion based on an elaboration of what was culturally believable. The problem of historical continuity was posed, the incorporation of contextual mimeses and popular motives was advocated, and common knowledge became a viable resource for architectural persuasion: "Architecture does not become more involved with representation, since it always is, but the 'real' represented and the verisimilitude sought after are easier and more concrete ... more realist and more intelligible as a collective discourse." J. Silvetti, "On Realism in Architecture," in *Harvard Architectural Review* I (1980), 15. Machado and Silvetti's theorization of "type" in relation to genre, doxa and verisimilitude thus sought an "ideological mutation": a strategic adoption of an accessible system of signification, more effective in engaging the social discourse of architecture in the cultural debate since "the idea of 'type' implies, first of all, a minimum level of intelligibility for forms based on the architect's and beholder's experience, which in turn will make architecture 'believable.' " Ibid. 23.

[43] Rodolfo Machado, project description for Country House in this monograph, 47.

[44] For example, that of Leon Vaudoyer's winning project for a ménagerie in 1783. In the Country House, the first floor of the building consists of four rooms and four exterior annexes organized according to a strict bilateral symmetry and functionally or semantically qualified by a diagonal chain of "attributes." On the second floor the same strategy is executed, but the furniture semantically reinforces the function of the attributes and further problematize the traditional notions of function and expression, which are understood to be naturally communicated by architectural form.

architect's personal and lasting encounter with a work of sixteenth- century architecture, Villa Montecchia. "This act of designing Country House is then a tribute," writes Machado, "a loving reenactment, a new mise-en-architecture. It ignores those features of Montecchia that are found bothersome; it exaggerates or repeats those that are especially pleasurable."[43] The general layout of the house also recalls typical partis of the Prix de Rome in the late-eighteenth and early-nineteenth centuries.[44] The structural and grammatical functionsof the type are most explicit in the plan where a rigorous symmetry conveys a sense of organic coherence. The plan thus allows the viewer to rationally intuit the building through its compositional armature and to articulate a system of formal relationships or syntactic equations between its major components. This armature is rhetorically reproduced in a series of perspectival drawings depicting the four major rooms of thehouse. The drawings are identical in their layout; they all share the same perspectival parameters, orientation, and focus: the attribute occupying the corner. The repetitionof the perspectival configuration establishes a paradigmatic nexus among the different spaces and reproduces the syntagmatic structure of the plan. In both planimetric and pictorial modes of representation, the typological configuration of the building, with its exacerbated symmetry and redundancy, structures, redistributes, channels, and also amplifies the connotative fields of the different elements such as the rooms and their "attributes."

Silvetti's House on the Island of Djerba (Fig 11), a project from the same period as that of the Country House, is another example of a typological framework articulating and orchestrating polysemous utterances. Although immediately intelligible in the calligraphic simplicity of its form, the house appears to be totally unprecedented: a solid cube enveloped by a colossal staircase. A closer look at the drawings, however, will point to an unmistakable affiliation with a particular genre, most strictly realized in Palladia's Palazzo Thiene: a monumental and ceremonial space shaped by a thick "wall" of subservient rooms. This generic affiliation allows the recipient to construct an interpretive framework from a set of generic expectations. The recipient can accordingly decipher the contradictory assemblage of cube and stair: an allegorical confrontation between architecture and building, order and function, culture and the vernacular.

The logic of types also structures Machado and Silvetti's Carnegie Mellon University Center (Fig 12). The architects write, "Mixing the rich spatial strategy of John Soane's Bank of England and the uncompromising plan-

ABOVE. Jorge Silvetti, House on the Island of Djerba, 1977

ABOVE. Machado and Silvetti, Carnegie Mellon University Center, 1987

ning rigor of Diocletian's Palace and Ferdinado Fuga's Albergo dei Poveri, our proposal ... can be seen as a contemporary contribution to the old, but small, family of programmatically complex and dimensionally large buildings."[45] Ten distinct buildings, rendered as more or less independent types, are coordinated by a non-hierarchical gridded plan. What seems in elevation to be a quasi-picturesque blocking together of typal elements—towers, loggias, roofs, and the like—in plan is dissolved into or emerges out from a matrix: a kind of engendering plate for the multiple programmatic elements of the project that is analogous, in a sense, to the implied structuring matrix "behind" the photographic paper of a photomontage.

Unlike standard notions of type, which view architectural forms as autonomous from their use, the typology operative here requires that both the functional program and the physical form exist together, on the same conceptual plane, as preparatory material arranged and distributed by this plan matrix. It is as if there are functional as well as formal data out of which the architecture and its programmatic effects emerge, saturating the matrix. But what should be underscored here about the Carnegie Mellon University Center is that the vocation of producing, staging, and joining together the forms and programmatic events is taken on precisely and literally by the seams of the project—that system of spaces I have called the matrix. It is a different sort of system than mere circulation or structural grid, for it is also the major public space (comparable to the complex street

[45] Rodolfo Machado and Jorge Silvetti, project description for Carnegie Mellon University Center in this monograph, 81-82.

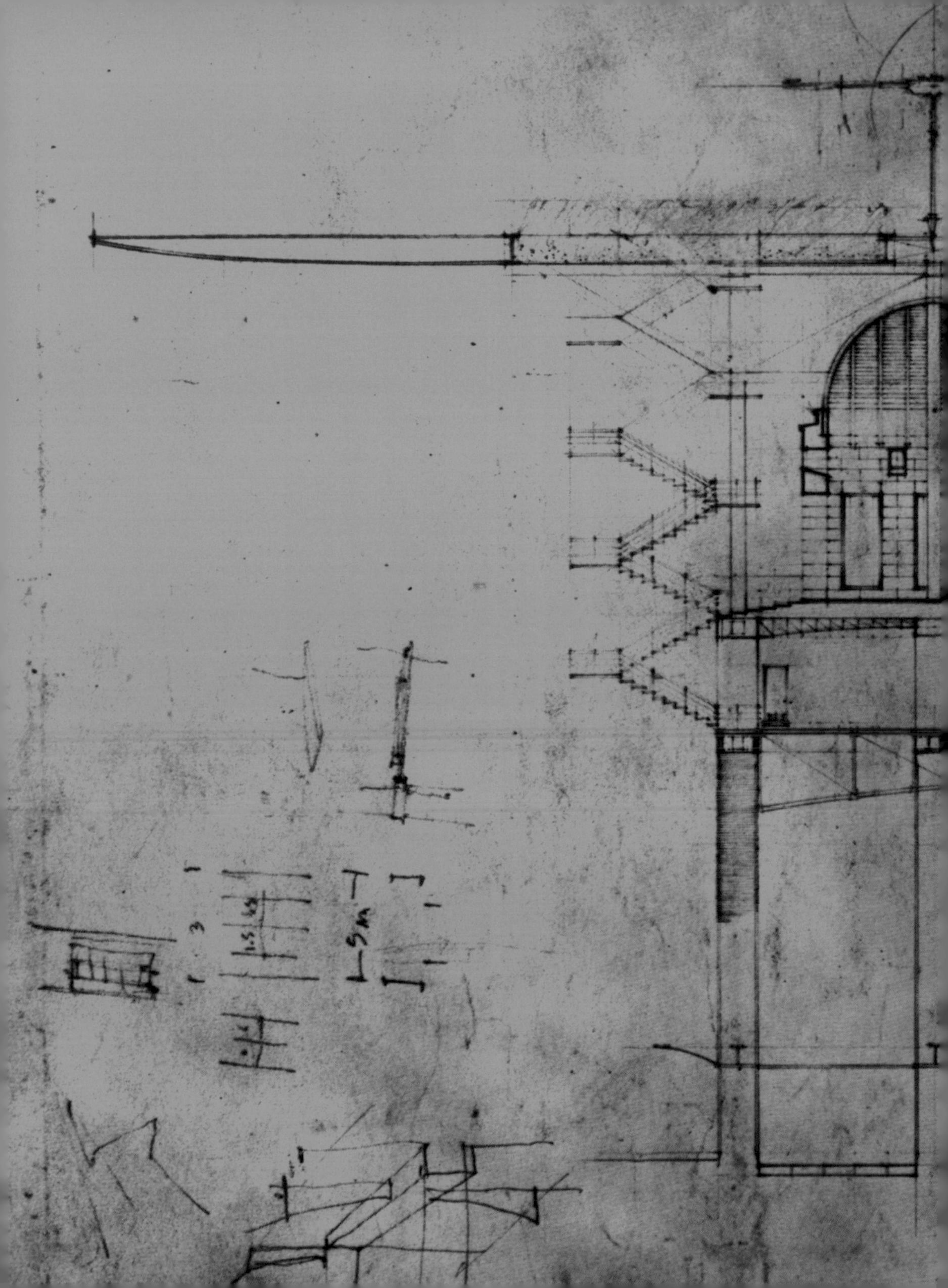

> "The montaged work thus ruptures the supposedly indissoluble unity of form and content that is placed on history by ideology. But the montaged work also rejects the critical modernist (formalist) retreat into the opacity of the medium as a necessary step in countering the distortions of ideology."

grid in the Proposal for the Nordbahnhofgelande in Vienna), the primary catalyst for student life, as well as the stitching that conjoins other spaces of varying degrees of publicness (from classrooms to dining halls to athletic courts). At Carnegie Mellon, perhaps more radically than at any other project, the architecture seems divided from itself by its simultaneous participation in so many different spatial systems. Like the laminated spaces of anamorpic painting, incompatible architectural types seem impossibly copresent. They articulate a diagram of potential occupations, a dispositif or distribution apparatus for differential forms and functions from incommensurable architectural registers pressed together into a single tissue—a montage.

THE POETICS OF MONTAGE

The distinctive and characteristic coherence achieved in montage by means of typological frames and armatures provides a new functional context for signification, a catalytic chamber and sounding board for the anticipated semantic slippages within and across the montaged elements. Commenting on Duchamp's ready-mades, Claude Levi-Strauss describes a similar reorganization of meaning:

You then accomplish a new distribution that was in the realm of the possible but was not openly effected (in the primitive condition of the object). You make then, in one sense, a work of learning, discovering in the object latent properties that were not perceived in the initial context; a poet does this each time he uses a word or turns a phrase in an unusual manner.[46]

The reference to poetry in Levi-Strauss's comment is neither accidental nor metaphorical: the montage process he describes reproduces the mechanisms of the poetic function as analyzed by Roman Jakobson.[47]

[46] G. Charbonnier, *Entretiens avec Claude Lévi-Strauss* (1961). Translated and quoted in Jorge Silvetti, "The Beauty of Shadows," Oppositions 7 (1979), 51.

[47] Jakobson and Levi-Strauss shared this particular understanding of the poetic function and actually collaborated on a project, "Les Chats," to test and articulate it. Their work on the poetic function has had a considerable influence on Machado and Silvetti's formative years. See Michael Hays's study in this collection.

[48] R. Jakobson, "Closing Statement: Linguistics and Poetics," in *Style and Language*, Thomas A Sebeok, ed. (1960), 358.

[49] T. Eagleton, *Literary Theory, An Introduction* (1983), 99.

According to Jakobson, metaphor and metonymy characterize the polarity of the two-fold process of selection and combination in which the linguistic sign is formed. Jakobson contends that the poetic function of language draws on both the selective (paradigmatic) and combinative (syntagmatic) modes as means for the promotion of equivalence. "The poetic function projects the principle of equivalence from the axis of selection into the axis of combination."[48] And in Terry Eagleton's more accessible formulation, "When we speak or write, we select signs from a possible range of equivalences, and then combine them together to form a sentence. What happens in poetry, however, is that we pay attention to 'equivalences' in the process of combining words together as well as in selecting them: We string together words which are semantically or rhythmically or phonetically or in some other way equivalent."[49]

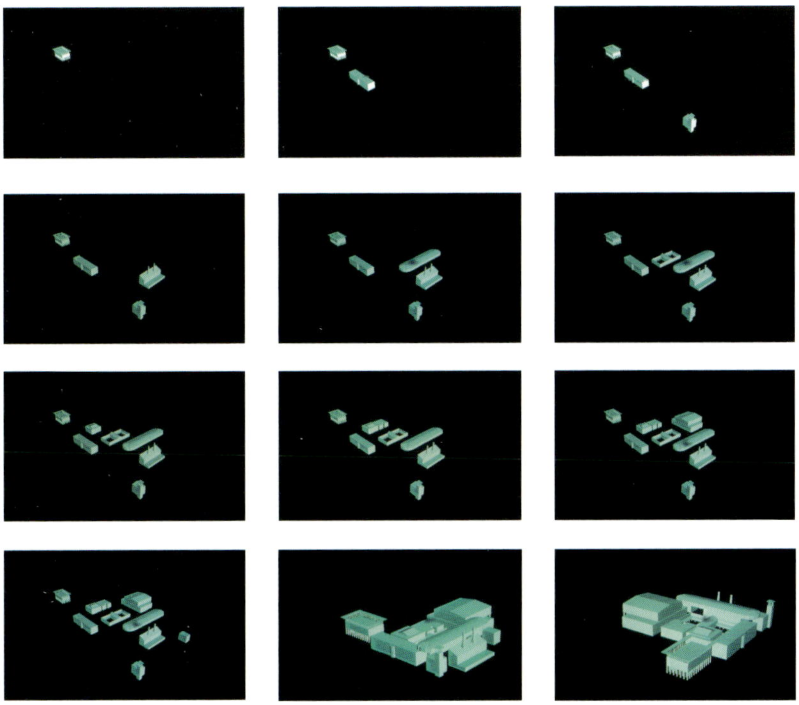

ABOVE. Carnegie Mellon University Center, accretion of constituent parts

This is precisely how Machado and Silvetti self-consciously proceed in composing their architectural montages: significant elements are selected according to resonant semantic and formal characteristics and then combined into configurations that allow for or produce systematic relationships among the parts. They activate, amplify, and confront their connotative fields so as to transform their signification, that is, to foreground and restructure the conventional relation between signifier and signified.

In contradistinction to the postmodernist pastiche where "mythification ... institutes a new signifying system in which its form remains almost untransformed, but by subtle accents, a new content covers the object,"[50] this montaged architecture is defined by Silvetti as a "signifying system in which the content is itself a signifying system: that is to say, the form and the content of the original object are both, in turn, the content of another form (the transformed object)."[51]

Accordingly, this montaged architecture continuously shakes the ideological ossification of its linguistic material in an endless battle against naturalized (mythological) meaning by breaking apart the abstracted, mythical sign and reinscribing it in a countermythical system, generating new significations in the "clash and condensation of its various levels."

Nowhere is the poetic function of montage more evident that in the project for La Porta Meridionale in Palermo (Fig 13). Following is an excerpt from Machado and Silvetti's description of the project:

We have "guided" Palermo's via Maqueda to its logical destiny, the mountains in the south, in order to follow a historical imperative as well as to help definitively organize la Conca d'Oro; we have used the program of a contemporary public park (Parco del Maredolce) to provide a place for leisure ... and to indicate a simple and clear order for urban growth and natural preservation. We have given the city another monument, il Belvedere della Corona di Palermo, which, in its excessiveness as a belvedere with easy automobile access, makes the city once again intelligible, manageable, and human insofar as it gives back to the citizenry the power to possess their city ... .

[50] J. Silvetti. "Beauty of Shadows," 52.

[51] Ibid.

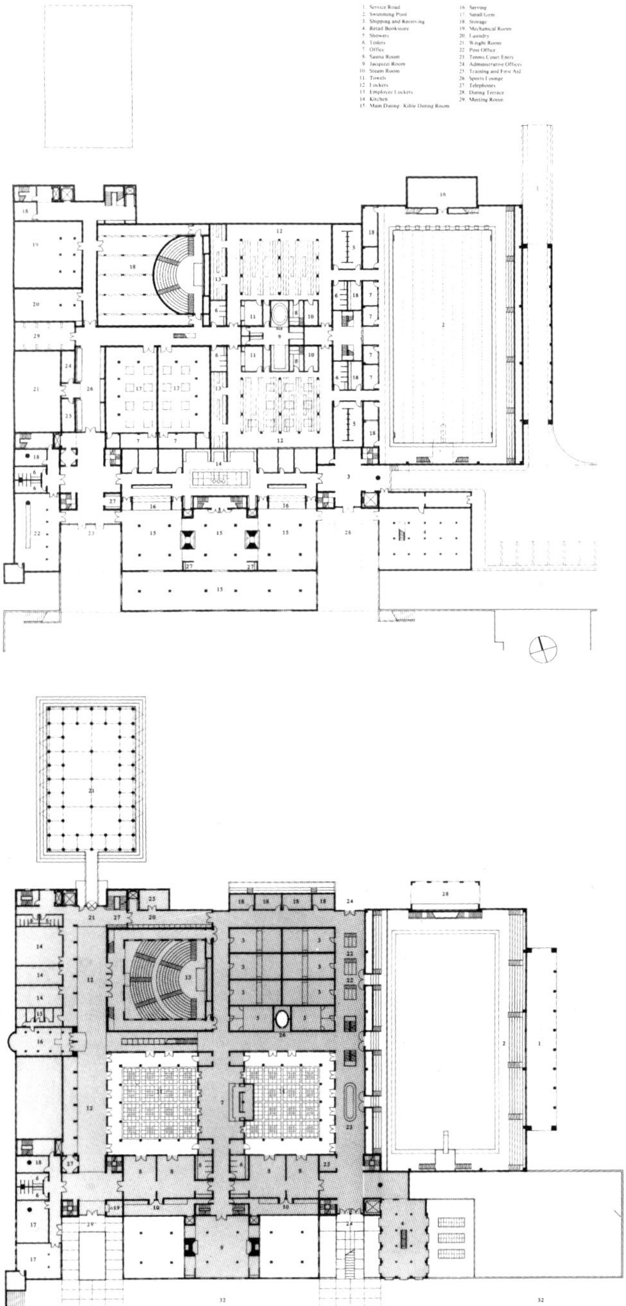

ABOVE. Carnegie Mellon University Center, floor plans

ABOVE AND NEXT PAGE. Carnegie Mellon University Center, perspective views

We designed three buildings and planned two parks. These are laid out along a new street that is the continuation of the all-important via Maqueda. Via Maqueda continues into via Oreto, which continues into via Coronata. There it ends (as it should) against the mountain. This functional, circulatory, and geometric continuity is emphasized. But via Cordnata is a building, blue and gold, is a road running between the brick retaining walls of the park, is a large ramp going through a building; it becomes a tower.[52]

If this description is recast in terms of montage procedures, the project is then revealed as a set of appropriated objects—identifiable types or icons, complex signifying entities—linearly assembled into or "grafted" onto a monumental avenue. The syntagm of the resulting construction, which is via Coronata, totally obscures the disjunctive processes of its formation—appropriation, distortion, and recombination—and effectively, but momentarily, integrates the disparate elements into a functional and plausible whole.

Plausibility is further substantiated by means of an "obstinate corporeality of things" achieved in "technical veracity and proficient detailing."[53] Therefore, via Coronata, the newly fabricated whole, presents a resolved image of an unprecedented but possible reality, while simultaneously threatening to shatter it again, under the tenuously suspended weight of its repressed contradictions, into autonomous and irreconcilable fragments. The fragments thus endlessly oscillate between the restructuring and conciliatory influence of the new context, the superordinate whole, and the disjunctive, liberating effect of their inherent contradictions. Allegorically, via Coronata counters the processes whereby architectural icons or types are naturalized and devalued in mythifying architectural practices by critically rehearsing and strategically reorienting their disjunctive operations.

In structuralist parlance, each firmly integrated and syntactically inflected part participates in the syntagmatic (horizontal) chain of association while simultaneously engaging a network of paradigmatic (vertical) relationships. When two parts—for instance, the ramp and the tower—are equated because of their spatialcontiguity or structural equivalence

[52] Rodolfo Machado and Jorge Silvetti, project description for La Porta Meridionale in this monograph, 141-42.

[53] Ibid. 142

ABOVE. Machado and Silvetti, La Porta Meridionale Administration, Recreation, and Transportation Complex, 1987. View of the Crown of Palermo.

(the tower is aligned with the road and, when viewed frontally, appears as a mere extension of via Coronata), a sharper awareness of their formal and functional similarities and differences is produced. The collisions and resonances of previously unsuspected associations trigger a semantic avalanche among the assembled parts: the contours are blurred, the identities are confounded, the semiotic integrity of the signs are shattered, and, finally, the type is reinvented.

One particular event in via Coronata, the cloverleaf of the Porta Meridionale, now deserves greater attention. This event marks the intersection of via Maqueda/via Oreto (now renamed via Coronata), a historically and urbanistically prominent artery, with the beltway around Palermo. The proposal avoids the predictable gate-type building, considered "inappropriate, nostalgic, and ineffectual."[54] Instead, the cloverleaf is appropriated from the typology of infrastructural engineering and reinserted in this context "framed by walls that render it as a freestanding object building."[55] The architects describe the object as follows:

The various ramps and elevated roads are constructed as solids of traditional Sicilian building materials: local tufa stone and Caltagirone tile and balustrades. The building's floor is a flat inverted pyramid finished in glazed ceramic brick. Via Oreto, (via Maqueda) runs undisturbed through the building until it meets the mountains.[56]

Again, the characteristic operations of montage are here performed, isolating and appropriating the cloverleaf from its original context of megalopolitan superhighway.

The confiscated type is recast in a different architectural language-one associated with local monuments—without, however, being significantly altered in its formal structure or function. This operation once again recalls standard Surrealist strategies that aimed to dramatically unfamiliarize the apprehension of banal objects by changing one of their characteristic features. The transformed type is reinserted as an intersection on a major artery and then reframed as a significant event by surrounding monumental walls. Behind a unified and resolved image evoking the simplicity

[54] Ibid.

[55] Ibid. 142-44.

[56] Ibid. 144.

ABOVE. Via Coronata, Porta Meridionale cloverleaf

ABOVE. Via Coronata, ramp leading to belvedere

and realism of the monument, the reinvented cloverleaf finally presents a heterogeneous content that imposes upon the viewer an *oeuvre de connaissance*.[57] The viewer thereby "encounters a decentralized text that completes itself through his or her reading and comparison of the original and subsequent layers of meaning that the text/image has acquired."[58]

But material, too, is part of the technique of montage. Upon entering the cloverleaf we experience an abrupt change in the materiality of the road. As the smooth ride on black asphalt is suddenly interrupted by vibrating tires upon shimmering blue and gold tiles, we are immediately shocked into a new recognition of a strange but familiar object.

Our initial feeling of disturbance gives way to apleasurable sensation of intellectual complicity between the architect[s] and ourselves after we have, not without effort, succeeded in disclosing the building's arcane messages. The object appears as a revelation, not of sacred but of heretical nature because it confronts us with a subversive meaning whose opaque effect proposes and obliges us to perform a certain intellectual task of deciphering. The object cannot be consumed, but must be interpreted; indeed, we must wander along the same path the architect followed; we must work with it.[59]

And so, the montaged via Coronata as a whole performs very much like the belvedere that, concluding its chain of events, rehearses its critical functions. Recalling that belvederes usually look out on nature, Roland Barthes claims that the Eiffel Tower makes the city into a kind of nature by virtue of its very position of a visited outlook: "To visit the Tower, then, is to enter into contact not with a historical Sacred, as is the case for the majority of monuments, but rather with a new Nature."[60] In a similar fashion, via Coronata's belvedere offers to the panoramic gaze of the visitor the city of Palermo as a simulacrum, an object already prepared,

[57] "The image of the monument is, perhaps, what everybody can grasp more easily, and it is because of this that we will use its realism as an indication of simplicity." Massimo Scolari, cited by Silvetti in "On Realism," 23.

[58] B. Buchloh, "Allegorical Procedures," 52.

[59] J. Silvetti, "Beauty of Shadows," 51.

"exposed to the intelligence, but which he must construct by a final activity of the mind."[61] Barthes gives a name to this activity: "decipherment." Similarly, in the belvedere projected for Palermo, the "incomparable power of intellection"[62] assigned to the panoramic view allows the built world to be not only perceived but also deciphered. The belvedere and via Coronata thus perform analogous functions. They both distance the viewer from habitual vantage points or automated modes of perception in order to inculcate in the viewer a new attentiveness about a reality that, henceforth, can be experienced, deciphered, and conquered—that is, can be repossessed.

[60] R. Barthes, "The Eiffel Tower," *The Eiffel Tower and Other Mythologies* (1979), 8.

[61] Ibid. 9-10.

[62] Ibid.

NEXT PAGE. La Porta Meridionale, site plan

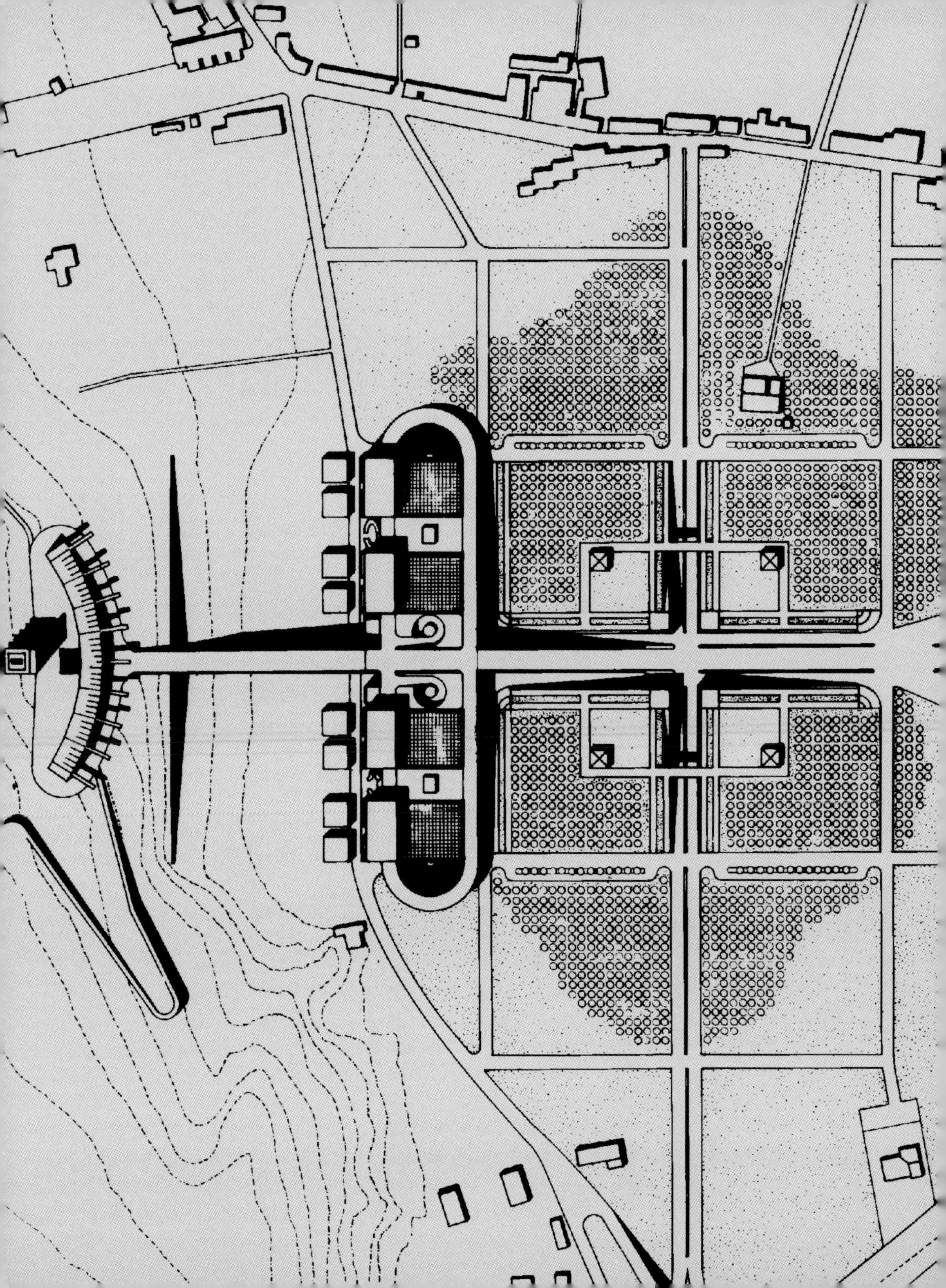

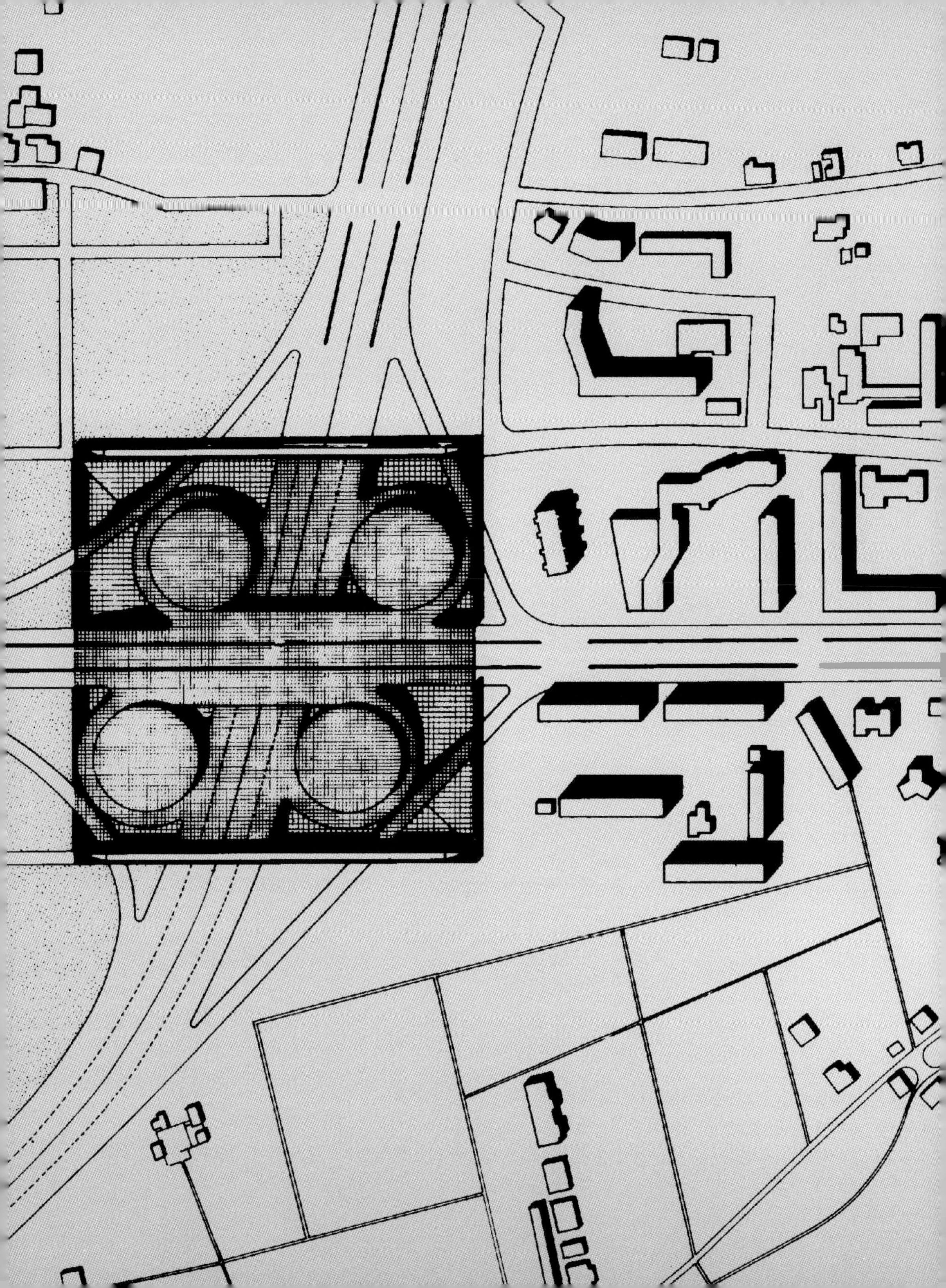

- PART THREE
BUILDINGS

Each essay in this section is dedicated to a single building. It is recognized for its critical contribution to the field or for a pivotal role it plays in shaping the contours of a particular practice. The architecture is examined in detail and in broad cultural context. Material and formal attributes are shown in their capacity to condense ideas in concrete and meaningful ways while the conceptual ambitions of the architecture are framed in relation to a wider cultural debate.

- THE VIRTUAL MONUMENT: LIBERTY BELL CENTER BY BOHLIN CYWINSKI JACKSON

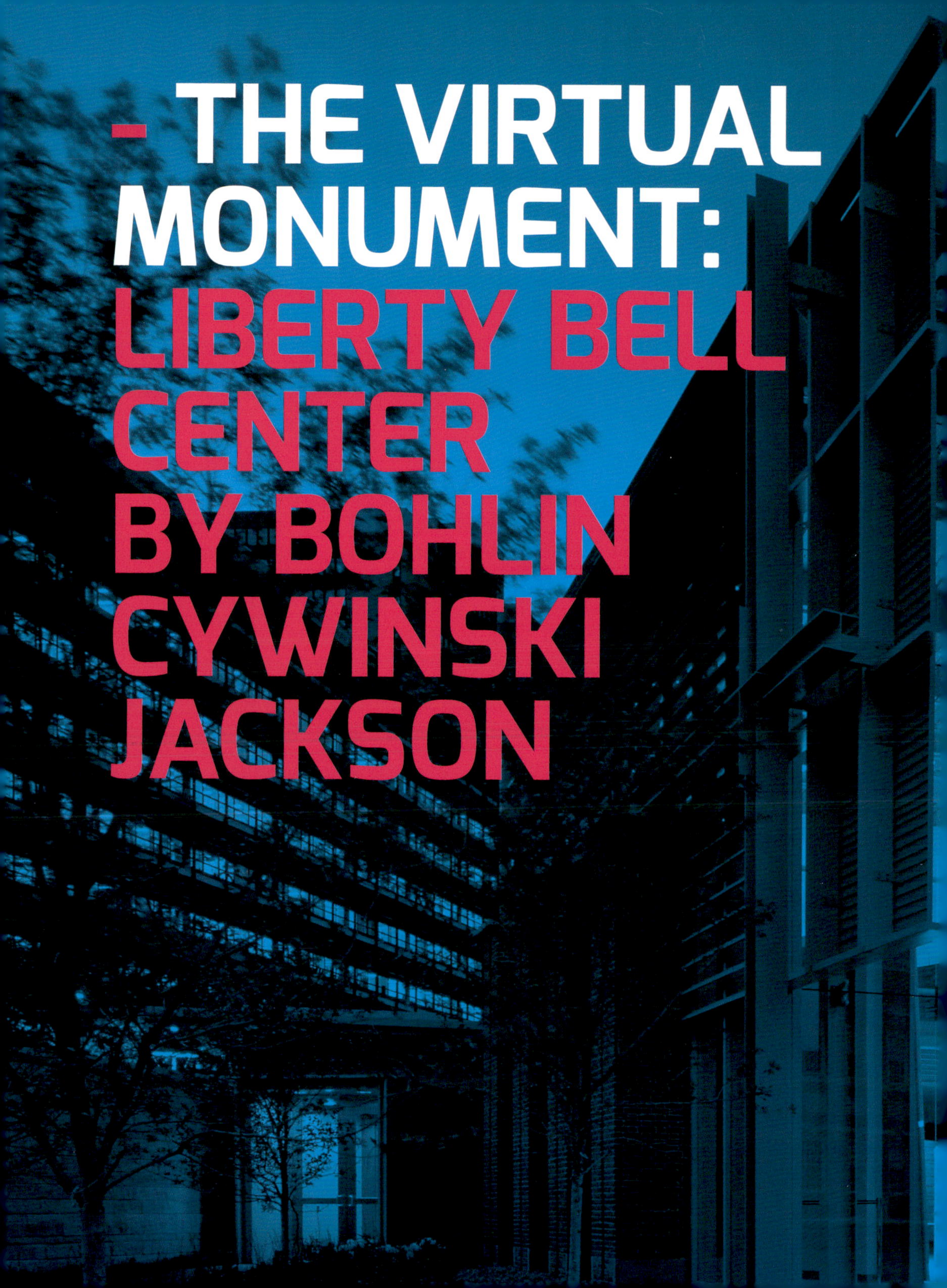

ORIGINALLY PUBLISHED IN **LIBERTY BELL CENTER: BOHLIN CYWNSKI JAKCSON**, RODOLPHE EL-KHOURY ED., ORO EDITIONS, 2005.

ON OCTOBER 3, 2003, THE LIBERTY BELL CENTER, the new home of the Liberty Bell, was opened to the public. The building, designed by Bohlin Cywinski Jackson, is one of the highlights of Philadelphia's reconfigured Independence Mall, and the latest achievement in a long planning and building process that continues to unfold with the maturation of Independence National Historical Park.

Lawrie Olin, one of the key players on the planning team, gives a detailed account of the process in this book, while Richard Sommer provides an historical perspective on the mall's evolution and the building's present-day context.

As noted by Bernard Cywinski, the architect who led the design team, the building seeks to embody the ideas that drive the master plan as well as the values we associate with the bell. This is a relatively small building, dedicated primarily to the display of a single historical artifact. But given the importance of the Liberty Bell, and its resonance in the international community, such aspirations are not misplaced or unexpected. Cywinski explains how ideas are translated from the ambitious program to every aspect and detail of the building.

OBLIQUE VIEW

The architects' intentions are perhaps best evidenced by the way in which visitors encounter the Liberty Bell and Independence Hall. Mitchell/Giurgola's pavilion, the former home of the Liberty Bell, offered a frontal view of the hall as a distant backdrop to the Liberty Bell, displayed on axis in a glazed hall. The Bell Chamber in Bohlin Cywinski Jackson's building is positioned and designed to yield an oblique view of Independence Hall behind the bell.

Both buildings effectively exploit a familiar rhetorical device by displaying the bell with a direct visual connection to Independence Hall in the background.

The shift from frontal view to oblique view is a small but critical difference. It is analogous to a much-studied shift in the evolution of scenography, from one-point to two-point perspective. Thanks to ingenious designs by the Galli-Bibienas, the family of scenographers who dominated the European scene for several generations, the taste in stage-set design shifted very rapidly in the early eighteenth century from static frontal views,

ABOVE. Typical snapshot with author

ABOVE. Typical snapshot with tourists

well illustrated in Serlio's familiar genre studies, to a Baroque model where scenes are set obliquely, in dynamic tension with the proscenium.

The Galli-Bibienas' scena per angola was much admired and immediately adopted on the European stage, especially in Italy. In retrospect we attribute its success to a resonance with emerging theatrical practices that reflected fundamental shifts in the Baroque worldview.

CONNECTED SPECTATORSHIP

The "oblique view extended the space of the stage virtually into the auditorium, bringing the scene closer to the real world. With the Galli-Bibienas, the action that was tightly bound and framed by the proscenium was allowed, at least conceptually, to spill into the world of the spectator.

In Serlio's scenographic model, the implicit assumption is that the viewer is looking through the proscenium at a world that is separate and different. It functions as a window into another fictional realm that is governed by different spatial/temporal laws and representational conventions.

The framed oblique view implies continuity between what is behind and what is in front of the frame. It imitates a visual structure commonly found in cities where public squares, streets, and buildings interlock in mutually framing perspectives.

On the Baroque stage, theatrical representation is highly stylized, but the oblique introduced a touch of naturalism in its imitation of urban experience. The frontal view places the stage and auditorium in polar opposition; the oblique engages them in a visual dynamic that is modeled after chance encounters in the city. The theatrical structure implied by the former is predicted on separation, both physical and conceptual, while the latter strives for connection.

The visual structure of Liberty Bell Center is most literally theatrical in the bell chamber. The theatrical model is evident in the anamorphic geometry of the room, which optimizes the staged view by means of a forced perspective (proscenium) framing a two-point perspective (scene).

Thanks to the oblique view, Independence Hall is experienced as part of the display in the foreground rather than a detached backdrop. It is dynamically pulled into the space of the exhibit, to directly engage with the bell in one continuous urban scene.

The connectedness is also enhanced by the hall's proximity to the bell. The close-up, exaggerated by the frame's accelerated perspective, restores a monumental quality to Independence Hall that was lost in the over-scaled park.

ABOVE. Drawing of a stage set for tragedy by Serlio

ABOVE. Drawing of stage set by Galli-Bibiena

"The framed oblique view implies continuity between what is behind and what is in front of the frame. It imitates a visual structure commonly found in cities where public squares, streets, and buildings interlock in mutually framing perspectives."

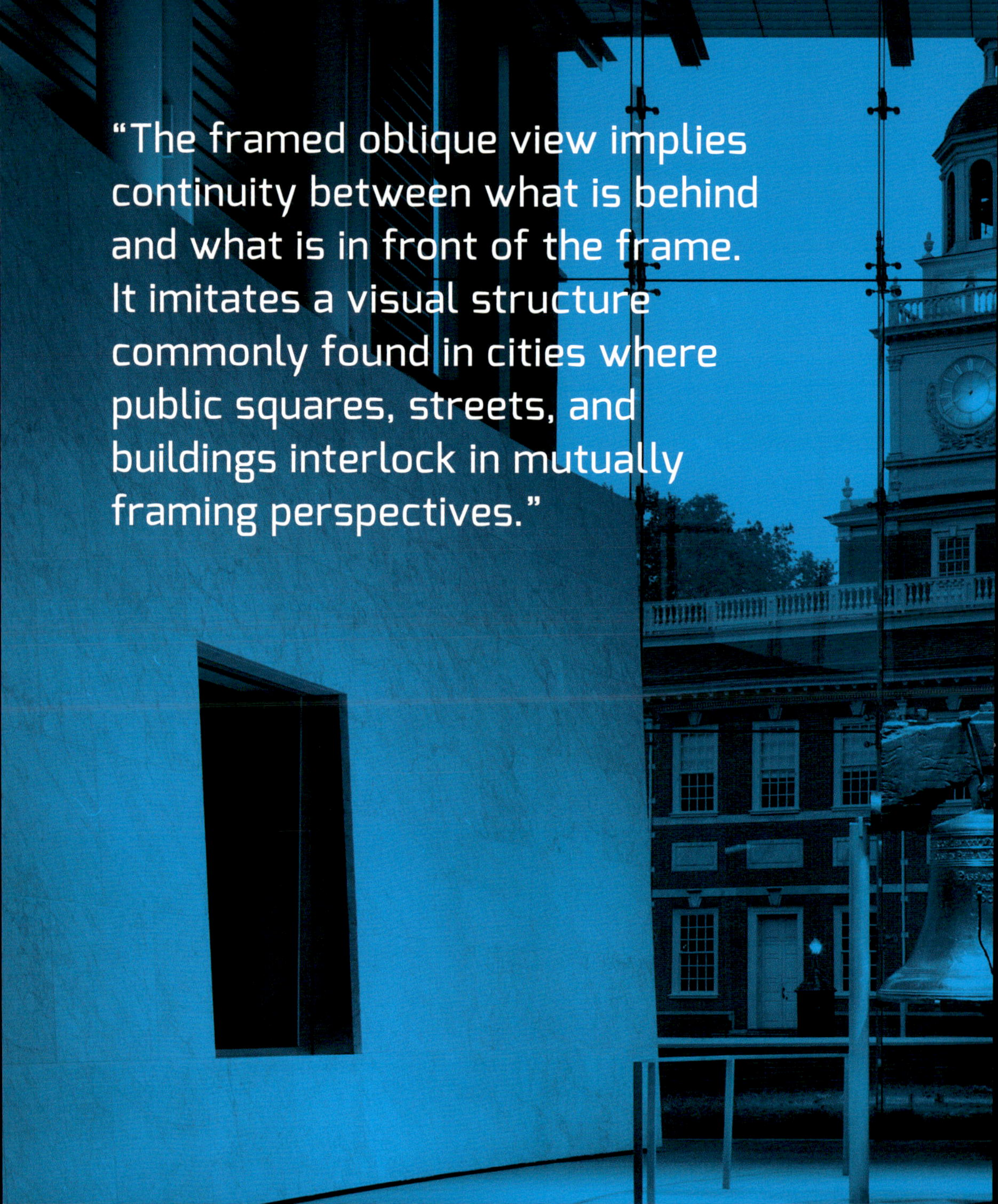

ABOVE. The Liberty Bell Chamber viewed from outside

The connection is sustained throughout the building thanks to the glass curtain wall and the lightness of the support structure. Even in the exhibit space where common wisdom is prejudiced in favor of hermetic environments, the architects opted for transparency. Content, in conventional museological practice, is best delivered without interference. Bohlin Cywinski Jackson and Ueland Junker McCauley Nicholson, the exhibit designers, chose to open the building to the city and welcome interference from everyday life. They take this risk because they are committed to the ideas of openness, accessibility, and connectedness that drive the master plan.

The undulating granite wall strikes a contrasting note in this transparent environment. The design process is telling with regard to its conceptual origins and purpose in the built scheme. One of Cywinski's early sketches shows an excavated space, dipping down into the ground like an archaeological dig, perhaps exposing the foundation of the buildings that previously stood on the site. The sketches place the main exhibit gallery between heavy retaining walls, within a material and spatial density that is entirely at odds with the airy transparency of the built structure. The dense heavy, and coarsely textured stone wall—as well as gently sloping paved floors—are vestiges of the excavated chamber. Both communicate a haptic sense of rootedness, a grounding in the particular conditions and archaeology of the site while the transparent curtain wall and the lucid super structure optically resonate with a universal agenda: they evoke the realm of reason and abstraction. This ambivalence is found elsewhere and in different registers of experience. It is also evident in the ambiguous parti, combining the universal order of the grid with the willful demarcation of the linear plan

RELATIVE VIEWS

The dynamic tension in the scena per angola was also better suited to evolving literary sensibilities of the Baroque. It coincided with a departure from rigid classical archetypes in favor of more nuanced and conflicted characterizations—a reflection, no doubt, of structural transformations in the social fabric.

This is the time when Europe was still assimilating the material and psychological impact of the New World, as well as notions of an ever-expanding universe. The discovery process paved the way for new hybrid genres and relative frames of reference. There is only one correct frontal view in line with the axis of symmetry; there are an infinite number of oblique views each with a unique perspective on a given scene. This fact also accounts for the overwhelming success of the scena per angolo in the eighteenth-century Italian opera house. In comparison to most European stages that catered principally to the privileged view from the royal box by aligning the vanishing point of the stage design with the position of the sovereign, the Italian scene was less hierarchical, and its audience less rigidly stratified. In Italy's theaters, the oblique view looked right from all angles; it is, in a sense, a democratic view.

In contrast to Serlio's stable and homogenous tableaux, the Galli-Bibienas' angled compositions spoke of complex and varied elements dynamically held in a delicate and provisional balance. They also evidenced a shift from the assumed authority of a privileged and fixed view to the multiplicity of partial and relative revelations.

Bohlin Cywinski Jackson's Liberty Bell Center and Galli-Bibienas' stage set designs belong to very different worlds. The cultural and political circumstances behind their inception couldn't be more different. Yet they share a common intuition: the impulse to present the world as a partial, dynamic, and malleable construct.

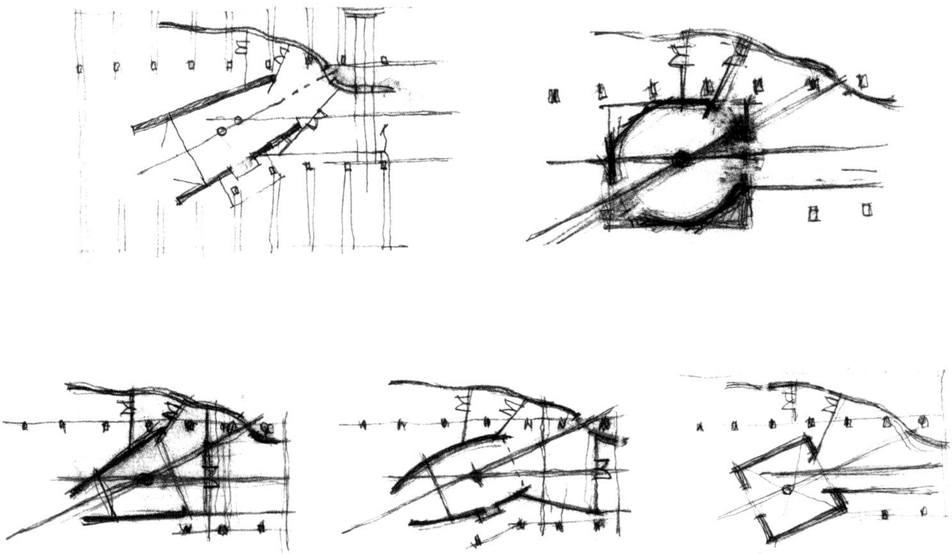

ABOVE AND NEXT PAGE. Sketches exploring the geometry of scenographic sequence and display

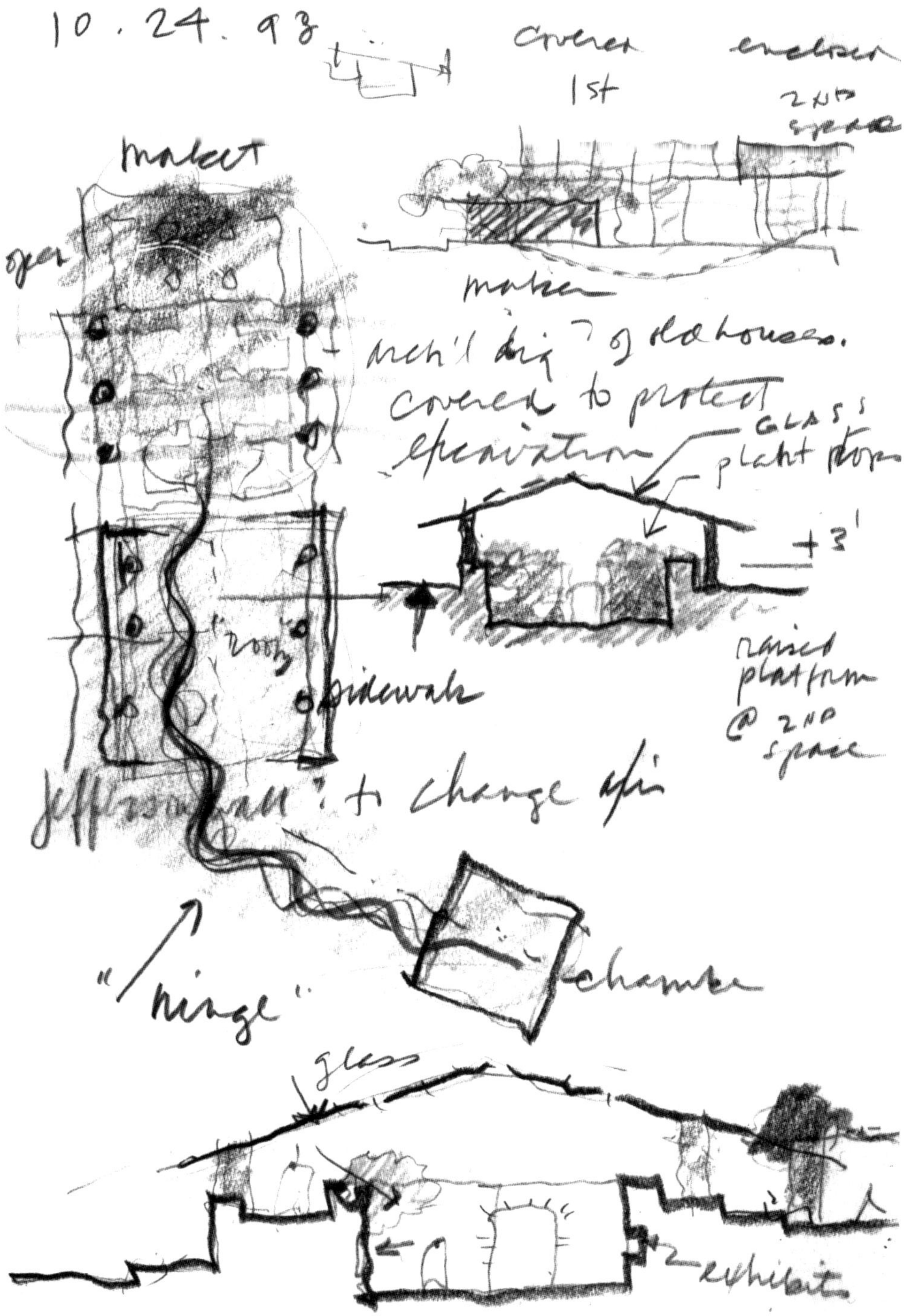
10.24.93
covered
enclosed
1st
2ND space
market
open
market
covered to protect
GLASS
+3'
raised platform @ 2ND space
sidewalk
to change
"hinge"
chamber
glass
exhibits

“In contrast to Serlio’s stable and homogenous tableaux, the Galli-Bibienas’ angled compositions spoke of complex and varied elements dynamically held in a delicate and provisional balance. They also evidenced a shift from the assumed authority of a privileged and fixed view to the multiplicity of partial and relative revelations.”

ABOVE. The Liberty Bell seen from outside

Instead of the proper axial composition that would automatically telescope and naturalize the historic artifacts in a ready-made and fixed relationship, the Bell Chamber offers an arbitrary—or arbitrated—view, one among many possible others, in which bell and hall are brought into strategic and provisional alignment.

The deliberate yet fleeting alignment suggests allegorical readings of dynamic and institutional forces at play in a democracy. Also, as stated in Richard Sommer's essay, it "provokes the idea that symbols are malleable and, more important, that history may still be in the making."

VIRTUAL ARCHITECTURE

The highly charged bell/hall scene concluding a carefully designed procession through a chronologically arranged exhibit is the building's—

and perhaps the site's main destination. The procession, which is guided by the stone wall, is occasionally punctuated by perpendicular view corridors aligning with the urban grid. The sporadic intrusion of the cross axis overlays the open-ended and field-like condition of the city over the directionality and purposefulness of the linear exhibit, rehearsing again the dialectic at play in this building—and, by allegorical extension, in the course and making of history.

The lateral counterpoint diverts the visitor's attention sideways, to the urban surrounding, but doesn't distract from the main purpose and destination of the building. It is dramatically unveiled as one leaves the linear path and enters the Bell Chamber. This is a precisely orchestrated transition that the architects calibrated in countless studies.

The scene, the raison d'être of the building, has an iconic quality that visitors are compelled to record in a photograph, preferably including themselves in the shot—I had this inevitable impulse when I visited the building and, luckily, the architect was there to take the snapshot himself!

The composition, which no doubt will be reproduced in millions of photographs taken at the very same spot every year, is striking in its compositional and conceptual clarity. The bell is in the foreground, occupying the lower half of the field, graphically silhouetted against the brighter background. Independence Hall fills the whole frame behind, with the bell tower sitting exactly above the bell in the upper half of the picture.

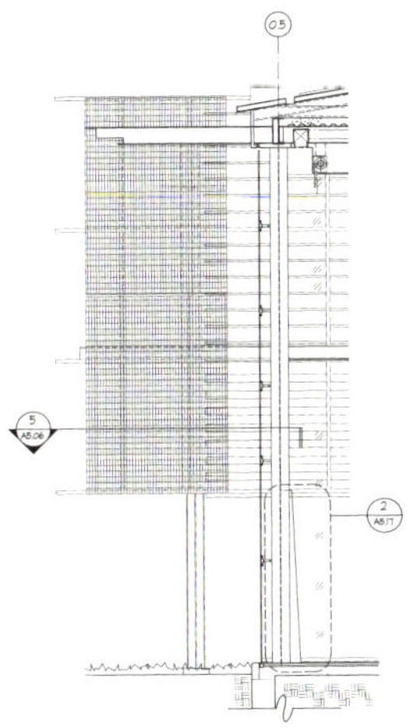

ABOVE. Details of the framing and shading apparatus

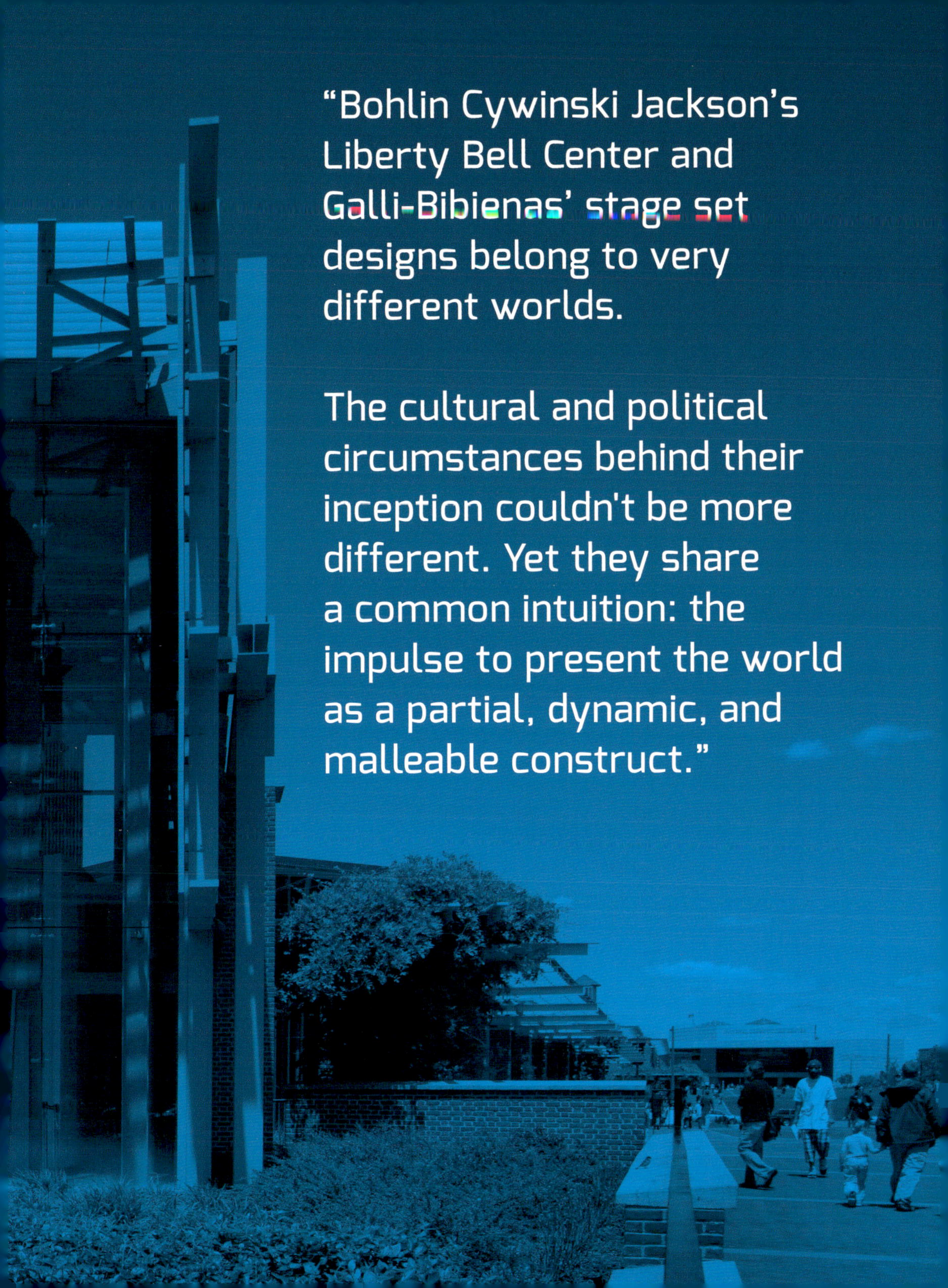

"Bohlin Cywinski Jackson's Liberty Bell Center and Galli-Bibienas' stage set designs belong to very different worlds.

The cultural and political circumstances behind their inception couldn't be more different. Yet they share a common intuition: the impulse to present the world as a partial, dynamic, and malleable construct."

ABOVE. Undulating wall leading toward the Liberty Bell Chamber

FOLLOWING SPREAD. View of the Liberty Bell Chamber from the exterior

An office tower with a giant corporate logo looms ominously on the right of the bell tower. In the axial view of Giurgola's pavilion, it stood behind the hall, dwarfing the monument with its overwhelming size. In the oblique close-up it is displaced to the side and reduced in scale. It is a manageable and welcome addition to the symbolic scene, a meaningful flitch that adds yet another shade of complexity to the mythological palette.

The bell, Independence Hall, and, most likely, the visitor, are all framed by architecture, which here assumes a self-effacing character. Up to this point the architecture is articulate to an extreme, obsessively crafting every connection with exquisite intricacy. In the Bell Chamber, the purpose and destination that it was set up for, it is uncharacteristically mute, a neutral frame that is meant to construct relationships rather than an elaborate architectural setting. Compare this scene to an exterior view of the chamber, and you get a good sense of the restraint and minimalism that were painstakingly invested in its design and construction. The machine-like exterior bristles with structure, layered revetments, and shading devices. It is a complex apparatus that is designed to make the bell/hall/subject scene possible and deceptively effortless while remaining unobtrusive.

In comparison, the chamber's interior is an exercise in deferential neutrality where subtle planimetric and sectional inflection are meant to enhance the framing function, rather than add formal intricacy. The Bell Chamber, in effect, is a giant camera that is meant for the production, recording, and dissemination of the bell/hall/subject scene—and the nuanced values that it captures in the angled view.

As an instrument of mass communication, we may think of it as the visual analogue to the Liberty Bell, an instrument that had served the same purpose aurally.

We may also recall that "chamber" and "camera" are, etymologically speaking, the same. The fact points to the camera obscura origin of the modern camera but also, obliquely, to the instrumental and cognitive role of architecture in shaping our understanding of the world.

In the Bell Chamber/camera, architecture is distilled to an abstract and quasi- immaterial art, dedicated to constructing intellectual relationships as much as to building material objects. This architecture is perfectly suited for the colonization of virtual space. The architects may indeed be said to have devised a virtual extension to the Liberty Bell Center, destined for countless photo albums, books, and magazines. Considering the ubiquity of media representation and their prodigious rate of proliferation, this virtual architecture has arguably a greater presence and impact in the world. The architects of Liberty Bell Center understood and exploited this fact.

Bohlin Cywinski Jackson designed and built two homes for the Liberty Bell. First, the actual building on the mall is a handsome structure that is replete with the fine tactile qualities that have earned the firm's international reputation. This building excels in situating the bell in its particular historical and physical context and is epitomized by the stubborn materiality of the stone wall; a substantial and singular feature in counterpoint to the optical logic of the building, with its impenetrable and tactile presence.

There is also another building, a virtual construct that was tailored with no less precision and ingenuity for the universal resonance of the Liberty Bell. It is based on optical effects and is implied in the building's dematerialized features. The virtual building with characteristic structure, the oblique view, is likely to supplant the first with the dissemination of media representations—to become the Liberty Bell's privileged home in the collective imagination.

We have Bohlin Cywinski Jackson to thank for the complexity and richness that is now built into the iconic representation, home of a most cherished symbol.

- NO OBSTACLE: MARTYRS' SQUARE AND OTHER ROOF-SCAPES BY KUTH RANIERI ARCHITECTS AND RODOLPHE EL-KHOURY

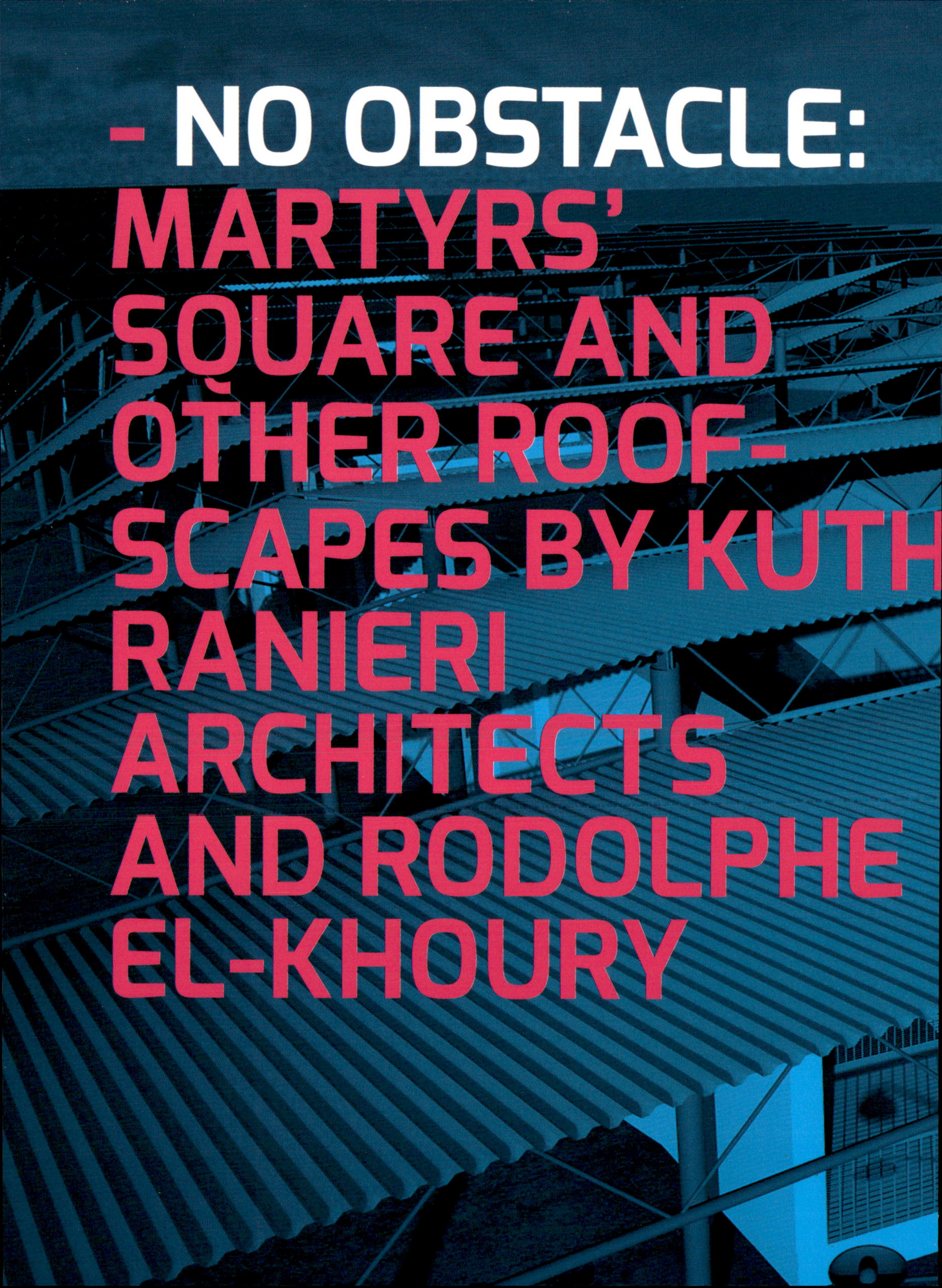

ADAPTED FORM AN ESSAY ORIGINALLY PUBLISHED IN **KUTH RANIERI ARCHITECTS**, PRINCETON ARCHITECTURAL PRESS, 2008.

THE ROOF OCCUPIES A RELATIVELY MODEST position in contemporary architectural theory. While plan, elevation, and section have their advocates and continue to provoke debates on their role and status in the production of architecture, few if any argue on behalf of the roof or a reflected ceiling plan. The roof does crop up in recurrent debates on style where the traditionalist commitment to the vernacular is pitted against the ahistorical rationalism of modernist architecture. Without fail, the emphasis in such discussions is on iconography—flat versus pitched roofs—and the issues debated are relevant only to residential architecture.[1] Roofs still make grand architectural statements in houses, but they are practically invisible in large institutional buildings and are usually reserved for back-of-the-house functions as well as mechanical equipment.[2] Yet the changing attitude toward environmental controls and their dedicated infrastructure may lately be pulling the roof into greater visibility. The roof is increasingly valued, not merely as a repository for expensive air-conditioning machinery but most importantly as a solar interface.

What follows is a commentary on projects in which roofs take center stage.[3] They serve critical functions in regulating and sustaining comfort zones within and around buildings, yet they also have structuring roles on many levels and in many aspects of architecture, both symbolic and performative.

The Martyrs' Square project, submitted to an international competition in Beirut, Lebanon, proposes a new vision for the historic site, including a detailed program for the urban surface and underground. The project's centerpiece is an oversized canopy that extends from the heart of the city to its northern waterfront. The competition called for the rebuilding of the existing venerated square—the epicenter of the old capital—as well as

[1] The debate reached a fever pitch in Weimar- era Germany when it resonated with political intentions, dividing the opposing camps along the same lines.

[2] Diller Scofidio + Renfro's Museum of Contemporary Art in Boston provides a good example of the disenchanted roof. The building is attentively detailed, particular care having been lavished on the articulation of the ground. The roof is an entirely different matter: it is treated with utmost indifference and could very well be that of a speculative office building. This attitude toward the roof is typical. The neglect is particularly disturbing here because the crude roof design irremissibly clashes with the sophistication consistently exercised elsewhere.

[3] The projects discussed in this essay are products of a collaboration between Kuth/Ranieri Architects and myself on competition projects from 2003 to 2005.

ABOVE. Martyrs' Square: elevation drawing

the surrounding blocks. It would be a landmark project in the ongoing reconstruction of the city center after Lebanon's protracted civil war. The vast site had been prepared for development: bulldozed, excavated, leveled, and serviced. As one of the most important developing areas in the city, it had also recently gained global notoriety because of widely circulated photographs and news reports showing immense crowds covering the entire field. It was this massive public demonstration that precipitated radical changes in the country.

With images of the oceanic crowd blanketing the open field fresh in mind, the burden of architectural responsibility weighed on every line of the proposal—delineating (and confining) the public realm. Therefore, bringing development to the site and giving definitive shape to the square became a difficult proposition in this physical and political context.

Growth in Beirut's business district is inevitable and indeed necessary for financing the reconstruction process. Yet development of this site, which had just enabled the most potent transformative act in the city's recent history, risked a troubling, but perhaps avoidable, problem: the physical and regulatory compartmentalization of the unobstructed open field into discrete areas. Any partitioning of the area through design, indeed any differentiation of the ground at all, could compromise the freedoms that this open field promised with every unscripted public event.

In lieu of a comprehensive master plan, the Martyrs' Square project proposed flexible strategies for the occupation of the ground and a single, albeit gigantic, object: a roof structure stretching from one end of the

site to the other. The roof was designed in detail, while features of landscape and urban design were left open to interpretation and change. The roof is a finite, concrete object. It was to be built gradually in phases that anticipated the waves of development, though the form was set and precisely described. Other aspects of the project were meant to evolve through open-ended processes that invited public participation and welcomed unexpected outcomes.

The roof structure consists mainly of rectangular corrugated metal panels that are tessellated in finely orchestrated patterns and supported on slender, tree-like columns. The roof extends along the central axis of the site in a continuous strip of varying width. It covers the entire original square, narrows to a thin canopy to shade a path along an archaeological site farther north, and reemerges in its full magnitude as a roof for a ferry terminal. It shelters a variety of programs but also serves as a unifying formal element that ties various episodes into an urban sequence extending deep into the city.

With flocking panels that glide above the square and only occasionally touch down in fleeting contact with the ground, the project is ostensibly at odds with current preoccupations in architecture and the pervasive investment in landscape. The ground here becomes secondary to a superstructure that is persistently and deliberately detached from the landscape. While trendsetting buildings such as Foreign Office Architect's Yokohama Ferry Terminal reached unprecedented extremes in integrating building and ground, thus transforming architecture into a built landscape, in Martyrs' Square the roof and ground remain physically, if not functionally, separate.

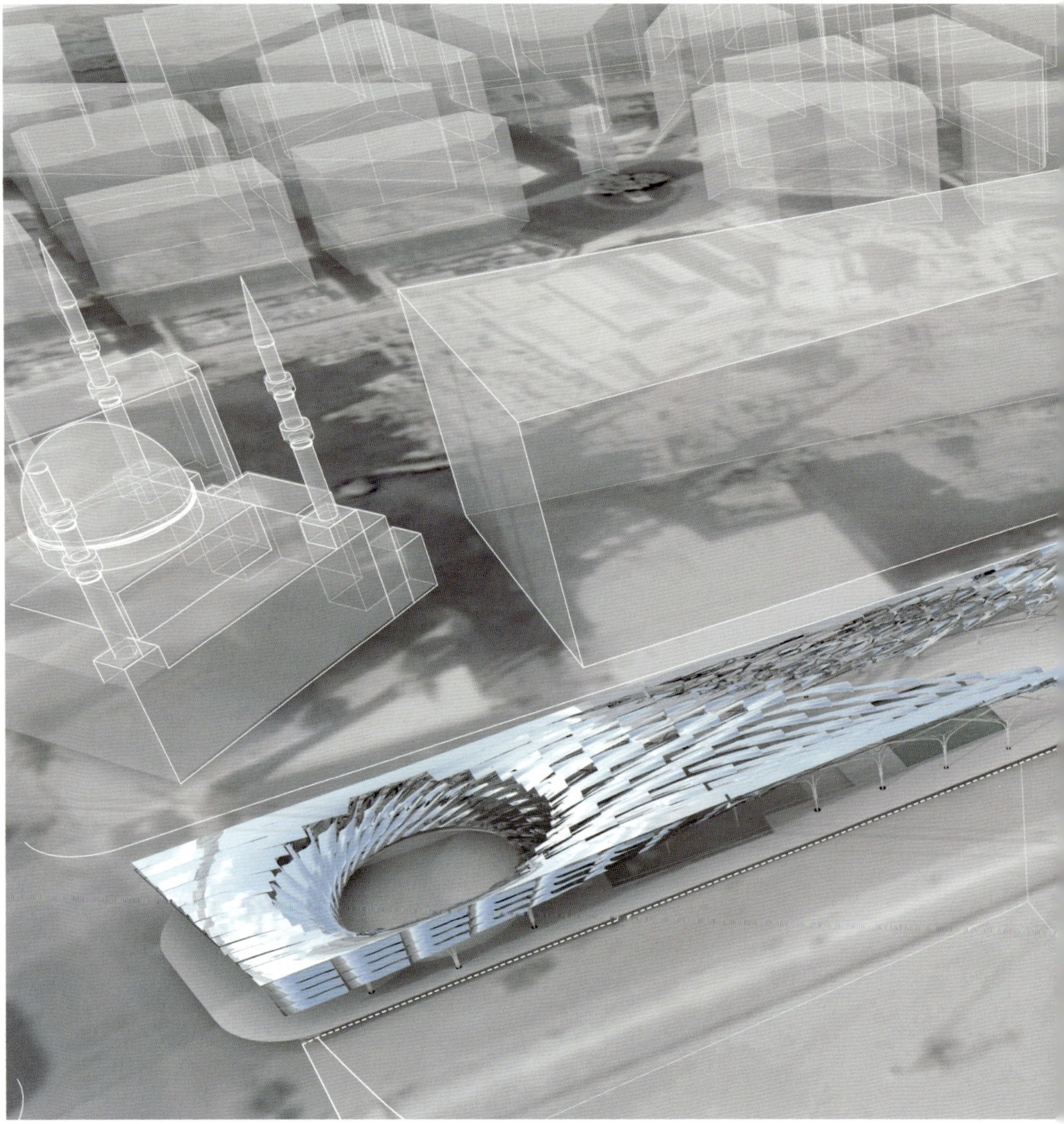

ABOVE. Martyrs' Square, bird's eye view

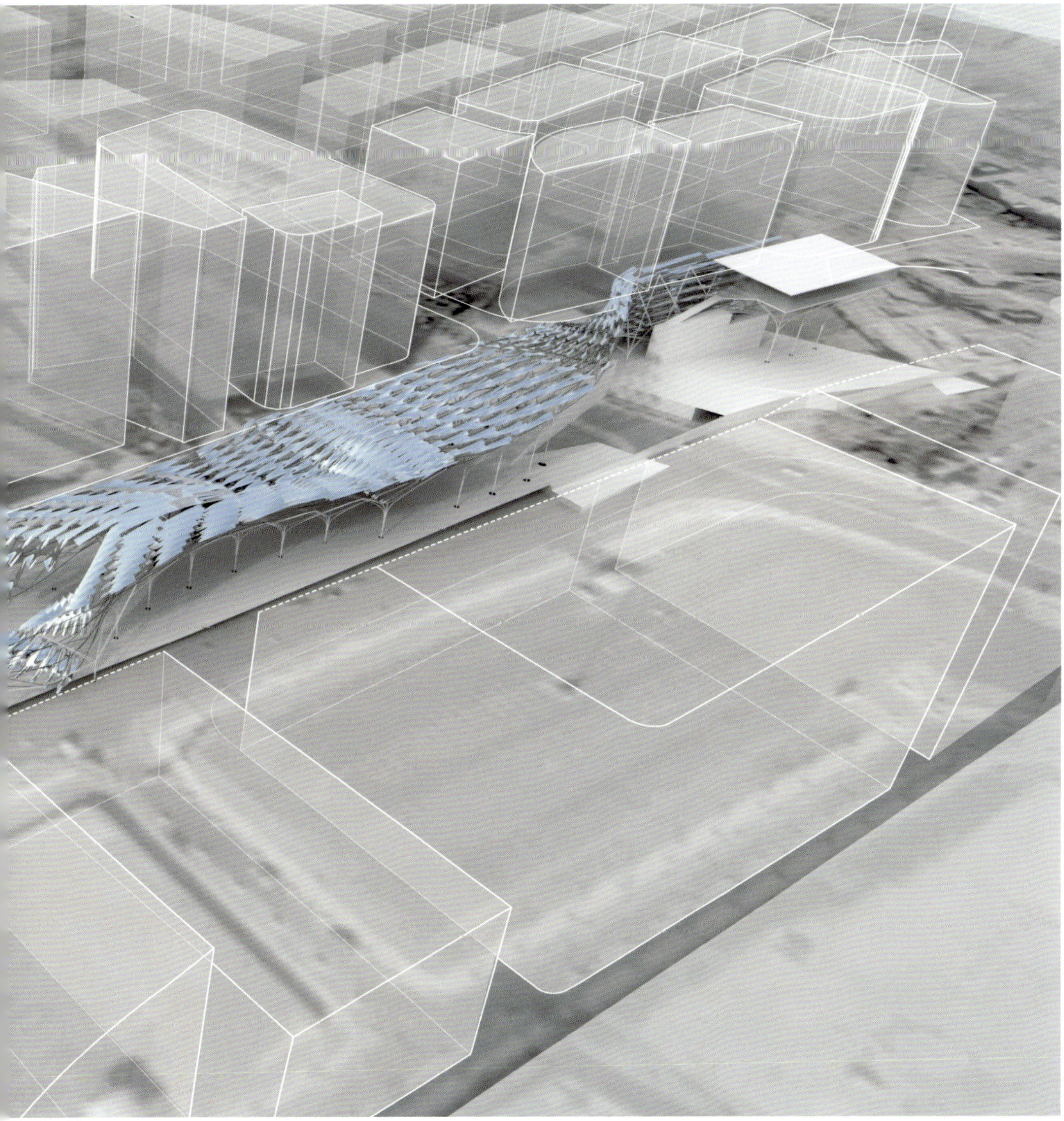

"In its sheer materiality, as an opaque object in an open landscape, architecture is the obstacle to the utopia that Rousseau yearns for but can only glimpse in the momentary freedom of the free-flowing and un-walled festival."

We may see in Martyrs' Square—and in several other projects from the Kuth Ranieri Architects/Rodolphe el-Khoury team—an exception to an otherwise consistent dedication to landscape and its capacity to immerse the architectural object in the vital currents that traverse the city. More relevant yet is to recognize common theoretical threads that align the roofscape of Martyrs' Square with the logic of landscape. The common genealogy in which the stubborn fixity of architecture is pitted against the informal, dynamic process it contains should clarify the ideas behind roofscapes and their place in the current architectural debate.

The common thread is a persistent philosophical theme that found its most ambitious formulation with Jean-Jacques Rousseau. In 1755 Rousseau became an overnight sensation with the publication of the *Discourse on the Origin and Basis of Inequality Among Men,* in which he outlined the main themes of his political philosophy. He singles out one foundational act in a mythical history of decline that accounts for many of civil society's ills: the building of the first fence. The wall (i.e., architecture) is what separates and excludes. It lies at the root of discrimination and repression among peoples. Rousseau's antipathy toward architecture, the artificial obstacle to free-flowing interaction and communion among human beings, sharpens in his critique of the theater. The festival, the countermodel he describes, stands as pure presence, performance that undermines the distinction between spectator and spectacle, spectator and spectator, to achieve an unmediated communion of souls in an obstacle-free environment.

As a frame to the spectacle—an agent of the structural separation between subject and object—architecture stands as a paradigm of mediation. The obstructive compartments of its exclusive interiors erect still more barriers to collective communion. In its sheer materiality, as an opaque object in an open landscape, architecture is the obstacle to the utopia that Rousseau yearns for but can only glimpse in the momentary freedom of the free-flowing and unwalled festival.

Rousseau's metaphors of the festival resurface, almost intact, in British postwar architecture, with the most potent renditions being found in Fun Palace and Archigram's Instant City. They are pushed to an absurd extreme in Superstudio's imaginary landscapes where Rousseau's vision climaxes in an epiphany of near-total emptiness. They also prefigure the Situationist project, leading directly to the worlds of artists such as

Constant (in his New Babylon world city) and later to the work of the Office for Metropolitan Architecture (OMA).

A closely related thematic may be found at the core of Rem Koolhaas's work, starting with *Delirious New York*. In this iconoclastic reading of Manhattan, architecture comes off as decorative packaging. It is an epiphenomenon and sometimes an obstacle to the economic and social processes that animate the city. Koolhaas followed up this critique with a series of projects that sought a rich orchestration of events within and around buildings. They explored compositional methods that emphasized programmatic relations, advantageous marriages as well as friction that may be—provoked by strategic proximities. Instead of defining and delineating use within clearly demarcated compartments, Koolhaas proposed fluid programs on magma-like surfaces, seamlessly linking buildings and urban spaces. In a competition project for the Jussieu Library, the ubiquitous surface spirals up several levels to constitute a vertical landscape, serving as a potent model for much of the ramp-based architectures of the last decade. These range from literal translations of buildings into horizontal fields with seamlessly shifting programs to more rhetorically driven versions where the idea of a continuous ground surface is captured in a formal style, as evidenced in Diller Scofidio + Renfro's Institute of Contemporary Art in Boston.

The impulse behind the dispersal of the autonomous architectural object, and more specifically the immovable vertical wall, into a horizontal field is also what motivates the roofscapes of Martyrs' Square in Beirut, the Malama Learning Center in Hawaii, and the Museum of Contemporary Art at the Luther Burbank Center for the Arts in Santa Rosa, California (MOCA).[4] These projects invest in the roof—a surface customarily hidden from view and reserved for mechanical equipment—as a primary material,

[4] A similar impulse drives Kuth Ranieri's interest in kinetic architectures: movable walls, plus partitions and cabinetry on tracks, allowing users to freely reconfigure their own living spaces. The Lodi Bunkhouse, for instance, features in its external envelope large, operable sections that radically effect the flow of space and people through the building, transforming the central hall into a public street at the touch of a button.

[5] Robert Levit links the current architectural interest in differentiated components and populated surfaces to a symbolic impulse that seeks to figure contemporary forms of social organization: "The variable cell, with its looser affiliation to a whole, suggests an analogy to the social world: a world of endlessly diverse individuation marked by a declining willingness or ability of diverse individuals to imagine themselves in relationship to a social whole except through sheer arbitrary assembly." See R. Levit, "Contemporary Ornament: The Return of the Symbolic Repressed," *Harvard Design Magazine* 28 (Spring/Summer 2008), 70-85.

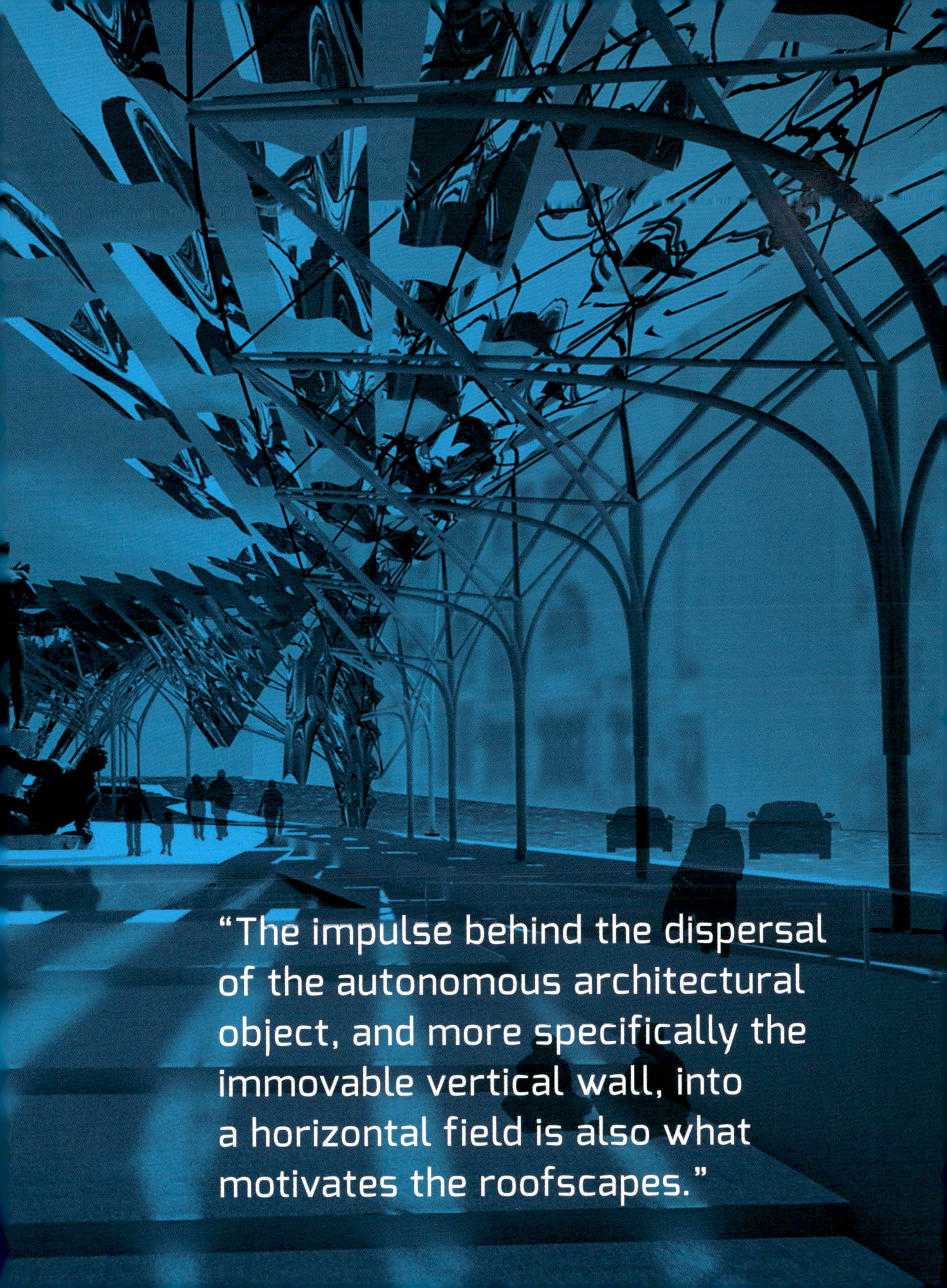

"The impulse behind the dispersal of the autonomous architectural object, and more specifically the immovable vertical wall, into a horizontal field is also what motivates the roofscapes."

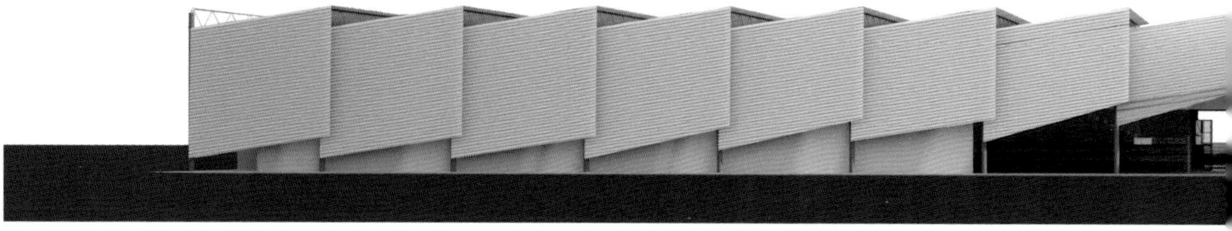

ABOVE. Malama Learning Center: side elevation drawing

an infrastructural and symbolic means to both enable and enrich life on the ground. The roof constitutes all that is solid and permanent. It supports, frames, modulates, and shelters activities below that are accommodated in less-formal arrangements. In Beirut, the ground plane is crisscrossed by complex, ever-changing activities that the sheltering roof facilitates and channels, rather than fixes or regiments. In Malama, the facilities under the roofscape are designed to adapt easily to the vicissitudes of the site and the institution; they are economical and generic wood-frame structures that can be repeatedly reconfigured for evolving scenarios of inhabitation. In short, the roofscapes in these proposals are inverted landscapes that organize the forces let loose on the ground.

While these projects invite an ad hoc and opportunistic occupation of the ground, they are anything but casual in the meticulous design and precise calibration of their roofs. Each roofscape thus comes to most effectively realize the project's representational ambitions.[5] It presents a differentiated yet unified figure that can readily stand as an imageable symbol for the complex aspirations and constituencies of today's institutions. As a piece of infrastructure that performs critical functions in the project's environmental program, the roofscape is also revealed as a demonstration of civic and institutional processes at work. Capitalizing on the roof—the building's primary solar face—as a site for architectural expression and innovation is a logical and defining move. The roofscape radicalizes a general current tendency

that recognizes the performative and figurative potential of the underutilized roof plane.

The roof as a charged locus of architectural content points back to canonical works by Ludwig Mies van der Rohe that generally sought to distill building into a question of roof structure. Colin Rowe described the National Gallery in Berlin as a flat dome, underscoring the rhetorical charge carried in the articulation of the exquisite flat roof. The cosmic reference aptly captures the transcendent quality in the classical perfection and universal resonance of Mies's roof. In sharp contrast, Beirut's roofscape is intently caught in the particular; its aspirations are decidedly earthbound.

The National Gallery seems to address its chaotic surrounding with calm indifference. In its tenuous connection with the landscape, Beirut's roofscape seeks to minimize interference with the action on the ground. Detachment here entails a subordination both to site and to the informal processes of everyday life.

As an autonomous object with a hermetic organizational and structural logic, the National Gallery presents a neutral backdrop to events unfolding separately below. The roofscape is a responsive structure that enters into dialogue with its surroundings, adjusting to the dynamics of the site that it seeks to influence and by which it is inflected.

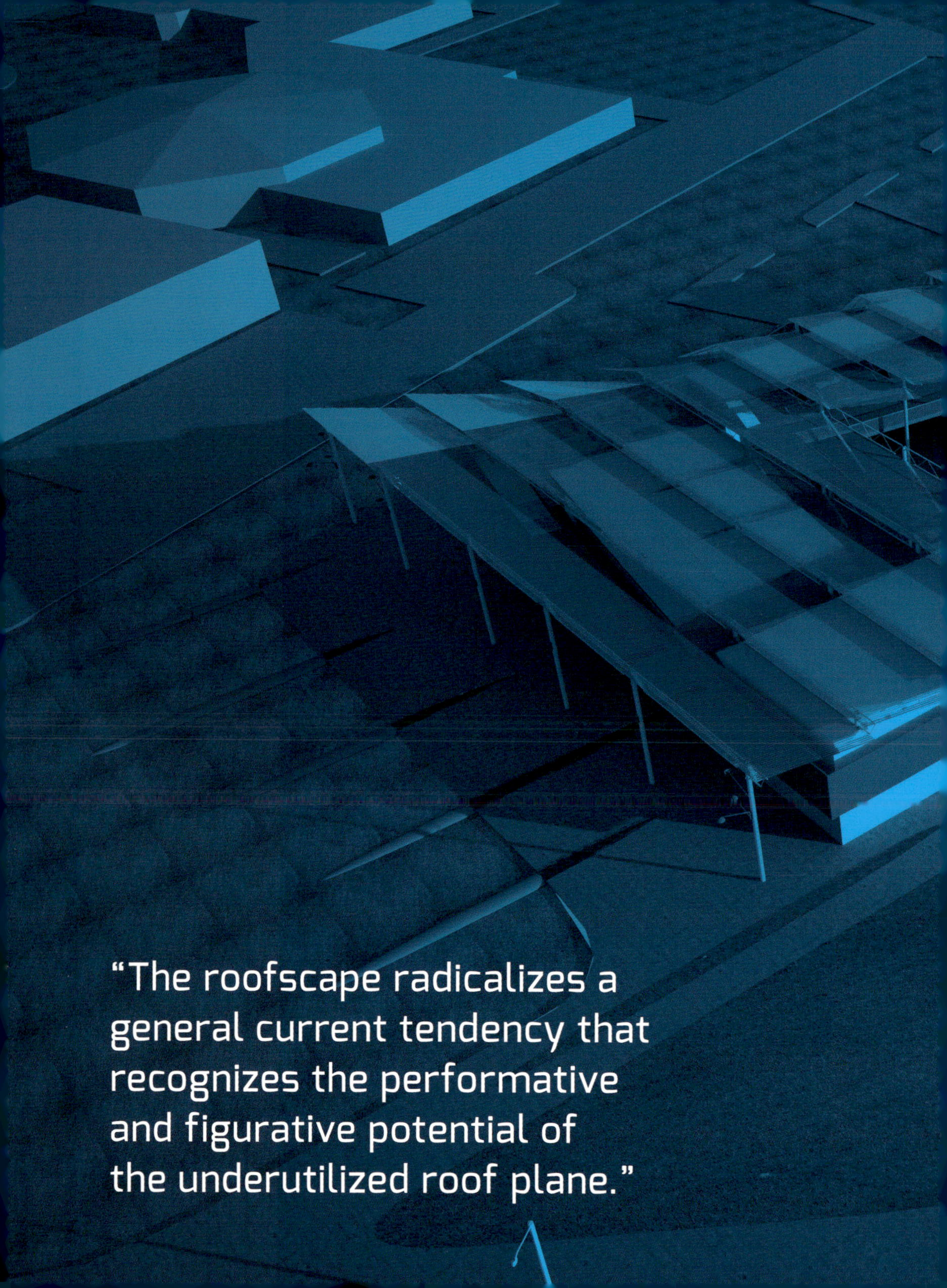

"The roofscape radicalizes a general current tendency that recognizes the performative and figurative potential of the underutilized roof plane."

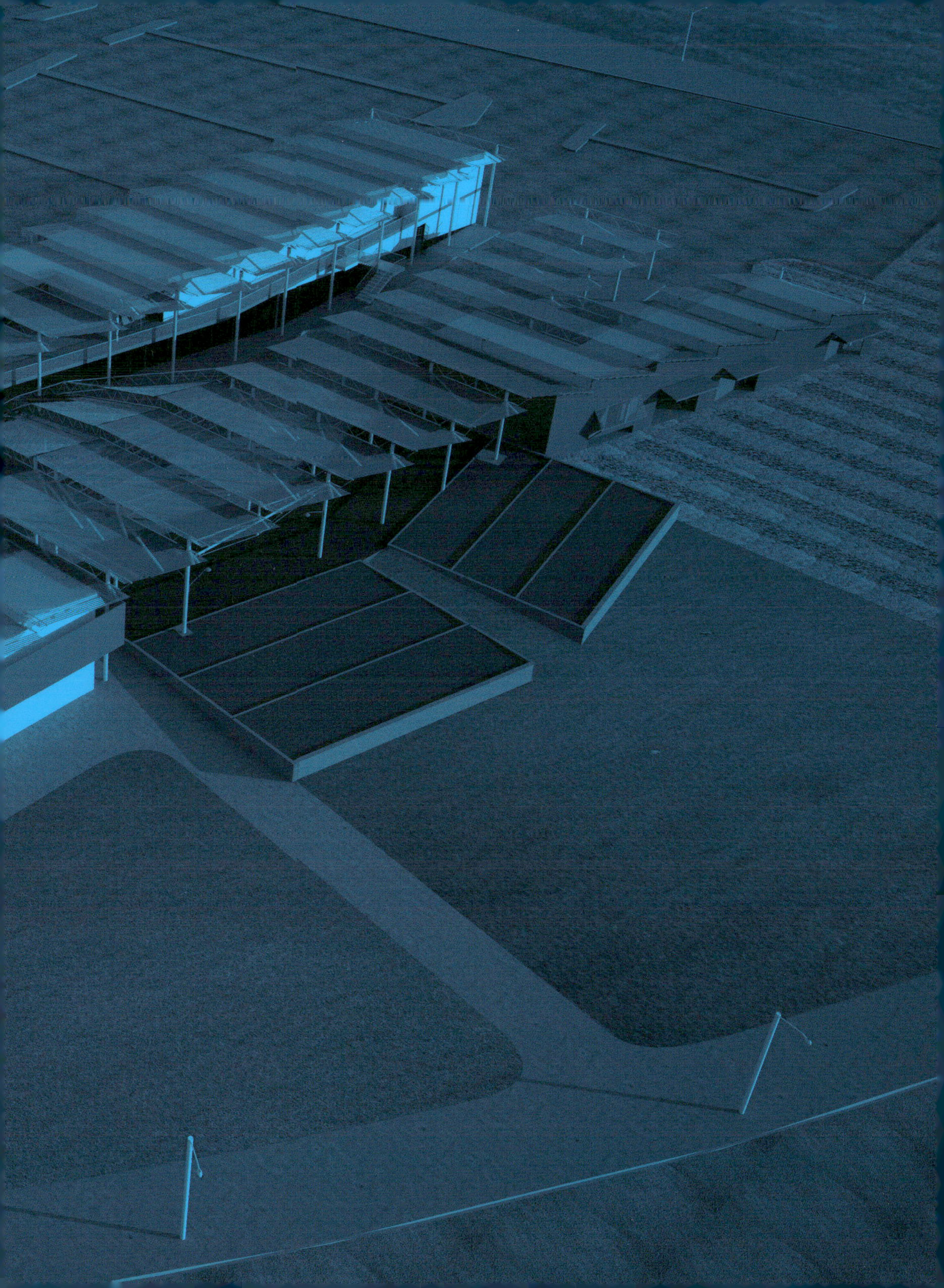

ABOVE. Malama Learning Center

The Convention Hall in Chicago is perhaps Mies van der Rohe's most radical project in the architecture-as-roof vein. Mies's famous collage, which condenses the architecture into two opposite horizontal fields (a relentlessly consistent space—frame above and a teeming crowd below), invites a comparison with Martyrs' Square. The two should sharpen the difference between a modernist conception of the building as an abstract universal frame with an optimized structure and the roofscape's symbolic and performative ambition: a localized and efficient architecture of differentiated parts that is enmeshed in the site's social and material ecology. The sinuous contour and intricately variegated form of Martyrs' Square contrast with the regularity of Mies's clearly delineated roof. They are inflected by the fuzzy logic of myriad external influences (natural and artificial) that continuously perturb its geometry. There is no indication of an exterior in Mies's collage. The only element that is other than building—that is, the crowd—is molded into the shape of a building: a perfect square.

Individual panels, tiled in shifting patterns, constitute the roofscape. It is a continuous surface formed by the aggregation of singular and highly individuated parts. Unlike Mies's space frame in which the standardized and mass-produced homogeneity of the constituent parts reinforces the structure's monolithic character—a totality whose individual parts are entirely subordinated to the overwhelming regularity of the whole- the constituent parts of the Martyrs' Square roofscape maintain their autonomy and identity with respect to the whole. They are highly differentiated, mass- customized elements. Each tile is a unique computer-designed and -manufactured product; all come together to constitute a larger figure, bearing inflections that are registered in larger strokes across the whole. The capacity for simultaneous differentiation and conformity allows for nuances in performance and efficiency that respond to local conditions while consolidating action at a larger scale with greater symbolic and environmental ambitions. Given the nature of today's crowds (Beirut's must be a prime example) in which individuals congregate as a "multitude" with shared experiences of alienation rather than as a "people" with a common identity—and considering the complex ecological dynamics that environmentally conscious architects now face at every urban site—the roofscape, as explored in Martyrs' Square, at the Malama Learning Center, and at other projects, is well equipped to take on new challenges and opportunities in the twenty-first-century city.

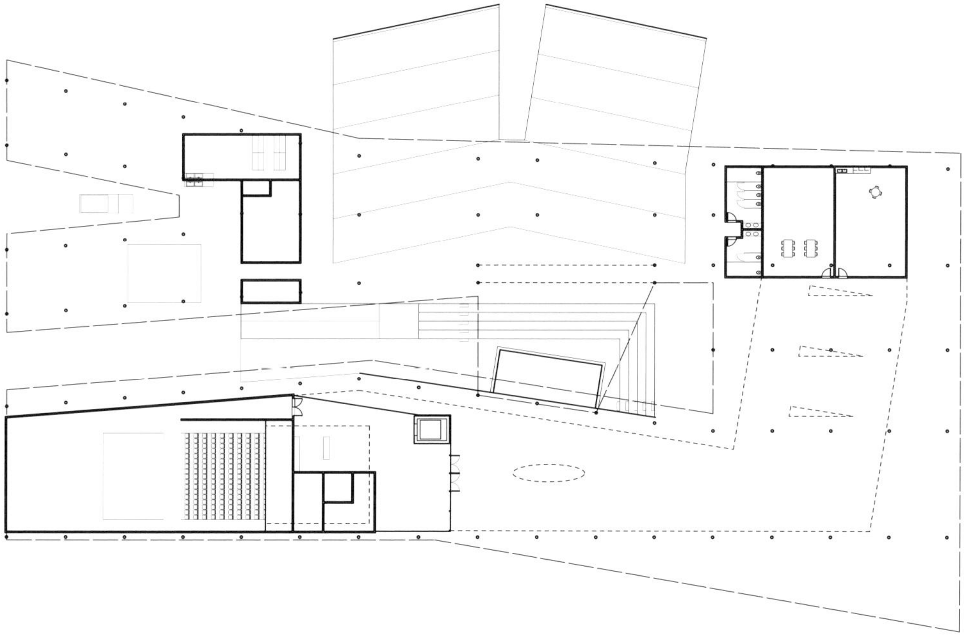

ABOVE. Malama Learning Center, ground level plan

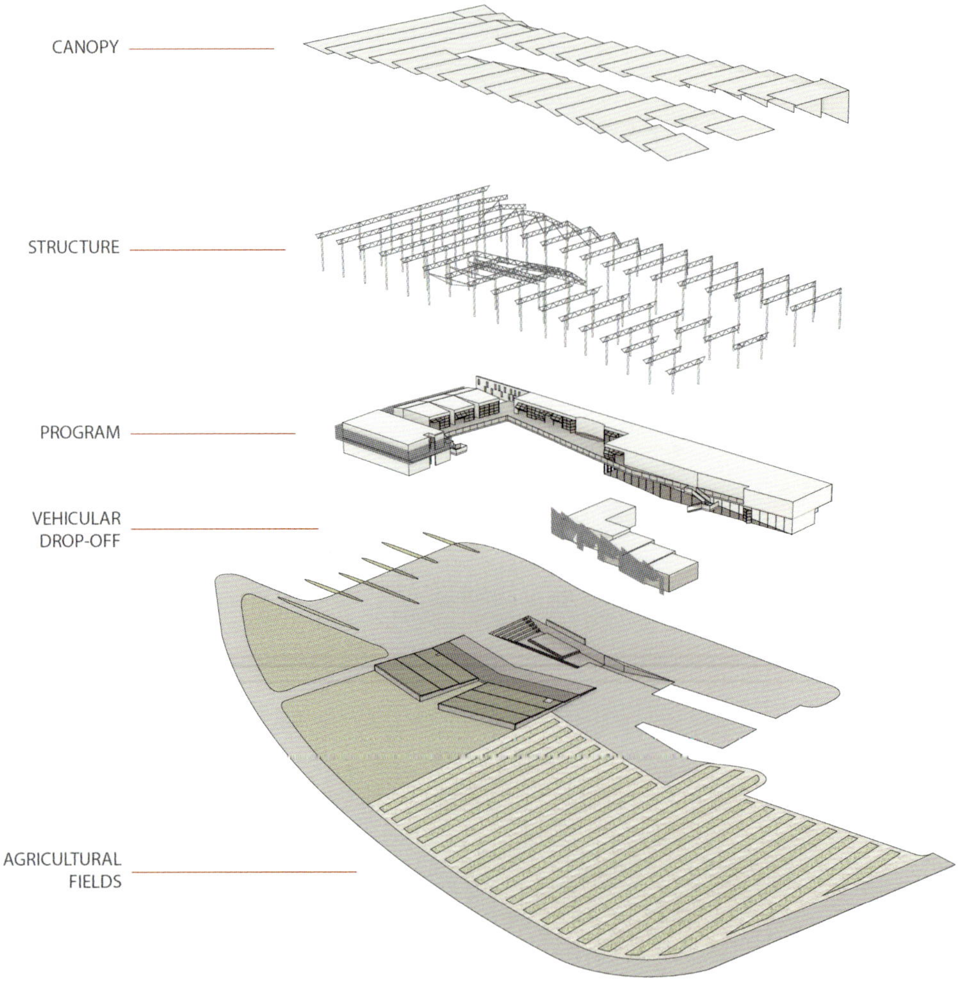

ABOVE. Malama Learning Center, landscape and building systems

ABOVE. Malama Learning Center: shaded amphitheater

ABOVE. Luther Burbank Center for the Arts

ABOVE. Luther Burbank Center for the Arts

- OFFICE VILLA: GROUPE FRÈRE CNP HEADQUARTERS BY PHILIPPE SAMYN AND PARTNERS*

ORIGINALLY PUBLISHED IN **RODOLPHE EL-KHOURY AND MARK PASNIK, GROUPE FRÈRE CNP HEADQUARTERS BY PHILIPPE SAMYN AND PARTNERS**, PRINCETON ARCHITECTURAL PRESS, 2003.

*WRITTEN IN COLLABORATION WITH MARK PASNIK

THE GROUPE FRÈRE CNP HEADQUARTERS epitomizes the unapologetic modernity, technological sophistication, and rigorously rational approach that are characteristic in the work of Philippe Samyn. It is not so typical in its resonance with an ancient building type. In its geometry, its situation in the landscape, and its formal qualities, the headquarters is consistent with the classical villa, a typology not commonly associated with sustainable technology, advanced curtain-wall systems, structural lightness, and other preoccupations of Samyn's work. Nor presumably is the villa readily associated with commerce, professionalism, global networks, or other aspects of an international holding company.

Yet the typological conformity is played out with great study and seriousness, while the qualities of the ancient villa—its original purpose as a peaceful retreat, its promotion of leisure, enjoyment, relaxation, and fantasy—are translated into a hyper-modern conception of corporate efficiency. The translation is not always smooth. It is a pretext for imagining a place that is full of sharp contrasts and contradictions: its rural location compared to the global markets the building serves; the opulence of its art and landscape program in contrast to the efficiency of the building systems. At many levels, the project capitalizes on such tensions, dialectically negotiating the rational imperatives of contemporary high-tech architecture with the symbolic associations of a typological origin.

The use of historic referents is of course a staple of postmodern architecture and perhaps best illustrated in the work of Robert Venturi. His architecture explicitly makes references to historic precedents in more or less literal quotations spanning across history: Baroque broken pediments, modernist strip windows, an Ionic column, and a populist television antenna are some of the motifs in his eclectic repertoire. In the Guild House (1960-63), one of his early buildings in Philadelphia, Venturi placed the gold-anodized television antenna atop the building to create, in his now notorious words, "a symbol of the aged, who spend so much time looking at TV."[1] Samyn positions a satellite dish in the same honorific position, transcoding, as it were, Venturi's gesture into architectural terms now relevant to the world of global business.

Regardless of the undoubtedly self-conscious nod toward Venturi, to mistake the CNP Headquarters for a historicist building is to ignore Samyn's entire oeuvre and miss its significance as a work that defies classification

[1] R. Venturi, *Complexity and Contradiction in Architecture* (1990), 116.

ABOVE. Dupuis Publishing Company

and challenges the expected opposition of the rational to the symbolic, the engineered to the artful. For Samyn, who is more interested in facts than ideology, pastiche is by no means a relevant technique. We see in projects such as the Houten Fire Station (1998-2000) in Houten, the Netherlands, and the Dupuis Publishing Company (1994-95) in Marcinelle, Belgium, simple and elegant designs that are ostensibly rooted in the mathematics of engineering, the exigencies of program, the geometry of statics, the logic of environmental systems. Beauty, in this architecture, is a function of objective truths; the self-evident clarity of rational thinking and the rules of physics are its main driving forces. Another set of latent forces is manifested in the CNP Headquarters: the building's geometry is not solely rationalized by structure and program. It is also rooted in the idealized proportions of the humanist villa, in a tradition that relates form to natural harmonies and human proportions. By investing in this tradition and the villa ideal, Samyn brings a cultural/historical dimension— with all of its semantic connotations and mythic implications—to bear on geometry. In the CNP, Samyn's usual preoccupations converge with a symbolic agenda that seeks a mytho-poetic resonance in the lucid facts of engineering without literally quoting from historical referents.

If the CNP evokes the classical villa, it does so in the abstract realm of geometry, in the fundamental traits of its very conception rather than in applied iconographic references. The affinity is evident in the design process itself. Samyn's sketches, for instance, clearly demonstrate his concern with proportioning and relational systems at the earliest stages of the design. The ubiquity of the ordering grid is consistent with modernist rationalized methods. But there is more Palladio than Durand in the recurring circle in the square motif of the schematic plans. The building's generative—if not metaphysical—power is fueled by classical ideals as much as modernist methodology.

ABOVE. Houten Fire Station

The firm's early presentation drawings tellingly treat plans, elevations, and sections as a single composition, much like in Palladia's idealized representations of the Veneto villas, published in *The Four Books of Architecture* (1570). In Palladio's drawings, plans are superimposed over elevations. Samyn expands this technique, surrounding his plans with four drawings—a section and three elevations. These iterative sketches establish the interrelationship of façade and plan, the consistent compactness of the building, and the comprehensive proportioning of rooms. As a consequence, the design shows remarkable formal similarities to the villa type in massing, geometry, order, symmetry, axial configuration, proportion, and precision.

The main building is part of a larger complex formed by a gatehouse, a long drive leading to a motor court, formal gardens in the front, and a rolling landscape in the back. The resonance with the tradition of the villa is unmistakable. Historian James S. Ackerman traces the villa as a building type to Roman origins in two competing models, "compact-cubic" and "open-extended." The former were singular that stood formally separated from the landscape, often made of light-colored materials and seen as foils to the natural world. The latter were sprawling compounds that engaged their environment and blurred distinctions between building and landscape.[2] Later Renaissance architects such as Palladio maintained the polar opposition of building to landscape employed in the compact-cubic model while beginning to establish ordered, classicizing relationships between the villa and its garden. Thus, wings that reached out to the grounds often flanked the main volume in a U-shaped formation, and the landscape itself was defined in structured geometries along a principal axis.

[2] J. S. Ackerman, *The Villa: Form and Ideology of Country Houses* (1990), 18-26.

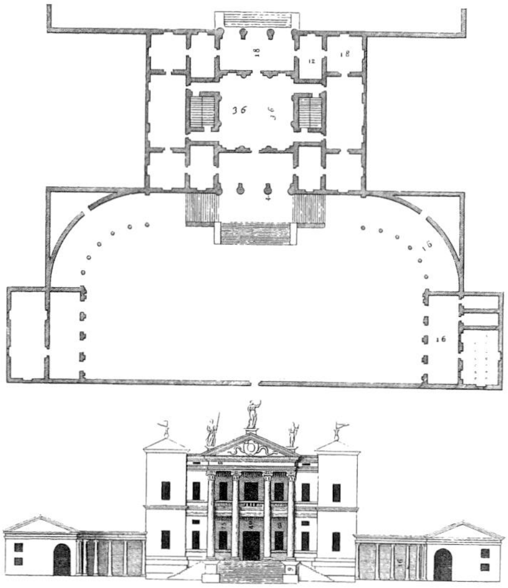

ABOVE. Villa by Andrea Palladio for Count Oleardo and Count Theodoro de Thieni at Cignona, from *The Four Books of Architecture*, 1570

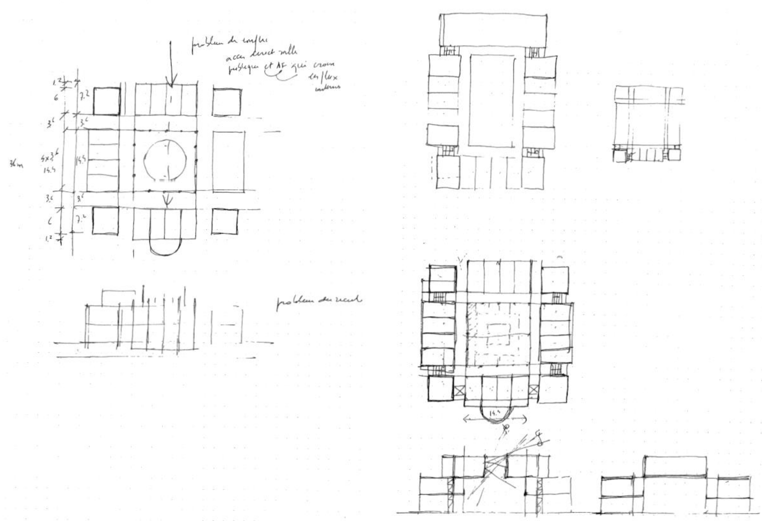

ABOVE. Philippe Samyn's diagrammatic sketches on grid paper, showing the building volumetric and geometric organization

The CNP Headquarters draws heavily from these traditions in its free-standing cubic volume, light-colored material, axial symmetry, and commanding position over both the strict formal gardens and the more picturesque grounds. The site is organized along a diagonal axis that runs precisely north-south and originates in a densely wooded corner of the property; this axis passes through the center of the cobblestone motor court, the entrance and lobby, between the elevators, through the boardroom, and into the picturesque landscape. It intersects a pair of secondary axes that run perpendicular. The first extends from the gatehouse along the roadway and is marked with a sculpture by Niki de Saint Phalle; entitled Nana, it is a brightly colored figural timepiece made from lacquered polyester on a metal frame, which rotates hourly on its cylindrical base. The second crossing occurs where the main axis meets the building's east-west circulation system—passageways that extend outward to the boundaries of the site along gravel paths on the lawn.

Samyn's building is in keeping with the hybrid nature of the Renaissance villa, where a main central block is often complemented by flanking wings that contain the agricultural functions of the country house. Early sketches proposed a scheme with an enclosed central court. In conceiving this space, the architect recalled his childhood school's *préau*, a covered vestibule surrounded by galleries that served as the animated heart of the institution.

The CNP of the courtyard eventually migrated frontward. Although it is in fact an indoor lobby, it performs much like an open courtyard that has later been enclosed and roofed over with a lightweight structural system. Its diagonal struts are bolted to concrete-filled steel columns and splay outward in a manner reminiscent of Violet-le-Duc's nineteenth-century iron structures. The diagonal and its structural logic are consistent with Samyn's own quest for light and efficient constructions, in this case resulting in only four columns interrupting the large double-height hall. A similar logic is one of the most persistent motifs in Victor Horta's architecture, such as the Maison du Peuple (1896-99) in Brussels—an architectural icon that still captures the imagination of Belgian architects. In Samyn's building, the transparency of the courts front wall compared to the opacity of the side volumes creates the impression of two flanking wings on the east and west sides of the enclosed lobby court, and a main body to the north. The organization is parallel to the hybrid villa: the central block contains the main aspect of the program—the boardroom and an apartment for the company founder, Baron Albert Frère

"If the ambition of the villa type is to balance aspirations for work, contemplation, pleasure, relaxation, health, and entertainment, then Samyn's building is the villa par excellence, a building that derives its unique character and great strength from the tensions inherent to the villa type itself and the vitality of its competing desires."

ABOVE. Aerial view of the grounds

—while the flanking wings house the working spaces and offices. The CNP Headquarters indeed exhibits characteristics of the two villa types: it is both compactly cubic and embracingly U-shaped. The double resonance is reinforced by the building's surfaces. Its envelope is entirely clad with ultra-clear glass produced by the company Saint-Gobain and previously used at the Grande Bibliothèque de France. For the opaque panels, the glass is acid-etched outside and coated with enamel behind. Seams are minimal, and the aluminum mullions are barely noticeable.

The effect reinforces the buildings' ambiguous allegiances. On the one hand, the front elevation presents a flawlessly smooth and materially homogenous surface that gleams with high-tech sophistication and affirms the systematic logic of cladding regardless of any concern for typological identity. On the other hand, the alternating A-B-A pattern of opacity and transparency adds a sense of symmetry and hierarchy to the structure—the abstract volume becomes a villa. The cubic type, recalling Renaissance structures like the Villa Medici (1485) at Poggio a Caiano (by Lorenzo de' Medici and Guilano da Sangallo), is dominant in daylight when the contrast between the impenetrable sides and transparent central bay is moderated by the reflective qualities of the glass. The U-shaped type of Palladia's winged villas emerges especially at night, when the hall is exposed behind the glass wall: a central block with two wings flanking a court.

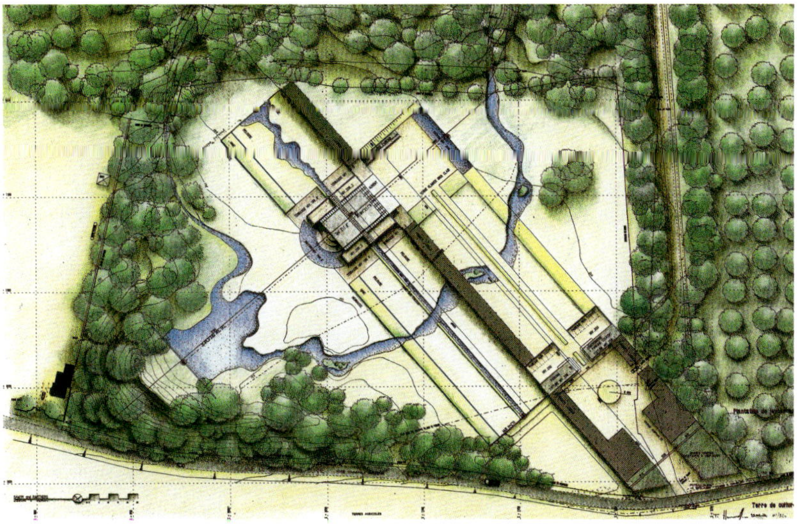

ABOVE. Sketch study for the site plan showing the building's, orientation along a diagonal axis that runs precisely north-south

Inside, this impression lingers. The central block is rhetorically emphasized by the two glass towers of the elevators flanking the boardroom entrance and a symmetrical staircase leading into the space itself. In plan, the building evokes models such as Lord Burlington's Chiswick House (1727-29), where symmetrical flights of stairs lead up to the main portico of the house. This platform provides the opportunity to view back across the landscape from which one arrived. But Samyn has inverted this familiar device. The stairs here lead downwards, giving the podium at the top of the stairs a view to the north, across the boardroom and forward into the landscape.

The view of the landscape beyond, framed by the boardroom in the foreground, has a dramatic effect with obvious allegorical resonances. The boardroom is contained within the largest and lowest of three apsidal forms located at the rear of the building; it provides a sense of visual control over the landscape, a panoptical effect suited to the company's

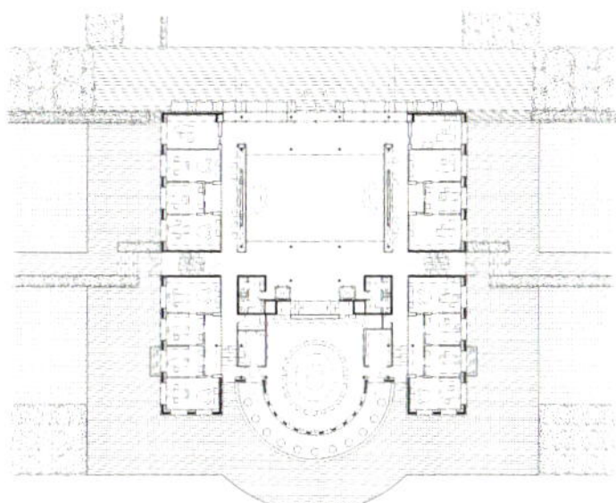

RIGHT. Drawing composite of the CNP Headquarters, superimposing the plan, section, and elevations

nervous center. Control here extends to the virtual realm with state-of-the-art communication infrastructure and audio-visual interface. The boardroom predictably offers the seigniorial command over the site while remaining refreshingly unguarded and accessible, being neither physically isolated nor detached from the rest of the complex by layers of controlled spaces or security stations. Indeed, it is immediately adjacent to the most public location in the building—the lobby court—and screened merely by a sliding glass wall and retractable privacy partition. Its proximity to the collective center of the building—at the intersection of primary circulation paths, with elevators flanking the entryway—reaffirms the openness and accessibility of the company's leadership. The transparency here is both literal and allegorical.

The building envelope strengthens the tensions between contemporary and historical allegiances observed in the plan. The embodiment of the ideological nuances of architecture in the most pragmatic of elements, such as fenestration and mechanical systems, is a staple of Samyn's work, perhaps most literally demonstrated in the Château Groenhof (1996-99) in Malderen, Belgium. In this project for a private residence, the new addition partially enshrouds a typical French Mansard-style mansion, resulting in a double-layered façade: the high-tech, machined, and repetitive skin of the addition slipping in front of the nineteenth-century, load-bearing masonry mansion. The contemporary layer, separated by less than ten feet from the existing façade, contains solar screens, photovoltaic panels, steel, and wood. The new structure cautiously and delicately engages the historic building, while observing principles of conservation. It can be altered or reversed without damaging the original. Tensions between past and present, history and modernity are staged didactically, in the spatial confrontations of the two surfaces and their respective figurative and performative differences.

The CNP building's envelope is similarly layered with ambivalent tendencies: an emphasis on sustainable design and a sensitivity to historical precedents. Their interplay is here more subtle, blurred, conceptual. The client requested a stone-clad building, but Samyn, in his usual insistence on light, energy-efficient, and resource-saving solutions, opposed the idea. Instead, he exploited the versatile uses of glass and cutting-edge cladding technology to translate the phenomenal qualities of stone masonry into a new medium: a glazed double skin with a capacity for stately thickness and density.

The headquarters' double skin is finely calibrated for energy-efficient ventilation with layers of operable shading screens that adapt the building envelope to daily climatic conditions—reducing solar heat gain in the summer months and minimizing heat loss in the winter. At the lobby, the skin comprises two outer layers of glass separated by forty-five inches from one inner layer. It is designed as part of an air displacement system, whose main supply vents are embedded in the volumes along the sides of the hall. The air is absorbed into the double skin at gaps in its base, then cycled through to a collection point at the top of the wall, and finally re-circulated to heat the basement and parking level. The configuration results in enormous environmental benefits, helping to create a building that is significantly more energy-efficient than typical commercial structures. In the office wings, the outer enclosure is also double-glazed, with the inner skin set back twenty-seven inches; it consists of suspended sliding glass and operable shades, allowing office occupants to respond to climatic changes with great flexibility and control. The inner and outer skins are seamlessly integrated with each room's ventilation system, which expels air from above the window frame and collects it at the base of the double skin.

The high-tech features of the double skin and its ecological virtues are flaunted in the front, in the layered curtain wall of the central bay. The flanking bays are mute, presenting an impenetrable flatness that is in sharp contrast to the filigree of glass and steel. While the cladding pattern and material are consistent across the elevation, the opacity on the sides conveys a sense of density and solidity.

This virtual solidity is further emphasized on the east and west elevations, where the double skin is treated like a thick wall, with a deep section exposed around window openings. The hollow-yet-solid looking wall has a masonry-like effect, which is due to the phenomenal thickness, to the deep shadows cast on the blinds behind, rather than to any figurative hint or quotation. The ultra-light glass cladding is not meant to deceive; yet the sense of solidity and density is persistent. The evocative window type once again hints at Palladia with its familiar Serliana motif of sidelight, center bay, sidelight. In this case, the manually operated sidelights pivot laterally to an open position, slipping out and away from the center bay so as to expose the thickness of the double-skin envelope and emphasize the "punched-window" effect.

ABOVE. View of the south façade

What is hinted at in the front, in the tripartite composition of glass cladding, and further emphasized on the sides, in the thickness of the double skin, is clearly spelled out in the back. As if less restrained in the more private realm of the "backyard," the latent volumetric characteristics of the building are here literally deployed: two wings flank a main block, complete with a central rotunda à la White House. The whole is clad in the same system of transparent and opaque glass panels, which, in a tour de force of versatility, flawlessly adapts to the classical character of the composition and the circular geometry of the central bay.

The classical flavor is here dominant and the strict bilateral symmetry, although consistent on all sides, is more rhetorical. The back, perhaps ironically, has the most formal of elevations but the formality is that of a domestic typology. The building elsewhere evokes the villa ideal in relatively abstract terms; in the back, there is no mistaking the classical typology.

In the various adaptations of the cladding system we thus see a progression from corporate to domestic identity, from the abstract rationality of the front, to the corporeality of the side elevations, and finally to the conventions of a grand but still familiar domesticity in the back.

The domestication of the corporation continues inside. At the most literal level, an executive apartment for Albert Frère is nested above the board room, occupying the upper two floors of the central volume. Stylistically,

ABOVE. View of the north façade

it is entirely incongruous, and, in fact, was completed by another design firm. When compared with the rest of the building, it is a surprisingly different world of marble, mahogany panels, and classical moldings. Nonetheless, it is in keeping with a tradition of secret chambers, hidden rooms, and other spaces for entertainment in villas and chateaux.

More substantial forms of domestication occur elsewhere, outside the strictly private and ultimately inconsequential apartment. Consider, for instance, the individual private offices that are created in lieu of the open loft space now typical of commercial buildings. They are symmetrically laid out in the side wings with a compositional and proportional precision that is unusual to conventional office planning; it is drawn instead from precedents in the humanist tradition of harmonically proportioned residences.

The doorways between offices show a concession to openness and flexibility with their eight inch-thick motorized wooden panels that retract into the wall to seamlessly connect contiguous offices. Their alignment is reminiscent of enfilades in a chateau, an effect that reinforces the sense of residential compartmentalization over open and multi purpose office space.

When closed, the frameless sliding doors pre serve the integrity of each room with a continuous wall surface and total acoustical insulation. In the sealed room the emphasis is on individual users in personal space; this is a private enclave equipped with independent and sustainable

“If the CNP evokes the classical villa, it does so in the abstract realm of geometry, in the fundamental traits of its very conception rather than in applied iconographic references.”

environmental controls for ventilation and natural lighting, providing a sense of individual autonomy within the larger corporate framework.

In light of this contrast a few questions arise: why the conflation of the domestic villa and the corporate headquarters? And how does the architect represent the corporate body through humanist ideals? Over its history, the villa has aspired to the ideals of country life: relaxation, health, leisure, contemplation, fantasy—not necessarily characteristics we associate with an industrial holding company. But the villa has broader and more complex associations, which are persuasively emphasized in the CNP building's dual identity.

Pliny the Younger hints at such complexity in his collected letters, which record some of the most important observations on ancient Roman villas. In describing his own Tuscan retreat, Pliny recounts its "lovely situation"and its restorative powers, claiming:

I can enjoy a profounder peace there, more comfort, and fewer cares; I need never wear a formal toga and there are no neighbours to disturb me; everywhere there is peace and quiet, which adds as much to the healthiness of the place as the clear sky and pure air.

He continues, stating: "There I enjoy the best of health, both mental and physical, for I keep my mind in training with work and my body with hunting."[3]

In Pliny's view the villa should not only cater to pastoral inclinations but provide the setting for a full and balanced life, embodying a quasi-utopian vision of a perfect equilibrium between body and intellect, activity and rest, business and pleasure:

Shut yourself up with your books in the peace and comfort of your retreat.... This is what should be both business and pleasure, work and recreation, and should occupy your thoughts awake and asleep![4]

The dialectic of work and pleasure is not limited to the villa's original Roman incarnation. From Palladio's sixteenth-century villas in the Veneto to Jefferson's eighteenth-century Monticello in the American South, villas are indeed often working farms. Palladio comments extensively on this balance of work and pleasure in *The Four Books of Architecture*, outlining the virtues and utility of a gentleman's country house, a place where, time will be passed in seeing and adorning his own possessions, and by industry, and the art of agriculture, improving his estate; where also by the exercise which in a villa is commonly taken, on foot and on horseback, the body will the more easily preserve its strength and health; and, finally, where the mind, fatigued by the agitations of the city, will be greatly restored and comforted, and be able quietly to attend the studies of letters, and contemplation.[5]

If the ambition of the villa type is to balance aspirations for work, contemplation, pleasure, relaxation, health, and entertainment, then Samyn's building is the villa par excellence, a building that derives its unique character and great strength from the tensions inherent to the villa type itself and the vitality of its competing desires. This villa wears its technological and ecological sophistication without pompous moralism. In every aspect of the design, down to the slick light switch featuring nickel buttons on a glass faceplate, the building affirms its "modernity," but modernity here is not an ideology that has to be argued rhetorically. The CNP is not designed to look modern; it is modern—it exploits the latest resources and most advanced knowledge to deliver the best and most sustainable performance possible.

The optimal performance sought by Samyn concentrates on benefits for the user above anything else. The building states its humanist agenda at every opportunity- in the large-scale structural moves as much as in the minute ergonomic details. The humanism of the building has to do with material as well as conceptual aspects that aim for comfort as much as dignity, never condescending to flatter the senses with opulent but facile effects. The genuine generosity in this building is a consequence of design rather than the use of rich materials. It is visible in the building's ambitious art program, which more than compensates for the economy in the material palette. Generosity, or, rather, humanity is also apparent in the commitment to natural lighting, in the enormous structural and spatial investments that maximize the building's impact and benefits. It is in the immense effort spent on ingeniously compacting mechanical systems in the tiniest possible spaces, while public rooms are oversized well beyond functional requirements.

Samyn's brand of architectural humanism is perhaps most evident in the way the office-villa negotiates corporate aspirations with individual autonomy. The private offices are designed as self-contained spaces; yet,

[3] B. Radice, trans., *The Letters of the Younger Pliny* (1969), 144, emphasis added.

[4] Ibid. 36

ABOVE. Château Groenhofg

ABOVE. View of the building's operable office windows, with a glass volume containing the staircase at center

formally as well as proportion ally, they are inscribed in a more comprehensive system of relationships that lends coherence and consistency to the corporation. The same dialectic is at play at a much larger scale, in the overall organization of the site. Symmetry and axial alignments convey a sense of institutional monumentality; they also emphasize the building's relationship to the landscape and establish an egalitarian pattern of access and use that privileges public space.

State-of-the-art building materials, systems, and technologies are exploited to optimize the building's performance and sustainability. But performance here is not limited to programmatic, structural, and environmental criteria. It is also addressed in its symbolic dimensions, as a means of cultural production. Herein perhaps lies Samyn's critical contribution to the contemporary architectural debate: The CNP Headquarters is a forward-looking building that tackles, with impeccable rigor and expertise, the critical challenges faced by architecture in a new global economy. It does so without losing sight of a cultural heritage that can still resonate with new forms and techniques. A case in point is the treatment of the side elevations, where the double skin is ingeniously designed to recover desirable effects of obsolete masonry construction while delivering the outstanding environmental performance of a modern material. This is one clear instance where the semiotic and rational logics converge. It is also symptomatic of a general design attitude that seeks to reconcile performative and representational ambitions. The CNP building may be one of the rare examples where a meaningful and productive synthesis is achieved from the positivist drive of modernity and the allegorical impulse of postmodern reaction.

[5] A. Palladio, *The Four Books of Architecture*, reprint of 1738 publication by Isaac Ware (1965), 46.

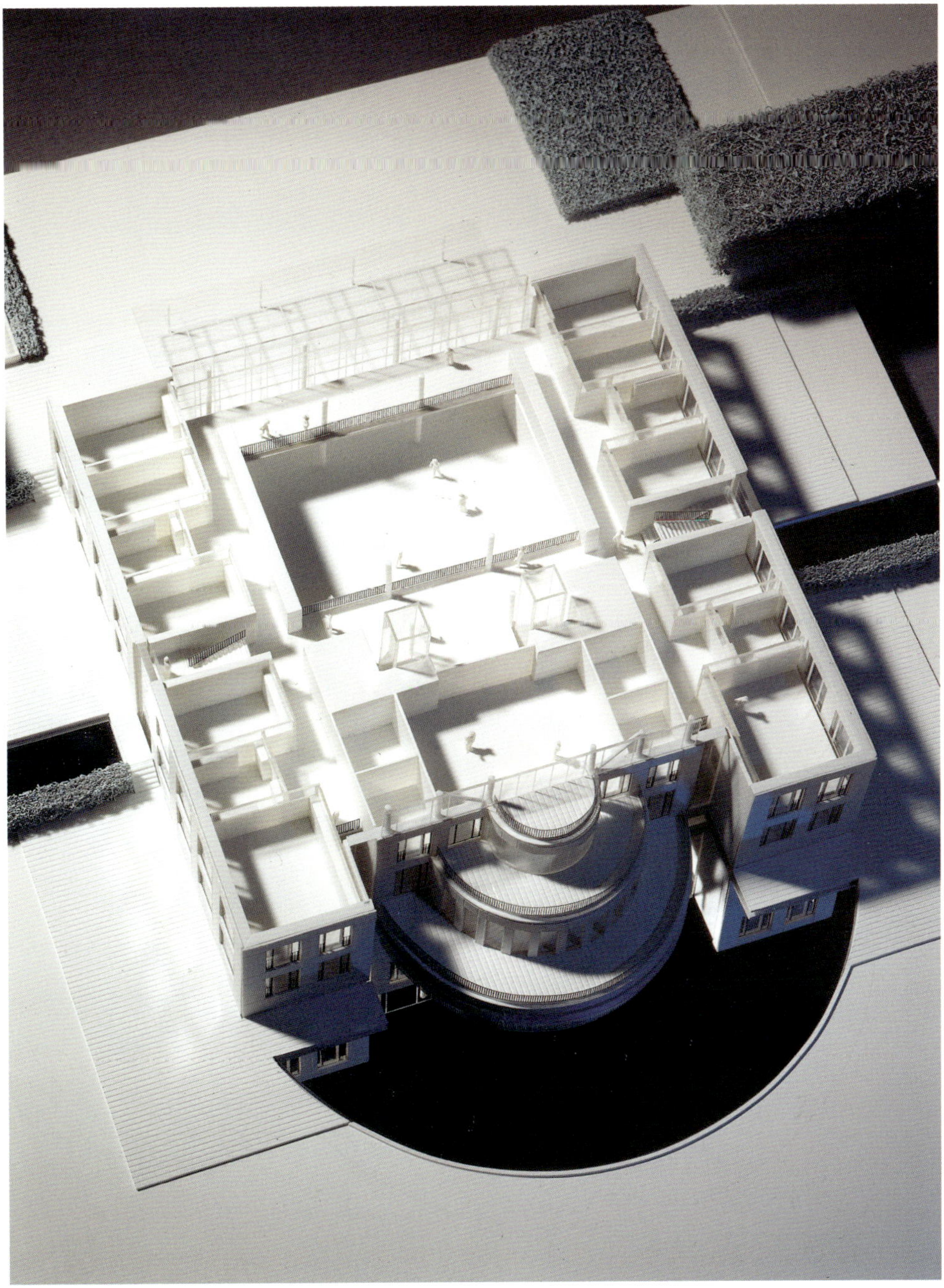

ABOVE. Cut-away model showing the organization of the first floor

- DIFFERENCE AND INTERACTION: FAYEZ S. SAROFIM RESEARCH BUILDING BY BNIM ARCHITECTS*

ORIGINALLY PUBLISHED IN **BNIM: SYMBIOSIS,**
ORO EDITIONS, 2008.

*WRITTEN IN COLLABORATION WITH ANDREW PAYNE

THE UNIVERSITY AS A PUBLIC INSTITUTION has undergone significant transformation since the philosopher Jean François Lyotard first heralded the emergence of a "postmodern condition" in a report written for the Quebec Conseil des Universités in 1979. Driven by a post-Enlightenment conception of the relationship between theoretical and technical realms of intellectual endeavor, new disciplinary agendas (semiotics, topology, cybernetics, systems theory, robotics, nano-engineering) and novel liaisons between already existing disciplines proliferate within this condition, leaving both humanistic and scientific sectors of the university community significantly transformed. What is more, this transformation is attended by an altered conception of the relationship between the university, as a public corporation, and private-sector interests. The result is a kind of vague epistemological terrain in which disciplinary boundaries are protean and the opportunities for unprecedented forms of collaboration between highly specialized knowledge sectors plentiful. If, at the time Lyotard penned his report, "language" was the privileged semantic locus for this disciplinary realignment, today it is "life," albeit a life reconceived in post-vitalist terms as self-organizing system, which seems to have assumed that role. The Italian philosopher Giorgio Agamben expresses the current intellectual ethos when he says, in an essay published some sixteen years after *The Post Modern Condition*, that "the concept of 'life' ... must constitute the subject of the coming philosophy."[1] Concomitant with this shift from language to life, one can observe the emergence of a bioconstructive paradigm in which traditional distinctions between living and artificial systems are progressively dissolved and in which life is increasingly conceived as informational complexity. The challenges and opportunities implied by this dissolution are arguably brought into focus by the Human Genome Project, with its promise of willfully redesigning the constituent elements of the life process in conformity with a perspective that collapses any distinction between biogenetic and informatic regimes. As the cultural theorist and philosopher of science, Eugene Thacker, observes, the adoption of this paradigm brings both philosophy and science into confluence with a diverse array of all technical fields and commercial enterprises, including genomics, patenting, GM foods, and pharmaceuticals.

Enter the Fayez S. Sarofim Research Building, home of The Brown Foundation Institute of Molecular Medicine for the Prevention of Human Diseases at The University of Texas Health Science Center at Houston.

[1] G. Agamben, "Absolute Immanence," *Potentialities*. trans., Daniel Heller-Roazen, (1999), 238.

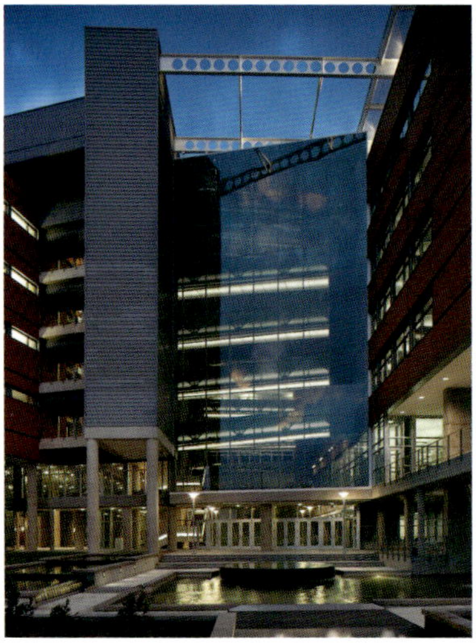

ABOVE. Fayez S. Sarofim Research Building, view towards atrium

ABOVE. Fayez S. Sarofim Research Building, typical lab space

A 6-story, 229,000-square-foot structure that incorporates wet and dry research laboratories, administrative offices, conference rooms, open spaces specifically designed for collaborative scientific discussion, a 200-seat auditorium and a large atrium for public events and ambient social interaction, the building takes its name from a donor who gifted the Health Science Center with $25 million for biogenetic research. The Institute's first director and presiding genius of the place, Hans J. Müller-Eberhard, was both a doctor and a research scientist whose career was deeply committed to cross-disciplinary collaboration. This commitment remains a conspicuous feature of the Institute in its current incarnation, which oversees research in a variety of areas, including human genetics, proteomics and bioinformatics. These few facts suggest the degree to which this building and the Institute it accommodates are products of that altered intellectual condition invoked above, with its conflation of vital and informatic regimes, its blurring of boundaries between erstwhile intellectual jurisdictions and its novel confluence of public and private interest. So the question inexorably arises: what sort of architecture would be adequate to this changed intellectual condition and the bioconstructive paradigm currently regnant within it?

[2] M. Polio Vitruvius. "On the Training of Architects." De architectura (On architecture), Book 1, c. 1, trans. Frank Granger (2002), 9–24.

Before responding to that question, it is worth observing that architecture was very early to the transdisciplinary ethos, and that its commitment to this ethos has implied, from the start, a nimble two-step between theoretical and practical, humanistic and technical agendas. A glance at Book One of Vitruvius's *De architectura* will serve to suggest just how far this polymathic spirit reaches down into the discipline. As for life, a preoccupation with it and its autopoetic properties can be observed at every step along the architectural way.[2] It is apparent, for instance, in Vitruvius's description of the efflorescence of the human building arts out of the primitive givens determining the life of the species it passes through Claude Perrault's late-seventeenth-century attempt to apply Descartes's newly minted physics simultaneously to the fields of medicine and architecture; finally, it serves as a thematic counterweight to twentieth-century fascination with industrial mechanization, a counterweight felt in projects as diverse as Le Corbusier's Unité d'Habitation and Eero Saarinen's IBM Thomas J. Watson Research Laboratory. What is more, architecture has been, among the cultural disciplines, the first to elaborate both a theoretical perspective on and practical responses to this bioconstructive paradigm, as is apparent in a range of topics that have animated the discipline over the past decade. To improvise a random sampling from a much larger constellation, that range may be thought to include: post-human architecture, cybercity, biomimicry, biopolitics, non-standard construction, autopoesis, self-organization, emergence, landscape urbanism, rhizomatic—as against arborescent—organization, complexity theory, the green building and the intelligent building. True to their profession, BNIM Architects has a long and distinguished history of cross-disciplinary collaboration, and although their work operates at some distance from the rhetoric associated with the constellation of contemporary topics cited above, their approach, developed over thirty-seven years of practice, represents a considered response to this bioconstructive paradigm. It is an approach that argues in intelligently pragmatic ways for a sustainable imbrication of natural and human systems aided by the most advanced construction technologies. Whereas the current neo-avant-garde, taking inspiration from the post-vitalist life philosophy of Gilles Deleuze, has attempted either to give figure to this emergent paradigm or, through the insinuation of hypersurfaced artifacts, to dramatically reshape the modalities of collective conduct associated with its ascendance, BNIM eschew grand rhetorical gestures, preferring to negotiate the most resounding effects of this intellectual and cultural sea-change by the most modest and pragmatic of means. Though deeply invested in cross-disciplinary collaboration and biomimetic

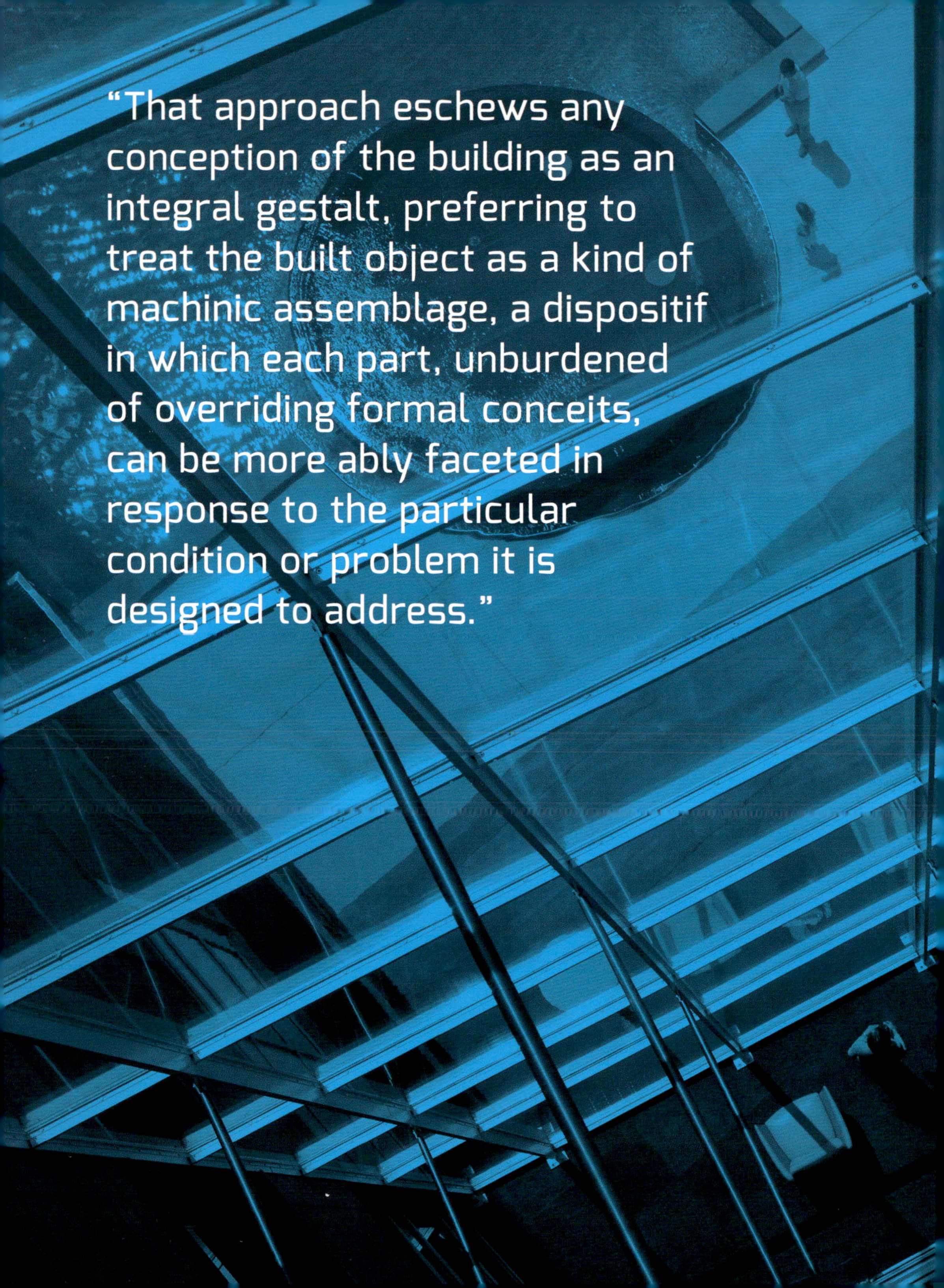

"That approach eschews any conception of the building as an integral gestalt, preferring to treat the built object as a kind of machinic assemblage, a dispositif in which each part, unburdened of overriding formal conceits, can be more ably faceted in response to the particular condition or problem it is designed to address."

integration of living and artificial systems, BNIM construe the architectural question provoked by the current state of university research as simply a variant on a very familiar one: how might a building most generously support the needs and aspirations of the community, of users living and working under this new condition, while at the same time optimizing the reciprocities obtaining between the animate and artificial systems supporting this use?

To judge from the built results, BNIM's response to their own question is twofold. On the one hand, what these postmodern knowledge workers most need and desire is a legible spatial diagram in which the provision of disciplinary specificity is recognized not as an impediment to, but rather as a necessary precondition of, meaningful collaboration between distinct jurisdictions, and in which the accommodation of such specificity is sufficiently flexible to adapt to the protean nature of contemporary intellectual endeavor. On the other hand, what they need and desire is a climatic filter for mediating and rarifying their experience of their surroundings. The result of that twofold response is a "vertical campus" whose lower stratum follows BNIM's preference for open, flexible public spaces, which combine the spatial intensity and social focus of a deliberately shaped interior with the freedom and atmospheric amenity of the exterior, and whose upper strata are then given over to accommodating the more specialized activities of the distinct research communities inhabiting the building in the most efficacious, flexible, and ecologically responsible manner possible.

Designed as the gateway to a new academic campus, the building internalizes the large open space that forms the heart of the projected campus. Here, the unfolding of the urban savannah is less interrupted than framed, giving discernible form and concentrated presence. This frame takes the form of the building's central atrium, which, inserted between the building's administrative and laboratory wings, serves as the link not only between interior and exterior spaces but also between lower and upper, open and secured strata in this "vertical campus." The atrium is, quite simply, the device that brings all the discrete parts of this machine into sympathy, and its presence dominates the distribution of space and program on the building's layered grounds.

The strategy of clear vertical stratification—as against a more complex imbrication of open and secured spaces—is consistent with the approach to institutional architecture that BNIM has developed. That approach eschews any conception of the building as an integral gestalt, preferring to treat the built object as a kind of machinic assemblage, a dispositif in which each part, unburdened of overriding formal conceits, can be more ably faceted in response to the particular condition or problem it is designed to address. In this case, the stratification of program allows both public and private spaces to be more precisely calibrated to their respective modalities of occupation, with the central atrium then serving as a spine along which these strata are distributed and by which they are brought into communication. Meanwhile, the various circulation devices (stairs, ramps, and bridges) that circumscribe and traverse the atrium serve to at once render movement between the building's two specialized sectors, research and administrative, more efficient and to provide exhilarating vistas onto the public scene below, thereby lending a measure of social drama to the professional routines of their users. It is along these generously dimensioned and extensively deployed devices that much of the casual mixing among the community's various constituencies will take place. They provide a mediate scale of social interaction between the privacy of the labs and offices and the public character of the ground floor, which includes a cafe, an auditorium, confer ence facilities, lobbies and service areas. These are designed to serve not merely those working in the building but the entire campus community. This floor is organized on a free plan that distributes program in a flexible manner perfectly suited to the diverse demands placed on it by the various communities availing themselves of its services.

This conception of the building as an infrastructural framework that accommodates a kit of specialized parts is also apparent in the approach to the building's façades, which are differentiated in response to both distinct climatic conditions and to the formal peculiarities of the gardens and lawns onto which they face. It is equally apparent in the variable floor elevations on the building's south wing, which serve to accommodate air distribution systems designed to minimize the energy cost of climate control. The result is a flexible building that avails its occupants of all that counts as amenity on the surrounding site, fosters both programmed and spontaneous collective interaction at all scales and provides the research communities working within it with lab spaces that are at once flexible and outfitted for the most specialized and technologically demanding forms of con temporary research.

FOLLOWING SPREAD. Fayez S. Sarofim Research Building: view from the street

– GENEROUS PRAGMATISM: SCHOOL OF NURSING AND STUDENT CULTURAL CENTER BY BNIM ARCHITECTS + LAKE | FLATO ARCHITECTS

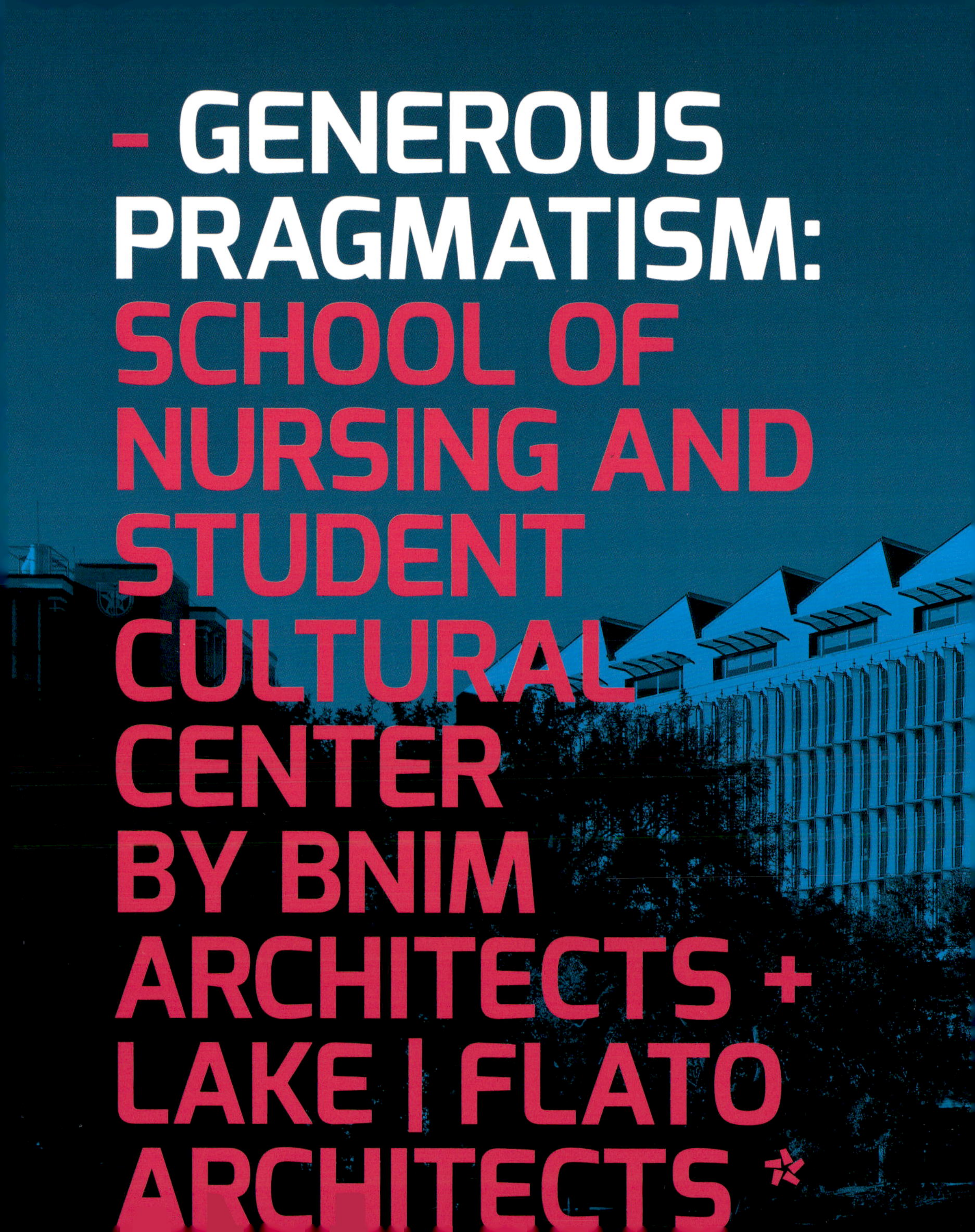

ORIGINALLY PUBLISHED IN **BNIM: NURTURE**, ORO EDITIONS, 2007.

*WRITTEN IN COLLABORATION WITH ANDREW PAYNE

BEHIND THE RECENT BROUHAHA CONCERNING the building as spectacle, the Bilbao effect, as it has come to be known, we can observe the emergence of a new pragmatism in contemporary architecture, a concern with how well buildings perform in response to the full range of social and ecological processes they are called on to organize. The work of BNIM Architects and Lake | Flato makes them implicit advocates of this pragmatism in which what a building can do matters as much as what it looks like. Their buildings are perhaps best described as instruments or devices whose function is to instill in their occupants an ethos of engaged propinquity in settings that bring the convenience and intensity of the artificial environment into intimate proximity with the amenities associated with the natural surrounding. What is more, their buildings perform this complex function in accordance with practices designed not only to minimize negative ecological consequences of construction, but also to ensure each building's ongoing contribution to the ecosystem in which it performs. In view of this ecological emphasis, we can be more precise about the building's instrumentality: they are biotechnical instruments, living machines. Having said that, what makes these buildings especially compelling is the way in which this ecologically spirited instrumentality, fashioned over fifty years of collective practice, is inflected by a generosity toward the lived character of organized human affairs. In these buildings, the minutiae of everyday life are treated not as obstacles to architectural invention; they are, rather, invention's justifying occasion. Far from being overlooked, the normative routines of contemporary professional existence are consistently embraced by BNIM and Lake | Flato as so many opportunities for bringing the built environment into a deeper attunement with our collective desire for convenience and delight.

Such commitments and inclinations enabled the successful collaboration with Lake | Flato, with whom they joined forces in designing the School of Nursing and Student Community Center at The University of Texas Health Science Center at Houston. Here, the synergy between like-minded firms produces one of the finest demonstrations of generous pragmatism: technical efficacy in optimizing performance coupled with an aesthetic commitment to sustaining everyday pleasures.

The aesthetic of the technical instrument is an aesthetic of self-effacement, and this building as biotechnical instrument is no exception to that rule. On first glance, it is a box set squarely on its site, a box among the many boxes that comprise the Houston landscape. This continuity with the idiom of its place is in fact a form of camouflage, however, for unlike the boxes that surround it, which are pretty dumb, this box is a clever box—clever enough to nest within its restrained massing a series of ingenuously simple devices for bringing organization, space, and light to the event of human congregation. Approaching the building on axis, one sees this aesthetic of self-effacement literalized in the void that penetrates the building's cube at its center. The insertion of this void has at least two effects. First, it nests an exterior space at the heart of the building's interior, emblematizing the building's larger strategy of engagement with its surroundings. Second, it transforms the building into a monumental frame or proscenium that serves to put the visitor, arriving from a landscape composed of parking lots and dumb-box building stock, in immediate contact with what is unquestionably the site's chief aesthetic amenity, the park lying on its north side. The "breezeway" that this piercing of the center of the building's interior volume provides also serves as a shaded space for public congregation, an alternative to the sun-exposed space of the park onto which it gives way. Hence, the breezeway serves as a device for putting otherwise disjointed things in a relationship of vital proximity to one another: events of arrival and events of occupation; artificial and living systems; interior and exterior spaces; openness and purposiveness; optical drift and spatial definition. In that sense, also, this device is emblematic of the architects' larger commitments, for in their version of the building as living machine, the mechanic operation always involves bringing two or more persons or things into a relationship of adaptive advantage. This relational strategy concerns more than merely placing the site's amenities at the immediate disposal of those occupying the building's

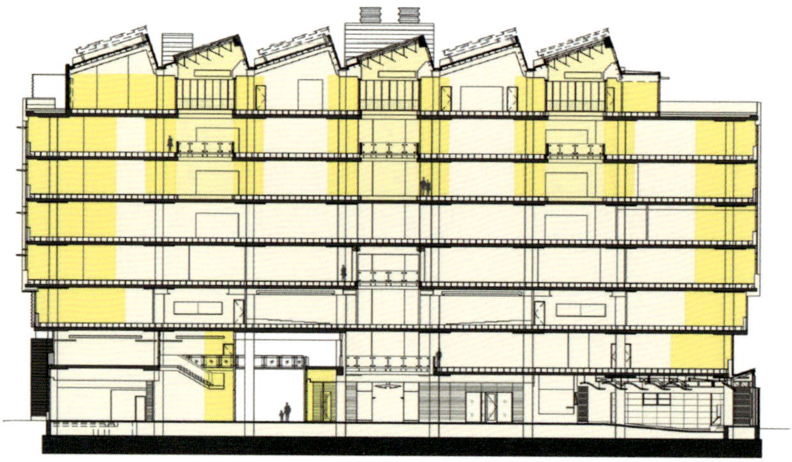

ABOVE. School of Nursing, section drawing showing demonstrating daylighting

ABOVE. School of Nursing and Student Community Center

ABOVE. One of the three atriums

interior – it also involves enlisting the building in a re-orchestration of the elements composing the urban context, establishing new relationships and hierarchical dynamics between those elements. In the hermetic and atomized landscape of Houston, where the operative logic linking persons and things remains largely hidden from view, the breezeway acts as a kind of urban ventilation system: a system for circulating light, air, and space, to be sure, but also for circulating common sense, a degree of collective intelligence concerning our relationship to our immediate surroundings.

The instrumental approach to built form is also apparent in the treatment of the School of Nursing's façades. That approach eschews any attempt to convey an integral gestalt, in favor of a faceted approach in which each elevation responds to the conditions peculiar to its orientation. Whereas the front elevation opens the building to the park as the site's chief amenity, the other elevations are designed to maximize and manage sunlight while limiting passive heat gain during the hot summer days. This strategy of employing the façade as a filter for letting in light and keeping out heat is repeated on the building's roof. Replete with a network of skylights and reflectors working to coordinate natural light and shade in the building below, this roof truly does manifest the oft invoked but seldom realized ideal of a fifth façade. On all elevations, the cubic massing of the building is echoed in a strategy of varied reticulation that, in keeping with the instrumental aesthetic described above, prizes the flexibility of operative configurations over more classical compositional strategies.

The advantages of this pragmatic strategy are immediately and powerfully felt on the building's interior. True to the aesthetic of self-effacement, BNIM

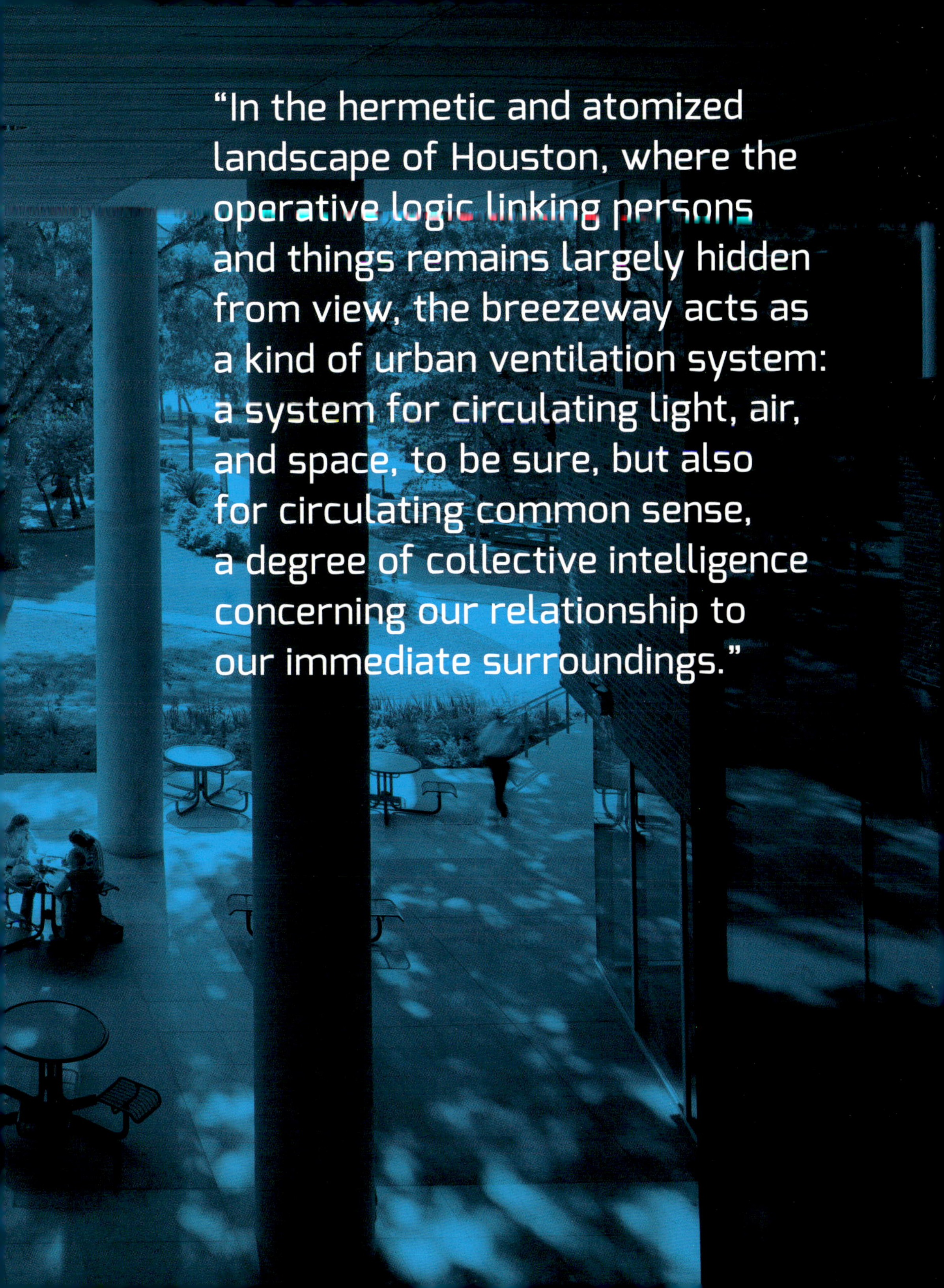

"In the hermetic and atomized landscape of Houston, where the operative logic linking persons and things remains largely hidden from view, the breezeway acts as a kind of urban ventilation system: a system for circulating light, air, and space, to be sure, but also for circulating common sense, a degree of collective intelligence concerning our relationship to our immediate surroundings."

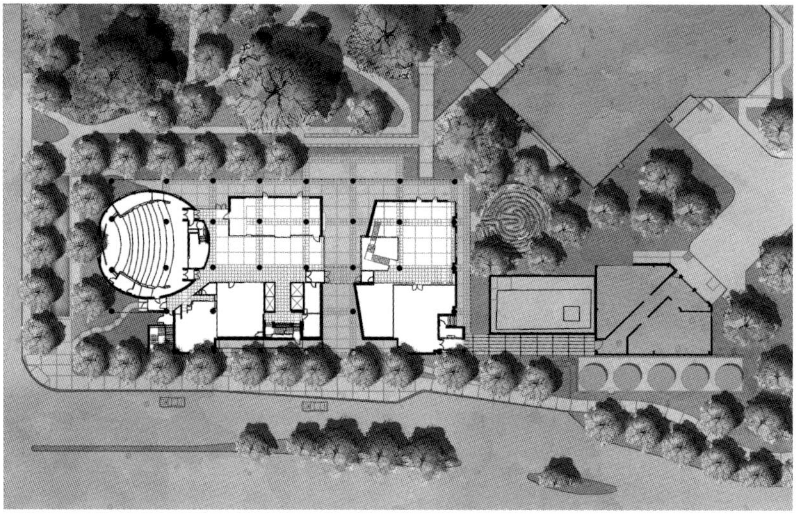

ABOVE. School of Nursing and Student Community Center, ground floor plan

RIGHT. School of Nursing and Student Community Center, façade with shading system

and Lake | Flato have taken pains to design not merely the built object, but the atmosphere it contains.

Using advanced digital simulation technologies, the architects have calculated the quality of light and its associated ambiance with a precision generally reserved for more tangible media like glass, steel, and stone. As a result, the most memorable feature of the building may be the most immaterial. Long after visitors have forgotten the self-effacing elegance of the object, they are likely to retain a strong impression of the atmosphere of airy transparence this object evinces and contains.

This emphasis on delivering natural light, so very apparent in the treatment of elevations, is echoed in the sectional strategy, which is organized around the provision of atria that extend deep into the heart of the building along both horizontal and vertical axes. It is in section that the box most fully reveals itself as a permeable framework penetrated by shafts of light. These strategies lend to the building a sense of openness and transparency that is simultaneously pastoral and urbane. This is a generous conception of the contemporary institutional building, one in which the vicarious social pleasures lining the daily performance of our professional routines are not cynically theatricalized—as in so much contemporary architecture—but rather, recast in the light of an entirely pragmatic and contemporary Arcadian ideal.

Texas Children's Hospital

– DIGITAL CRAFT: TONGXIAN ART CENTER GATEHOUSE BY OFFICE DA

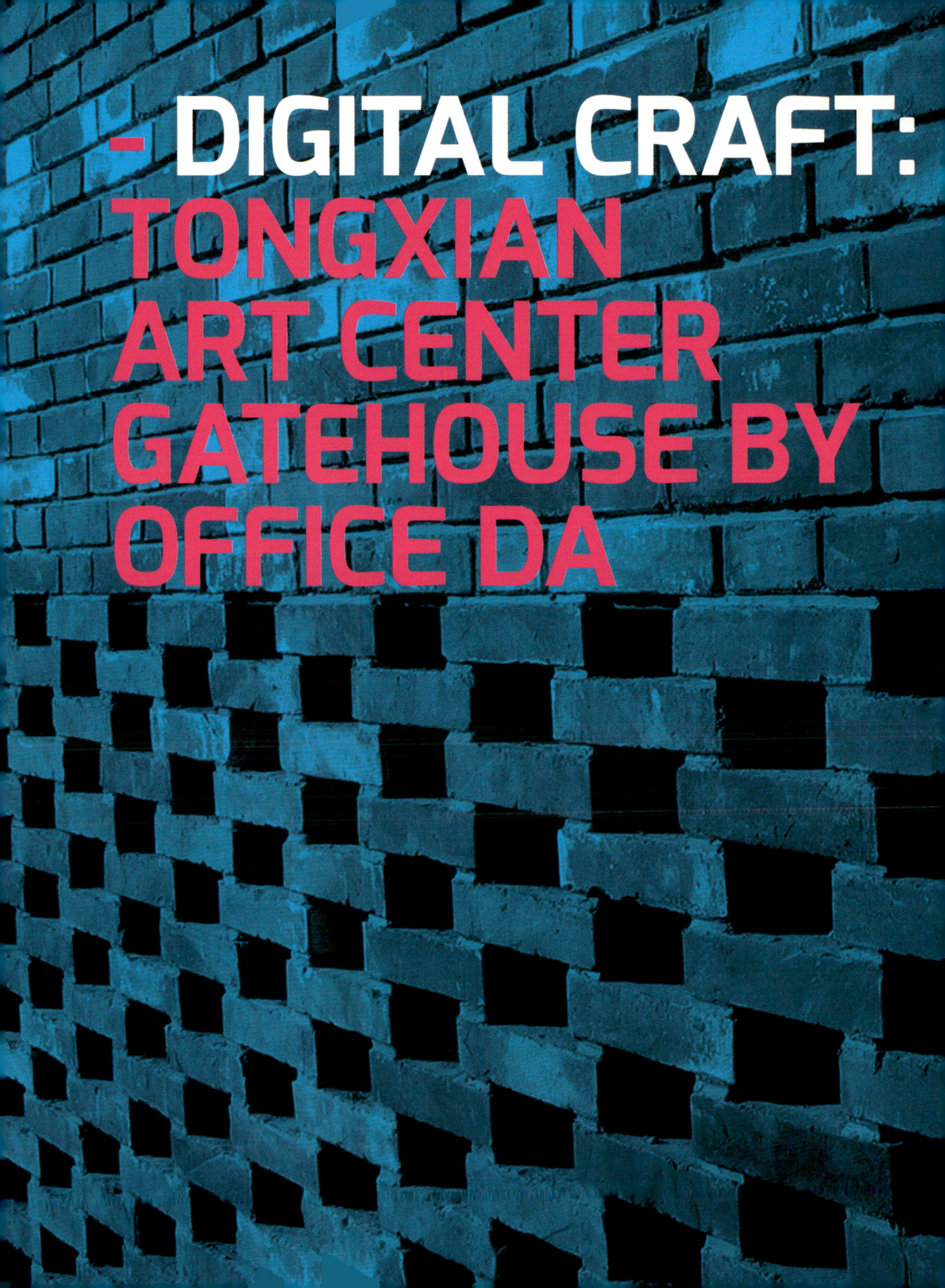

ORIGINALLY PUBLISHED IN **32 BEIJING/NEW YORK MAGAZINE,**
ISSUE 5/6, 2006.

THE GATEHOUSE OF THE TONGXIAN Art Center is the completed first stage of a larger project comprising galleries, studios, housing for visiting artists, and administrative spaces for a thriving artist community in a village thirty miles from Beijing.

This is an eloquent prelude to Office dA's ambitions for the main facilities, rehearsing the critical design moves at a modest scale but with a no less radical degree of innovation—as expected from the firm that has invested the same intensity and ingenuity in all its designs, from bookshelves to housing blocks. The Gatehouse provides a good snapshot of the firm's evolving trajectory with regard to design method, building materials, and technology.

In typical Office dA manner, the designers have imposed a limited material palette and various other constraints—geometric, structural, and programmatic—on the building so as to "provoke" invention. Invention indeed is necessary when the aim is to produce a generous architecture through fiercely reductive rigor and means.

The architects, for example, speak of "the entire building as having undergone a rigorous diet, its bodily mass suctioned to a critical minimum." The metaphor illustrates how a self-imposed space restriction necessitates the colonization of residual "fatty" areas under and above stairs. This is achieved by means of wall deformations that ripple across the building, implicating every brick in a chain of subtle inflection.

The deformations—which are also played out against other constraints, such as drainage—bear a familial resemblance to the curvilinear architecture that has recently proliferated with the help of the computer. But unlike formally complex propositions that bank on the promise—and fantasy—of infinitely plastic building materials to effortlessly flourish in the friction-free environment of digital media, Office dA's smart curves result from the painstaking negotiation of spatial abstraction with concrete building, matter with substance, quantities with qualities. Embedded within the complex geometry of the gatehouse is a seasoned knowledge of industrial bricks and Flemish bonds, as much as of digital computational techniques.

"Each building block in the Gatehouse is linked to the others and to the whole in a cascading play of cause and effect, putting the building in a state of virtual flux."

The building relies on both analogue and digital means-the conflation of low and high-tech is a staple Office dA strategy. They use common local standard materials and traditional methods of construction, requiring no specialized labor skills beyond local expertise. For the non-standard geometry of continuous deformation they use full-scale templates that are mapped and produced with digital modeling and CNC milling. Office dA exploits sophisticated digital tools to set up, at minimal cost, a guiding framework of vectors for an otherwise conventional construction process that capitalizes on local skills and resources.

The Gatehouse also converges with current practice in digital architecture in more subtle and significant ways. Consider, for instance, how the bricks are animated by a system of continuous deformation. Each building block in the Gatehouse is linked to the others and to the whole in a cascading play of cause and effect, putting the building in a state of virtual flux. The building does not move, of course; movement is embedded as potential, in the virtual responsiveness and pliancy of the structure, its possible re-deformation in response to a different set of constraints. The bricks are here suspended and interlinked in a pseudo-fluid state that is akin, in principle, to the parametric environment of digital models where all elements are dynamically embedded in a system of relationships.

That a brick building in rural China with an unmistakable artisanal character should align so closely with cutting-edge digital theory and practice testifies to the ever-impressive ingenuity of Office dA, as much as to the power of the digital paradigm in a globalized architectural practice.

ABOVE. Tongxin Art Center Gatehouse

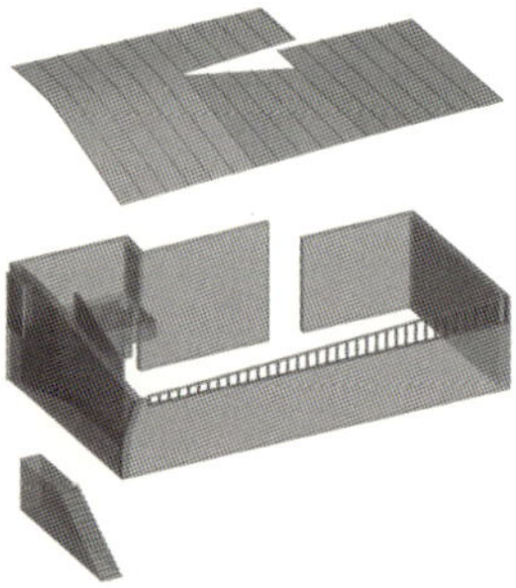

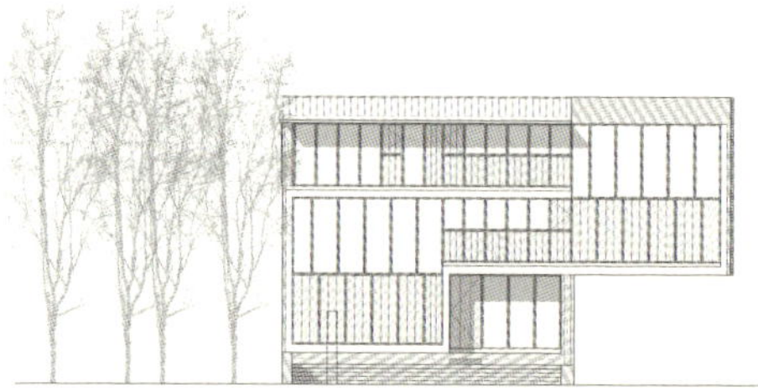

Tongxin Art Center Gatehouse, brick cladding detail

CREATIVE DIRECTION
BY LEO MALINOW

GRAPHIC DESIGN
BY YANINA ARABENA

COPY EDITING
BY BRIGETTE BROWN

PHOTOGRAPHIC CREDITS
Pages: 4-5 An Te Liu, 6 Courtesy of NADAAA, 20-47 Nic Lehoux, 48-61 Nikkol Rot for Holcim, 76-85 David Rokeby and Michael Awad, 94-95 Michael Moran, 100-101 Courtesy of Samyn and Partners, 114-131 Hervé Le Reste (except 126-127 Atelier Arcau), 132-151 James Steinkamp, 152-167 Courtesy of Höweler + Yoon Architecture, 168-179 Courtesy of Jaklitsch / Gardner Architects, 192-203 Aedas, 207-217 An Te Liu, 221-222 An Te Liu, 223-245 Courtesy of NADAAA, 297-317 Nic Lehoux, 342-363 Courtesy of Samyn and Partners, 364-385 Hester + Hardaway, 386-399 Courtesy of NADAAA.

OSCAR RIERA OJEDA
PUBLISHERS

Copyright © 2015 by Oscar Riera Ojeda Publishers Limited
ISBN 978-988-12249-5-8
Published by Oscar Riera Ojeda Publishers Limited
Printed in China by Artron Art Center

OSCAR RIERA OJEDA PUBLISHERS LIMITED
Unit 6, 22/F.,
Far East Consortium Building,
121 Des Voeux Road Central, Hong Kong
T: +852-5311-1625

Production Offices | China
Suit 19, Shenyun Road
Nanshan District, Shenzhen 518055
T:+86-755-8336-6138

www.oropublishers.com | www.oscarrieraojeda.com
oscar@oscarrieraojeda.com

All rights reserved. No part of this book may be reproduced, stored in a retrieval system, or transmitted in any form or by any means, including electronic, mechanical, photocopying of microfilming, recording, or otherwise (except that copying permitted by Sections 107 and 108 of the U.S. Copyright Law and except by reviewers for the public press) without written permission from the publisher.